Praise for

Final Engagement

"A refreshingly honest, much-needed account of the failures of U.S. policy in Afghanistan—and the effect those failures had on the warriors sent into harm's way to carry out this (lack of) policy. A must-read for anyone interested in the real-world consequences of Beltway chaos."

—MAURICE "CHIPP" NAYLON,
Marine veteran and author of
The New Ministry of Truth

"A gripping narrative that transcends the written word, striking deep into the heart of those who have stood on the front lines. . . . This book doesn't just tell a story; it evokes the very essence of sacrifice and victory, leaving an indelible mark on the soul."

—DR. TONY BROOKS,
Army Ranger veteran and author
of *Leave No Man Behind*

"Americans should read this book to understand better the service and sacrifices of those who served on a modern-day frontier between barbarism and civilization in Afghanistan. Christopher Izant sheds light on the courage, sense of honor, and dedication to duty of those who fought there as he lays bare the contrast between the true character of the war on the ground and the unreal depiction of it in Washington, DC."

—LT. GENERAL H.R. MCMASTER (RET.),
former United States National Security Advisor,
and *New York Times* bestselling author of
At War with Ourselves and *Battlegrounds*

Final Engagement

A Marine's Last Mission and the Surrender of Afghanistan

Christopher L. Izant

DIVERSION BOOKS

Diversion Books
A division of Diversion Publishing Corp.
www.diversionbooks.com

Diversion Books and colophon are registered trademarks of
Diversion Publishing Corp.

For more information, email info@diversionbooks.com

First Diversion Books Edition: August 2024
Hardcover ISBN: 9781635768725
e-ISBN: 9781635768701

Book design by Beth Kessler, Neuwirth & Associates, Inc.
Printed in the United States of America

10 9 8 7 6 5 4 3 2 1

Diversion books are available at special discounts for bulk purchases in the US
by corporations, institutions, and other organizations. For more information,
please contact admin@diversionbooks.com

The views expressed in this publication are those of the author
and do not necessarily reflect the official policy or position
of the Department of Defense or the U.S. government. The public release
clearance of this publication by the Department of Defense does not imply
Department of Defense endorsement or factual accuracy of the material. Please
direct any questions regarding this case to Mr. Paul J. Jacobsmeyer,
ph. 703-614-4912, email paul.j.jacobsmeyer.civ@mail.mil .

For the Fallen

Contents

Author's Note

On language: Pashto words and phrases are italicized in my own phonetic spelling of the southern dialect we spoke.

On names: Aside from public figures, the deceased, and the men of Alpha Section, who reviewed draft manuscripts and consented to the use of their true names, the names of the individuals in this story have been changed or limited to first name only to protect their privacy and, in many cases, their safety.

On memory: A decade has passed since the events in this story, but I have done my best to render a true account. I have relied on field notes, correspondence, my journal, trusted secondary sources, photographs, video footage, and conversations with others who were present to confirm the accuracy of these events. Any errors are my own.

On opinions: I have written this story in my personal capacity. The views expressed in this book are my own and do not reflect any position of the Department of Defense, Department of Justice, or any other component of the United States government.

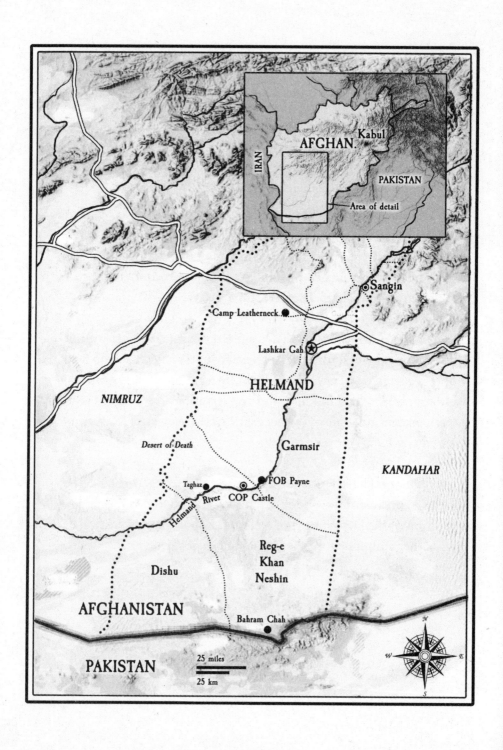

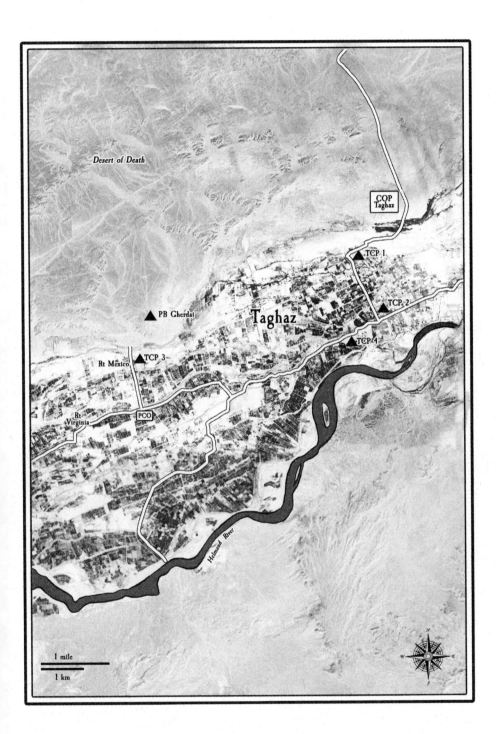

Desert of Death

COP
Taghaz

▲ TCP 1

▲ PB Gherdai   Taghaz   ▲ TCP 2

▲ TCP 4

Rt Mexico ▲ TCP 3

Rt
Virginia   PCO

Helmand River

1 mile

1 km

"Forward, the Light Brigade!"
Was there a man dismayed?
Not though the soldier knew
Someone had blundered.
Theirs not to make reply,
Theirs not to reason why,
Theirs but to do and die.
Into the valley of Death
Rode the six hundred.

—ALFRED, LORD TENNYSON, 1854

Preface

Surrender Revisited

This story needed telling. All the hot air and spilled ink that flowed in the wake of the Taliban's victory in Afghanistan in August 2021 did little to answer the painful questions of how and why they prevailed after all we had invested to prepare the Afghan National Security Forces (ANSF) to withstand the looming onslaught. The live broadcast of our chaotic retreat disabused the world of the notion that the military operations named Enduring Freedom and Resolute Support were anything but cruel antiphrases. But those dramatic final days were just the logical culmination of a long surrender that had begun nearly a decade earlier, when I was there. As a Marine Corps combat advisor to an ANSF unit in Helmand Province during the withdrawal of American forces, I witnessed firsthand how unprepared the Afghans were to fight on their own. Their impending defeat was obvious to anyone on the ground; but, as the last team to advise the unit, our orders were to abandon them anyway.

I first started writing before my deployment to Afghanistan as an outlet for the anxiety I glibly labeled "pre-traumatic stress disorder." It wasn't simply a reasonable fear of being sent into combat, but rather my distress at the possibility that—after years of investment and indoctrination into a culture that revered its combat veterans—I might *not* go to war. Once deployed, I continued to chronicle my experiences, partly as a mission log to reference when writing up awards for my Marines at the end of the tour, but mostly so my friends and family could have a record to keep their remembrance of me more complete and alive if they lost me in Afghanistan. If death was really like being an old book on a shelf, as Linda tells Tim O'Brien's narrator in *The Things They Carried*, I wanted my say in whom the reader resurrected. After I returned home, my attention turned to the life before me and my deployment journal sat in a folder, all but forgotten.

Then Kabul fell.

The speed of the Taliban's advance was shocking, but their resurgence was no surprise to anyone who had worked with the ANSF. In spite of the endless challenges, we seemed to have achieved some equilibrium in the later years of the war—the Afghan government controlled the provincial capitals, critical infrastructure, population centers, and key logistical routes, and the Taliban skirmished at the edges, harassing, waiting, and preparing. The situation resembled historian Thomas Barfield's "Swiss Cheese" model of Afghan central governance,[1] and it was critically enabled by a small coalition footprint of American contractors and Special Operations Forces focused on Taliban leadership and other high-value counterterrorism targets. But then the Trump administration negotiated for a complete troop withdrawal by May 2021 in a deal that excluded the Afghan government, shocking those of us who clung to a naïve hope that no American president would actually pull the rug out so precipitously and so recklessly. After all, the emergence of the Islamic State of Iraq and ash-Sham after the American troop withdrawal from Iraq was not ancient history. It wasn't history at all: it was still news.

Lesson not learned, President Biden followed through on his predecessor's promise. Before the withdrawal was even complete, an ISIS suicide bomber killed scores of civilians and 13 of the 5,400 American servicemembers who surged in to guard Kabul's airport and assist with the frantic race to evacuate Americans and our local allies before the Taliban could hunt them down. It was a sadly fitting end to the American mission in Afghanistan, the heroic efforts of the men and women sent to do right by our Afghan allies clashing against unrealistic planning of Defense and State Department officials in Washington. And as if to add an exclamation mark at the end of the tragic saga, some blundering swivel-chair commander killed an aid worker and his family with a Hellfire missile on our way out the door.

Grief, anger, confusion, shame—the emotions crashed in waves and pulled at something foundational, the way an under-tow vacuums away the sand beneath feet, once firmly planted, now tense and straining to stabilize. Reaching out to fellow vet-erans for balance, I learned I was not alone. We grieved for the Afghans and we blamed the Afghans. We grieved for ourselves and we blamed our leaders. For some, it was easier to coax ourselves into detached indifference, while others sprang into action to help our abandoned allies escape to safety. Disoriented, we grappled with nagging questions. Were we complicit in this defeat, or victims of it? What did it mean that, in the age of violently polarized politics, apathy toward the resurgence of the Taliban and the suffering of Afghan people was a common policy position of both the outgoing Republican and new Democrat administrations? What did this say about our worth as veterans of that war? What did it say about the value of our individual and collective sacrifices? We dared not equate ourselves with Vietnam veterans who were sent into a jungle of horrors and then harangued for it if they made it home alive. We were volunteers, after all. Still, we somehow felt akin. It was our turn to strive to make sense of our experiences.

Between calls, texts, and emails with other veterans, I reexam-ined what I'd written at the time in my journal and in emails to friends and family. What then had been frustrating, laughable, and depressing now seemed foreboding in hindsight. What armchair historians, politicians, and talking heads in the media reduced to political corruption, tribal culture, and the "graveyard of empires" tropes, I revisited in detailed account.

Writing had been an effective therapy before I deployed, so in the fall of 2021 I began again. With my war journal, emails, mission log, photographs, helmet-camera footage, conversations with my old teammates, a handful of publications I'd bookmarked over the past decade, and all the benefits of hindsight, I went to work piecing together this story. The process of constructing a narrative not only helped me harness my various conflicting thoughts and emotions; it also brought me a feeling of satisfaction that this story would be told, if only to those who cared to read it.

No one voice could ever speak for everyone who served as an advisor to the ANSF, much less for every veteran of the war in Afghanistan. As deployment experiences ranged from mundane office work to a daily gauntlet of violence, so, too, did the attitudes and beliefs of the men and women who fought there; the voices of cynics, careerists, cavaliers, and a spectrum of ideologies often filled moments of caffeine-fueled and boredom-borne banter. But questions of foreign policy and strategy were merely hypothetical to the individuals who bore the brunt of the fighting. Orders were not an invitation to conversation. We were there to do our job. And we all wanted it to mean something. In this way and perhaps others, Afghanistan was a collective experience. While I speak for no one but myself, I trust that other veterans will find that this story connects with their own in some small way. At least, the complete collapse of the ANSF demonstrated to me that my personal experience as an advisor was not the aberration I'd hoped it was.

So I offer this story to honor these American servicemembers, coalition partners, and our Afghan brethren—those who fought not merely with their boots on the ground, but with their bellies in the dirt—with an honest account of our lost battle to empower the ANSF to win their own war. To do so, I illustrate the immense

challenges we accepted; the investments we made; the daily brav-
eries that went unrecognized; and our earnest efforts to accomplish
our mission against the odds and under the clock. I also show why
I and many others voluntarily sought out these hardships and
how it felt to bear them in the face of a pervasive indifference that
denied us time and permission to succeed. Hard questions still
remain, and I don't pretend to know whether the ANSF ever could
have stood on their own, or how long or costly a commitment that
might have required of the American-led coalition. But I do know,
and will show you, just how reckless it was to leave them the way
we did, at the beginning of the end in Southern Helmand.

One

Evacuation

Our Afghans were in a firefight. And we had just left them. The machine gun disassembled in front of me was still caked in dust from the convoy across the desert to our new home at Combat Outpost Castle. I looked up at the black Motorola nested in its charger along the wall of our tent, as if eye contact would prompt something more from the radio. After a minute of tense silence, I returned to cleaning the gun.

Before long, Captain Quinn's voice came over the net calling me and Doc O'Connor to his tent. I grabbed my Navy corpsman and hurried over to get the initial report from our team's operations officer: a band of Taliban fighters armed with AK-47s, machine guns, and rocket-propelled grenades had ambushed an Afghan patrol in Taghaz. The attack left two Afghan patrolmen each with a gunshot wound to the leg. The Afghans initially applied tourniquets, but then removed them for some unfathomable reason, only to reapply them when the hemorrhaging resumed. They would be transporting the two casualties to us at first light, and we would help stabilize them until the medevac helicopters arrived. From there, Doc and I would be their escorts to a military hospital in the provincial capital of Lashkar Gah.

After three hours rumbling across the desert in an armored Humvee with red crescents stenciled on each side, the Afghans arrived with their wounded. Doc Matias and Doc O'Connor took those morning hours to transform the outpost's conference room into an improvised clinic, sanitizing tables to be makeshift beds, setting up IV lines, and staging all their medical equipment. The casualties came in on stretchers, followed closely by 1st Sergeant Amanullah. He was acting as the Afghans' only medic, since the other two were both absent: one in school for additional training, and the other home on leave. *Maybe Colonel Nasrullah has learned something about allowing both your medics to be away at the same time*, I muttered under my breath. But maybe not; our corpsmen were impressed at how 1st Sergeant Amanullah had effectively stopped the bleeding and prevented either casualty from going into shock throughout the night and the long, bumpy ride in the Humvee. Not bad for the "acting" medic.

The Afghan transport team placed the wounded patrolmen, Abdul Aziz and Nur Muhammad, on the tables prepared by Doc O'Connor and Doc Matias respectively. All the Marines present cleared out except for Captain Quinn, who wrote down information to send up in a casualty evacuation request, and me. I took notes for Doc O'Connor as he went through his assessment. Two other officers from our team stood at the door for crowd control, which ultimately failed as the district governor and other Afghan officials pushed their way through to watch our corpsmen at work. Doc O'Connor took a quick round of vitals, started the IV drip, removed an already-loosened tourniquet off Abdul Aziz's thigh, and uncovered the pressure dressings to evaluate the severity of the wound. The 7.62mm bullet had missed bone by about a quarter of an inch, but had split open the leg right where the calf muscle met the knee, taking out a solid bite. On the other table with Doc Matias, Nur Muhammad insisted that it was the very same bullet that had entered his right leg midway down the shin. In just twelve minutes, Doc O'Connor had completed his triage, patched up Abdul Aziz, and dictated a second set of vitals for me to record.

You could have been forgiven for thinking Doc O'Connor was a doctor. In truth, "Hospital Corpsman Third Class" was just too many syllables for the average Marine to verbalize, especially under stress. Chef-Doctor-Barber, the more descriptive of Zach O'Connor's unofficial titles, wasn't much better in that regard. So, like countless Marines before us, we bestowed the traditional honorific "Doc" upon the Navy corpsman we expected to save our lives, should the need arise. With the benefits of a childhood spent hunting in the woods of Michigan, a uniquely savage wit, and a previous deployment with the Marines, Doc O'Connor made us feel lucky to be in his capable hands, where Abdul Aziz presently found himself.

Abdul Aziz would be fine, Doc assured us, but Nur Muhammad's wound was more worrisome, since the bullet had entered his leg near the bone and made a sloppy exit out the other side. The potential complications warranted a medical evacuation to the Shock Trauma Platoon at Forward Operating Base (FOB) Payne, where the medical officers could take x-rays and perform surgery if necessary. Doc and I had already packed overnight bags for a trip to Lashkar Gah, so the change of plans made little difference to us. We strapped on our gear and met the Afghan ambulance out at the landing zone where the mortar platoon in charge of security at COP Castle had already set up a perimeter. Right on schedule, two Black Hawk helicopters, modified to support such medical evacuations, touched down in a swirl of dust and din. We deposited Nur Muhammad into the first bird, and Doc O'Connor hopped on with him; I followed Abdul Aziz into the second. The flight surgeon strapped me into a seat, and I passed off Doc's clipboard with the recorded vitals. A massive Army medic started working on Abdul Aziz as we lifted away, then the flight surgeon joined him and began cutting off all of Abdul Aziz's clothes. The roar of the rotors washed out all sounds of protest, but I could see Abdul Aziz's eyes pleading for them to stop and spare him the humiliation. I couldn't help but smile in amusement at the cultural clash between his Pashtun sense of honor and our standard lifesaving medical procedures.

When we landed at FOB Payne, a team of corpsmen rushed out to off-load the Afghan casualties from each bird while the Army medics on board bundled all the tattered uniforms and personal effects in trash bags. I shouldered my pack and followed the casualties to observe a fourth round of assessment outside the plywood clinic. Doc and I dropped our gear in a waiting room and met the casualties inside. A Navy surgeon spotted me and called me over.

"Hey, Lieutenant!"

I rushed across the busy emergency room.

"Are these guys ANA, AUP, or combatants?" he asked.

"Sir, these guys are ABP—Afghan Border Police, from the unit I advise."

It appeared that Abdul Aziz's continued resistance had raised some questions about his loyalties. After all, the medical staff at Payne were only informed on the Afghans' injuries, and the scraps of their ABP uniforms lay crumpled in garbage bags in the corner. I walked back to my bleacher seat and asked Doc to explain what we were seeing.

The surgeon pulled up a fresh x-ray on the screen, and Doc pointed out that the image was of Abdul Aziz's leg—he could tell from where the chunk was missing. The wound was too big to stitch up, but the flesh would grow back as long as the cavity was cleaned out thoroughly. Between rough scrubbing directly on the tissue and the burn of the sterilizing chemicals, Abdul Aziz was screaming and squirming—"like a bitch," as the surgeon explained his professional medical opinion.

Next up was Nur Mohammad. His x-rays revealed a million-dollar wound; the bones were completely intact, which meant the bullet had passed in between his tibia and fibula, miraculously missing both. With such good luck, we were told, both Afghan patrolmen would be discharged that same day. While they recovered on their cots, I took a short trip across FOB Payne to arrange for our temporary housing and to request transportation back to COP Castle. Then I returned to the clinic to debrief Abdul Aziz and Nur Mohammad on exactly what had gone down the prior day in Taghaz.

*   *   *

A small farming village nestled just below the *Dashte Margo*, the Desert of Death, Taghaz sat on the tip of the Helmand's "fishhook," where the mostly south-flowing river abruptly arched out to the west before turning back south. While not located on the physical border—the Durand Line, drawn by some British diplomat across Pashtunistan and Baluchistan in 1893—Taghaz was just about the southernmost strip of agricultural settlement in the province. All that separated Taghaz from Pakistan was about fifty kilometers of open desert and a dormant volcano. Down at the actual border stood the town of Bahram Chah, a market for weapons and drugs used by the Taliban as a staging area for launching operations in Helmand Province.

The decision to establish an American military presence in Taghaz was not an obvious one. Sending Marines to remote villages in Helmand Province, and Taghaz in particular, was the subject of much debate between Marine Brigadier General Larry Nicholson and his political advisor from the State Department, John Kael Weston, at the beginning of the 2010 troop surge.[2] Weston believed a creeping counterinsurgency effort that extended beyond the population centers that were critical to sustaining the Afghan government did little to meet the intent of the surge strategy. As no Afghan official had ever set foot in Taghaz prior to the arrival of the Marines in early 2010, Weston questioned the importance of sending Americans to patrol a village that the Afghan government itself, and the British military who had occupied Helmand before the U.S. Marines, both viewed as inconsequential.

But General Nicholson was not content merely to defend major population centers and give the Taliban free rein elsewhere. Following basic Marine Corps warfighting doctrine, General Nicholson wanted to strike the enemy where he was vulnerable and eliminate his sources of power. And, unlike his British predecessors, General Nicholson had enough Marines at his command to do so. Even remote villages that gave safe harbor to Taliban fighters, such as the river crossings of Southern Helmand, were, in General Nicholson's view, centers of strength for the Taliban. Places like Taghaz were the key avenues by which the Taliban brought fighters, weapons, and explosives from Pakistan to sustain their combat operations against the U.S.-led coalition and Afghan government. Unless the coalition was able to dismantle the Taliban's base of support, they would continue to attack and kill Marines.

The mindset was as Marine as Marine gets: if you have an enemy in your battlespace and the tools to fight him, that's what you do. As for the lower-ranking enlisted Marines and junior officers at patrol bases and combat outposts who actually engaged with the Taliban and local population, that's about all we were told, with some counterinsurgency doctrine peppered in for good measure. Even the larger picture made sense: the Taliban gave quarter to al-Qaeda, who had attacked America, and we were going to Helmand to kill them. By 2010—call them insurgents, terrorists, warlords, militias, or bandits—collectively, "the enemy" had been killing American servicemembers for nearly a decade, and that was enough to earn our wrath. It was an undeniably logical and satisfying purpose, and one for which Marines were willing to sacrifice their time, careers, marriages, limbs, and even lives. We took for granted that it was only valid for a limited time.

Even if we could have killed our way to victory in Afghanistan, forcing the insurgents to surrender and reintegrate peacefully with the central Afghan government, it would have taken far longer than the few short years prescribed by the Afghanistan surge. But that was not the strategy. President Obama had adopted the proposal of Army General Stanley McChrystal and sent thirty thousand additional troops to Afghanistan beginning in 2010, with three objectives: denigrate al-Qaeda's presence; take back control of key population centers from the Taliban; and invest in the development of the Afghan forces for an eventual transfer of responsibility for the security mission.[3] While Special Operations Forces focused on the first objective and the Marine infantry battalions in Helmand prevailed at great costs to accomplish the second, enduring success hinged on the trainers and advisors tasked with transforming the Afghans into an effective fighting force.

The strategy of the eighteen-month surge only permeated down to us at the ground level through the sense of urgency applied to our mission. We understood that the task of the infantry battalions was to beat back the Taliban and buy time for the Afghan forces to build competence to do so themselves. But while General Nicholson's expansive counterinsurgency campaign in Helmand may have been effective as a Marine operation, whether the fledgling Afghan forces would be able to sustain it in short order was an entirely different matter. The Taliban, who knew the clock was ticking on the U.S.-led coalition presence in Helmand, were waiting patiently for the changing of the guard and preparing to strike from their de facto sanctuary across the border in Pakistan. That far south and that far west, there was no Afghan National Army presence; defense of that frontier fell to the Afghan Border Police.

*   *   *

The Afghan Border Police did not police the Afghan border. At least, not in Southern Helmand Province. They were not really police. They were not really at the border. And they may have been as Afghan as Afghan ever was, but most would identify primarily by their tribe. The ABP units responsible for securing the border between Helmand and Pakistan paid little mind to their doctrinal "Blue Border mission" of enforcing the law at border crossing points. Instead, the ABP worked their "Green Border mission" of patrolling between points of entry. In practice, this meant the ABP in Helmand simply assumed the mission that the Marines handed to them: defending population centers to deny the Taliban a base of operations in Helmand through a patchwork of patrol bases and traffic control checkpoints (TCPs). If they made the occasional drug bust and arrest, all the better.

At least some of the ABP wanted to take the fight forward to the Taliban stronghold in Bahram Chah, and special operations raids there occasionally made a dent. But there was no plan or effort to seize control of that border town, and the ABP simply lacked the requisite manpower or heavy weapons to do so.[4] Like the rest of the Afghan forces, the ABP suffered from severe staffing shortfalls, demoralizing and underreported attrition rates, and the criminal patronage networks that pervaded every aspect of the Afghan government. Due to the dispersed and decentralized nature of its mission, the ABP was particularly challenged.

The ABP's 6th Zone, or regional command, was headquartered in Lashkar Gah. Two of its subordinate Kandaks—supposedly self-sustaining units equivalent to Marine Corps infantry battalions—operated more than fifty miles to the south in Khan Neshin District, with 1st Kandak based in Taghaz and 2nd Kandak twenty miles east at FOB Payne. Each Kandak was organized into company-sized units called Tolais, which conducted operations out of patrol bases and TCPs. Marine advisors paired up with the Afghans at every level, with a parallel chain of command.

The mission of our team, Border Advisor Team 1 (BAT-1), was to advise, train, and assist the 1st Kandak in Taghaz. We also were responsible for evaluating their readiness to operate independent of coalition forces.

When we arrived in October 2012, 1st Kandak was rated "independent with advisors," which was a generous way of indicating that the only assistance they received from the NATO coalition came directly from or through our team. That assistance was still significant, particularly with explosive ordnance disposal, casualty evacuation, and logistics. Since we could not build them a medevac helicopter and train a pilot, the articulated focus for our work with 1st Kandak was on logistics and maintenance of their headquarters facility, Taghaz Station, built with one million U.S. taxpayer dollars. Most urgently, the Kandak had been trying for months to get the 6th Zone command to send a truck to empty their septic tank, with no success. Nearly just as important, their vehicles were in a continuous state of disrepair with no trained mechanic on hand. Medical expertise was also a priority need. The Kandak had two fully trained medics, but they lacked any method of expediting critical casualties to higher levels of care, and they had no preventive care services to keep the ABP in fighting shape. These focus areas extended to the Kandak's three Tolais, where we also set goals to improve their battle tracking, operations planning, and counter-IED procedures. We knew our powers to fix these key issues were limited, but we trusted the judgment of the previous advisor teams, who indicated that these were areas where focused investment could yield appreciable results.

Stationed alongside 1st Kandak at Combat Outpost Taghaz, our team was the farthest-south and farthest-west Marine Corps unit in the country, well beyond the range of any friendly mortars or artillery. A giant aerostat surveillance balloon floated above the outpost when weather was cooperative, but it was not an armed asset. My section of the team was sent even farther south and west

of COP Taghaz, assigned to advise the Kandak's 1st Tolai at Patrol
Base Gherdai. Having planned for this in advance, every Marine
on my team carried an M203 grenade launcher and a bandolier of
40mm high explosive grenades. When I found myself on a larger
base, I frequently got questions from bewildered Marines who
noticed my weapon while standing in line for the chow hall or elsewhere: "Sir, why do you have a 203?" The weapon was ordinarily
fielded by an enlisted fire team leader with a rank of corporal, not
an officer whose primary weapon was the radio. Yet I felt it was
worth the strange looks and awkward questions. Unless we pre-
arranged to have aircraft accompany our patrols or managed to
call them in on request, we would have to drop our own bombs.

But we were not completely on our own. A Marine Corps
infantry battalion "owned" our area of operations and performed
the security mission for the outposts and bases there. Shortly after
our team moved in, 3rd Battalion, 9th Marines assumed this role
from their usual station in Twenty-Nine Palms, California. The
battalion commander, a lieutenant colonel with the radio call-sign
"Bobo-6," assigned a platoon to maintain security and logistics at
COP Taghaz. We had a lukewarm relationship with this platoon,
who went by "Carnage" on the radio: they essentially just stood
watch and ran the outpost while the advisors went outside the
wire on combat missions with the Afghans. Our advisor team
helped by pulling overnight shifts in the combat operations center
where we monitored video feeds and radio traffic; but other than
that, we stuck them with the mundane work and had all the fun
ourselves. Still, I heard no complaints from Carnage. In 2012,
Marines were just grateful to be on a combat deployment at all,
even more so if an infantryman could pitch his tent at an outpost
away from the brass at Camp Leatherneck, Camp Dwyer, or the
few remaining FOBs.

Bobo-6 made no exceptions to the battalion's mandatory
security posture for our advisor teams. This meant that each

convoy operation needed a minimum of three trucks, two
Marines per truck, and, of course, a Navy corpsman. The lead
truck also had to push a mine-roller—a giant metal rake jutting
out in front with wheels on the tines, weighted down to trigger any pressure-plate IEDs. Foot patrols required a minimum
of four Marines plus a corpsman, two metal detectors, two
backpack-mounted electronic radio frequency jammers, plus
our standard load of ballistic plate carrier vests, two radios,
ammunition, water, optics, pyrotechnic signals, extra batteries,
and the rest. For an ordinary infantry squad on patrol, it would
not be overly burdensome to spread some of this gear among a
dozen Marines (although they also frequently brought along a
mortar tube, a couple of machine guns, and plenty of ammunition for both). For an advisor section of four Marines, though,
who also all carried 40mm grenades, everyone was weighed
down by between eighty and one hundred pounds of gear. But we
could manage the weight. The personnel threshold was the real
limiting factor; it forced my section, Alpha, and the other on our
team, Bravo, to alternate between visiting our Tolais on advising
engagements and simply supporting one another with manpower.

So, while our team was co-located with 1st Kandak at COP
Taghaz, we could only visit the Tolais to train and conduct
operations together for a few days at a time, once a week. It
would be even more difficult once we relocated farther east
as the base-closure timeline reeled us farther up the Helmand
River. We also had to accommodate the ABP's own scheduling conflicts; Thursdays—the last day of the workweek in the
Islamic calendar—were blocked out for the Kandak to conduct
routine maintenance on its vehicles and equipment. Further limiting our ability to work with the ABP, our team only had four
of the eight interpreters we rated on paper, and they needed
frequent breaks to stay effective. Our team leader, Major Select,
kept his two favorites for the headquarters component of the

team, and gave Alpha and Bravo sections each one full-time linguist of our own.

Interpreters were the unsung heroes of the advising mission, but not all were created equal. Some spoke shoddy English. Some were opportunists looking for influence and prestige. Some were exceedingly sensitive about Marines calling them by the abbreviated slang "terp." Some didn't want to patrol. Some didn't even want to interpret. But the local Afghan assigned to Alpha Section was none of those. Young, humble, fearless, and fluent in both Dari and Pashto, Ahmed came from a small farming village outside of Kabul. When I first met him in October 2012, Ahmed was fresh off a short vacation at Camp Leatherneck, enjoying his first break from the daily grind since he initially embedded with Marine units in 2011. While he had access to a telephone there, he called his father and received a disturbing warning.

"Don't come home . . . the Taliban are looking for you here."

His father went on to describe how he had found a note in the gate around their family's garden. The Taliban wrote that they knew Ahmed was working as an interpreter for the Americans, and threatened that they would slit his throat and cut off his head if he did not quit his job.

> "Tell your son he can't be safe all the time; we will find
> him one day. If not today, *inshallah*, next week, next
> month, or next year . . . we will find him."

The Taliban delivered their next threat shortly after Ahmed joined my team. They sent it by way of his cousin, who worked for the NATO coalition at Bagram Airfield just north of Kabul. In a letter that they stuffed in the young man's pocket before dumping his headless corpse for Ahmed's family to find, the Taliban wrote:

If anyone works for the infidels, they will be killed like this man. We will cut off your head into pieces like this worker; very soon you will receive the interpreter's body with no head. Ahmed didn't listen to us. Wait for Ahmed's death.

As the Taliban terrorized his family with threats and murder, Ahmed stood steadfast on our side. So the intimidation continued.

A few weeks later, Ahmed's father was collecting firewood in their village when two menacing men armed with AK-47s and their faces covered in scarves drove up to him on motorcycles. They forbade Ahmed's father from working in the garden or fields of their village until Ahmed quit his job and returned home.

"Do you understand, or do we need to make you understand?" one of them challenged, with all the cringey machismo of an '80s-movie bully. For dramatic effect, they confiscated all the wood Ahmed's father had just collected, lit it afire, and told him to leave. So he did; the Taliban threat was clearly too dangerous for him to continue working in their village. Ahmed's family also had to shut down the education center where his brothers taught English and his sister taught math. If the threats continued, Ahmed's father told him, the family would have to flee Afghanistan.

Back in 2009, Congress authorized the Department of State to issue Special Immigrant Visas (SIVs) to Afghan nationals who needed resettlement due to an ongoing serious threat as a consequence of working for the U.S. military. Applicants seeking to take advantage of this benefit under the Afghan Allies Protection Act in 2012 needed to prove they met several criteria, wait for years to have their case adjudicated, and pray to get one of the only 1,500 visas allotted per year.[5] If there was ever a perfect example of the kind of situation or the kind of person Congress intended to qualify for a SIV, it was Ahmed. But he had to compile the proof of his protection in a multi-step process and then hop in line for adjudication, where the average wait time was several years thanks to bureaucratic inefficiencies, the cost and availability of medical examinations, and difficulty vetting people with common names and unknown dates of birth. With the Marines' withdrawal already under way, Ahmed had no time to lose; so, in between our engagements with the ABP and tagging along on patrols, he worked to assemble everything he needed for his SIV application. While Ahmed's service to the U.S. left him homeless, he clung to the promise of a new home in America. In the meantime, he had Taghaz.

TWO

Geronimo

Abdul Aziz was out cold on his hospital bed. Reclining on the next bed over, Nur Muhammad appeared to be conscious, so I approached him to get as much of the story as I could without the assistance of an interpreter. I strung together the obligatory burst of Pashto greetings—*salaamu alaikum, tsenga yey? Joori? Pakhayri? Sha yey?* etc.—and then Nur Muhammad began: A ten-man patrol had set out from TCP 3 heading south down Route Mexico. No one was in charge. There were no officers or even a sergeant in the group. I instantly recognized that this situation was exactly what I had advised them to prepare for during a meeting one month earlier, as if I had coordinated with the Taliban myself to prove a point.

For now I said nothing, and Nur Muhammad continued.

Just before the patrol reached the main bridge into town, the Taliban launched their ambush from fighting positions in a thick brush to the west that the ABP called the "jungle." Abdul Aziz and Nur Muhammad both went down during the initial machine-gun bursts. At the same time, the Taliban opened up on the Tolai commander's truck, parked across the road from TCP 3 where he was visiting with a village elder. More Taliban fired at TCP 3 from a second position in the farmland east of Route Mexico.

Between the three firing positions, Nur Muhammad estimated an enemy force of ten to fifteen Taliban, which I mentally reduced to six to eight after factoring in the ABP's tendency to exaggerate and the likelihood that the Taliban had moved around during the skirmish. According to Nur Muhammad, who lacked both a watch and the ability to tell time, the firefight began when the sun started to set and lasted almost two hours. No Taliban were killed or captured; the ABP were happy just to make it back to safety with their casualties. Though the gunfire was relatively light, this was not the pop-shot harassing fire that had become routine since our team moved from Taghaz to COP Castle. I sketched a rough schematic of the positions and landmarks in my notebook and showed it to Nur Muhammad to confirm that I had correctly interpreted everything in our Pashto conversation. He shrugged, never having learned to read a map. That ended the debrief.

Once Abdul Aziz and Nur Muhammad were picked up for transport, Doc and I caught a ride across the base and relayed the story to the captain who ran FOB Payne, known by the call-sign Wake Island 6. Wake-6 promised to squeeze Doc and me into their convoy to Castle the next day, assuaging my fears of being stranded at Payne indefinitely.

The next morning as I came out of our transient housing tent, I saw a man lying on the ground with a couple of other civilian contractors gathered around him. I dashed back inside.

"Hey, Doc!" I interrupted his packing. "There's a guy collapsed on the ground outside!"

He dropped what he was doing and we both ran out to see a junior corpsman who had joined the group squatting down to ask questions. All the man could manage to say was "chest pains," and that was enough for Doc to take charge. He hollered at a nearby contractor who was driving a Gator all-terrain utility vehicle and flagged him down to stop. The contractor was baffled but obeyed Doc's commands. After lifting his semi-conscious patient into the cart, Doc hopped in next to him, pointed in the direction of the Shock Trauma Platoon, shouted "go!" and they were off. Doc O'Connor conducted an initial assessment en route, detecting an irregular, faint heartbeat, then delivered the contractor to the medical officers at the clinic with a summary of his vital signs and symptoms. The doctors managed to keep the man from going into cardiac arrest, and he survived.

When we got back to COP Castle, I wrote up Doc O'Connor for an "impact" Navy Achievement Medal (NAM) based solely on his actions those past two days. Since it was my first award submission, I shared the draft citation with Captain Quinn to get his feedback. "Yeah, it's good," he counseled, "but you could hold off for now and try to get him an upgrade based on what happens during the rest of the deployment." I deferred to his judgment. After his previous deployment to Sangin District with 1st Battalion, 5th Marine Regiment, deference was indeed warranted.

*　　*　　*

Clad in iconic dress-blue uniforms in a Las Vegas hotel ballroom to celebrate the Marine Corps Birthday, the men of 1st Battalion, 5th Marines passed around beer-filled prosthetics of the wounded like hockey champions with the Stanley Cup. It was November 2011. The six hundred–some infantrymen of the battalion and a few hundred supporting Marines and Navy corpsmen had just battled through a hell of bombs, rockets, and gunfire in Helmand Province's Sangin District, the most violent place in Afghanistan at the time. Seventeen had given their lives and nearly two hundred were wounded over the course of their seven months' "bangin' in Sangin," as the commemorative T-shirts proclaimed. Despite their suffering, or maybe just because it was over, the men of 1st

Battalion, 5th Marines—"one-five" (1/5) for short—were in out-standing spirits. It would be months before their traumas surfaced in maladaptive coping mechanisms and heartbreaking tragedies; but in the meantime, the Marines of 1/5 were happy with their work in Sangin and even happier to be home.

On the day the last of the 1/5 Marines returned from Sangin to the battalion's home base in Camp Pendleton, California, I checked in with eight other new second lieutenants fresh out of Quantico, Virginia, where we'd spent the last nine months training for this moment. As new lieutenants in a salty and storied infantry battalion, we knew the challenge that awaited us when we each picked up command of a rifle platoon. My platoon in Charlie Company, I was told, had the most "personalities" and discipline issues. After crossing off all the names of Marines who would soon be getting out of the Corps or getting orders to another unit, I found myself staring at a roster of seventeen lance corporals and a private first class (PFC)—two of the three most junior ranks. Even at the ripe young age of twenty-three, I was older than all of them except the PFC, who had been a lance corporal but was demoted for accidentally firing off a burst from his machine gun while standing watch at an outpost in Sangin and, on a separate occasion, allowing a Taliban detainee to escape. I imagined that their collective attitude toward me would be skeptical, maybe even belligerent, depending on the degree to which they fit the rebellious lance corporal stereotype. Naturally, I anticipated some degree of harassment from this battle-hardened group that the company commander described as "in need of a disciplinarian."

The lieutenant I was replacing sat down with me to pass along his insights about each of the Marines with whom he'd just spent seven months at war. He chuckled as he fondly recalled punishing one Marine for some infraction by running him around the patrol base with his gas mask on during what turned out to be that Marine's last day with legs. As an outsider looking in, I was uncomfortable with his laughter about something as grave as a Marine getting blown up. It felt profane. But lacking any personal understanding of what they had gone through together, I had no choice but to reserve judgment and shake my head in bewilderment. It wasn't all laughs; one of my first, and most important, responsibilities was holding up my cell phone on FaceTime with that double-amputee, who called in from Walter Reed to virtually attend the battalion's memorial ceremony on a cold, drizzly November day. The deafening silence between the names of the fallen, barked three times in the ritual roll-call, pressed the weight of my new responsibility as a leader of these men deep into my bones.

After the intense fighting in Sangin, many of the Marines in the battalion and their family members especially were relieved to learn that 1/5 was next slated to deploy aboard naval vessels as the "ground combat element" of the 31st Marine Expeditionary Unit (MEU). The 31st MEU began and ended with training in Okinawa, Japan, and typically included some amphibious exercises and jungle warfare training with allied countries in the Asian Pacific. Devoid of the dreamy port calls of a Mediterranean cruise or the possibility of responding to whatever crisis might unfold while projecting force on warships in the Persian Gulf—experiences offered by other MEU itineraries—the shipboard tour nicknamed the "thirty-worst" left much to be desired for a new platoon commander.

While some of the returning Sangin veterans actively searched for orders to other units, and some were indifferent, I knew that the Marines of 1/5 and their families especially deserved a break. I felt privileged just to lead my score of lance corporals and my very special PFC, regardless of our future mission. But the more I got to know them, the more jealous I felt of their experiences, what they had accomplished, and their peace of mind just knowing they'd paid off their debts to society. It kept me up at night just wondering if I would forever be indebted to men like these, or if I could one day feel like I, too, was worthy.

Like every other newly minted Marine in 2011, I was keenly aware of the fact that combat deployments in Afghanistan were coming to an end. President Obama had announced as much that July, confirming that the withdrawal of U.S. forces from Afghanistan would begin on the schedule prescribed eighteen months earlier.[6] Feelings of impatience ran rampant across my training cohort in Quantico, as if we were in a race to get to the war before it was over. It was bad enough that Navy SEALs killed Osama bin Laden that May while my classmates and I waged a fictional battle against "Centralians" on "Quantico-like terrain" for a weeklong field exercise. As the news circulated around the muddy foxholes we had dug in our defensive position, every Marine's fantasy of pulling that trigger was shattered. "So can we just go home now?" came the quips, some more than half-serious. I even ranked my preferences for the occupational specialty I would be assigned with an eye toward deploying quickly; Low Altitude Air Defense Officer made my top five because the occupational training school was only six weeks long. I felt no particular affinity for Stinger missiles, and certainly did not imagine I would lead a team shooting down (then) nonexistent Taliban aircraft; but if that was my ticket to the theater, so be it. Even higher up on my preferences list was the infantry, and to my family's dismay, that is where I went.

*   *   *

As the son of two physicians in a suburb with safe neighborhoods, good public schools, and an older brother attending an Ivy League university, college was the only option presented to me. Even my interests in military academies and ROTC were written off as nonstarters when I considered my options after high school. With few exceptions, I gathered that my parents, peers, and teachers all viewed military service as a last resort for people without better options. Like every teenager yearning for independence, I argued with my parents; but I lacked the courage, maturity, and steadfast certainty to do something drastic to pursue that dream.

One semester of Jesuit education and three hundred miles of separation from my parents' sphere of influence gave me the space I needed to pick up the cross I had been eyeing all along. During my freshman year at Boston College, I took a seminar that helped me discern how to heed the call I heard to serve through reading and discussing ancient philosophies, biblical passages, and Christian literature. As my parents continuously emphasized to me, there was a variety of nonviolent and less dangerous ways to serve my country. But I was inspired by the Christian tradition of physical sacrifice and wanted to put my whole self on the line.

I asked the Buddhist professor who taught that seminar to complete one of the recommendation forms I needed to join the Marines. She voiced her ideological opposition but agreed to support me. "You know, my cousin is in the Marines," she offered, back when I was too ignorant of Marine Corps history to connect any dots. So, with the written endorsement of Professor Susan Mattis, first cousin to the famed four-star warrior-monk himself, I submitted myself before the Marine Corps. You would think from my family's reaction that I'd joined some violent gang. I guess, in a way, I had.

The ferocity of my parents' opposition confused me, given the generations of service in my family. Grandpa Frank was drafted into the Army in World War II and spent two and a half years in the New Guinea Campaign in the Pacific. Grandpa Bob served as a physician in Alaska's Aleutian Islands after the Navy paid his way through medical school.

Even further back, my great-grandfather Ralph served in France during World War I as a first lieutenant in the U.S. Air

Service, the early predecessor to the U.S. Air Force. He was shot down on an ill-conceived bombing run in 1918, when inclement weather forced the squadron to fly at a dangerously low altitude. His commander and pilot, Thorton Hooper, had ominously mused before the mission: "I know this is murder, but the swivel-chair commanders don't know it, and all we can do is to go and trust to luck."[7] Luck was with the attacking Germans, who downed five American aircraft and killed three of the pilot-observer pairs. Great-Grandpa Ralph was wounded, but Hooper managed to set their damaged plane down in occupied France, where they were taken prisoner and held for months. Great-Grandpa Ralph, who carried bullet fragments in his leg the rest of his life, returned home to his wife Anne Lincoln, my great-grandmother. She shared a common ancestor with the legendary commander in chief of the Union in the Civil War. After the war, they produced my grandmother and Ralph Jr., who went on to earn the Distinguished Flying Cross in WWII for his skill and courage navigating B-17s on bombing runs in Europe as a first lieutenant in the U.S. Army Air Corps.

With this history, it baffled me that respect for military service somehow skipped a generation. It was only after I signed my contract that I learned my mom, like Grandpa Bob, had also joined the Navy to finance medical school, but her tour was abbreviated. She was pregnant with my older brother when the Navy gave her orders to Guantanamo Bay. As an unaccompanied tour, this meant not only that my father was unable to join her, but also that she would have to leave her infant in the care of stateside relatives for two years. My mom had signed up to care for military families, not be separated from her own, so she claimed conscientious objector status, paid back the Navy for her schooling, and got out with an honorable discharge. Even if she had shared this backstory while I was still considering the military, the point was moot. I bore no illusions about how disastrous the military was to family life. But I was a single teenage male; at that point in my life, a wife and kids seemed more like a threat than a promise.

My father's reasons were more compelling. After my first three weeks of training at Officer Candidate School in Quantico, Virginia, I had a twenty-four-hour period of weekend liberty. My dad came down and picked me up for a night of binge eating and restorative sleep in a hotel room. The next morning, he drove us to Arlington National Cemetery, where we walked over to Section 12, grave marker 1688. This was the burial plot of Jonathan Goulder Izant, my dad's uncle and the namesake of his older brother. Second Lieutenant Izant had volunteered right after graduating college and fought the Nazis in France and Germany. After repelling fierce German counterattacks during the Battle of the Bulge and enduring weeks of intense urban combat, Lieutenant Izant was killed in action.[8] He was posthumously awarded the Silver Star—which, of course, was no consolation to anyone. This devastating loss of a beloved family member was a festering wound in the corpus of my family history for generations. Sorrow over this unspeakable tragedy, too painful to acknowledge, had hidden this hero from me.

Standing among the ranks of white marble headstones, I finally understood my parents' adamancy. My father's family had already paid the ultimate price, and he was willing to do everything in his power to prevent paying Uncle Sam another installment. While I felt my stomach turn for my late grandfather, the great-grandparents I never met, and all who loved JGI, learning of his legacy only entrenched my sense of obligation. Not that I harbored some "Lieutenant Dan" death wish, but I saw my own wartime service as a way to honor the family's sacrifice. They saw it as youthful folly.

It took some time, but eventually my parents became my biggest supporters, even joining a local Marine parents' group and attending their own Marine Corps Birthday celebrations every year. But they were the "support the troops by bringing them home" type; they honored—not understood and much less endorsed—my decision to volunteer for the fight. Their most fervent prayer was my greatest fear: that I would miss the war.

*   *   *

With the Afghanistan troop-level reductions beginning in 2011, few Marine Corps infantry battalions were slated to rotate through Helmand, and those that did would be relegated to just defending large bases before long. The remainder of the war in Afghanistan would be fought by Special Operations Forces playing intelligence-driven whack-a-mole and embedded advisors with the herculean task of building up the Afghan units into a capable security force. Several of my peers planned to try their luck at assessment and selection for Marine Forces Special Operations Command, known now as the Marine Raiders, but they would first need to prove themselves on the MEU to earn the battalion's endorsement, then undergo another year or so of intensive training. The advisor mission, on the other hand, offered a faster route to deploying and a crucially important role in achieving long-term success.

Advisors were critical to the endgame in Afghanistan, just as they had been in Iraq prior to our withdrawal there and continue to be in partner countries around the world. They've borne many names over the years—Military Transition Teams, Police Transition Teams, Embedded Training Teams, Foreign Forces Advisor Teams, etc.—all sharing the same mission of developing a local security force capable of fighting its own battles so Americans didn't have to. Failure to do so in Afghanistan meant one of two inevitable outcomes: we would continue to "send American boys nine or ten thousand miles away from home to do a job that [Afghan] boys ought to be doing for themselves,"[9] or everything we built would crumble apart once we left.

If a deployment to Afghanistan was a given, the choice between platoon command and an advisor billet would have been a no-brainer. But leading a platoon on an MEU versus advising in Afghanistan was a more complicated trade-off. With officer promotions pegged to time-in-service, and platoon commander billets mostly reserved for junior lieutenants, both positions were time-limited opportunities. It was one or the other. In total, I had spent a year just preparing to lead a platoon and I had finally made it. And after what my platoon of young Marines experienced in Sangin while I was still training, I felt not merely responsible for them, but indebted to them. They deserved the leader I aspired to be, one who mentored, taught, nurtured, disciplined, and inspired them to realize their potential. But they also deserved a successor, I rationalized, someone to carry on their work and ensure that their sacrifices would not be in vain.

The first opportunity to deploy as a combat advisor came about a month after I checked into the battalion. I was still far from comfortable with the senior officers in my company, and with my commanding officer in particular. I even hesitated to share my consideration of an advisor team with my peers. The community of Marine Corps infantry officers was small, and I did not want to start my career by appearing ungrateful or unhappy with my assignment. Especially because I wasn't: I thoroughly enjoyed working with my platoon and planning training events with the other company officers. So that initial opportunity passed as the positions all were filled before I felt comfortable enough to bring up such a delicate topic.

Late one afternoon in early 2012, while the senior enlisted staff and officers sat around the company office waiting for the armorers to confirm that they had all our serialized weapons and optics, Gunnery Sergeant Jolanski brought up an email. In his capacity as the senior enlisted Marine in the company in charge of administrative matters, he had received this message from the headquarters unit about to take over command for all the Marines in Afghanistan. It tasked 1/5 to source half a dozen spots on an advisor team heading to Afghanistan.

"Hey, Gunny, sign me up for one of the turret-gunner billets," I joked, since they were reserved for sergeants and more junior enlisted ranks.

"Actually, sir, there are some officer billets too. They'd probably love to have you with that language shit you got."

I was fairly certain that Gunny was mocking me; he had previously proclaimed that he hated new second lieutenants with a passion. But whatever his motivations for trying to get rid of me, Gunny's suggestion gave me the push I needed not to miss this second chance, and I immediately voiced my interest. I was in good company.

Despite just returning from the horrors of Sangin, there was no shortage of volunteers from 1/5. Over in Alpha Company, Alfonso "Fonz" Palacios put in his name for a driver/gunner billet. Corporal Palacios had first deployed to Afghanistan in 2008 as a turret gunner in a heavy weapons platoon with 2nd Battalion, 7th Marines. After blasting away Taliban rocket teams from behind the Mk-19 automatic grenade launcher in his armored truck, his next deployment was underwhelming: the 31st MEU. In 2010, as news spread of the extreme suffering of 3rd Battalion, 5th Marines in Sangin, Corporal Palacios reenlisted and requested orders to whatever unit was next deploying to Afghanistan. That was 1/5, heading into Sangin to replace 3/5. Then, Corporal Palacios volunteered to transfer from his initial assignment on the battalion commander's personal security detail to Alpha Company, which had suffered multiple early casualties, and joined their group advising the Afghan National Army. A second advisor tour and third deployment to Afghanistan was far preferable to another 31st MEU.

Several Marines in Bravo Company also put their names in for advisor team billets. The Company 1st Sergeant interviewed all the candidates to probe their motivations before deciding whom to send. Responses ranged from "avoid the 31st MEU" to "save enough money to pay off my car loan," but one Marine responded that he was a warfighter, so he wanted to be where the war was. This was Cory Malone. A charming rural twang, bright eyes, and a colorful sense of humor belied the terrors of combat that Lance Corporal Malone had endured. He served as his squad's point man, sweeping for mines with a metal detector at the front of 110 foot patrols in the most violent sector in Sangin. The Taliban repeatedly ambushed his platoon at ranges of under fifty meters from "murder holes" burrowed through the thick mud walls of the compounds that peppered the crop fields. On one occasion, Taliban machine-gun fire pinned down Lance Corporal Malone and his squadmates so effectively that they had no alternative but to rush across an open field in alternating bounds to assault the Taliban position head-on. Afterward, they watched in a mix of horror and relief as aerial surveillance footage showed a Taliban fighter dig up an IED that somehow did not detonate in that very field. Sangin was hell for Bravo Company, and there was Lance Corporal Malone, volunteering to go back.

Two other new second lieutenants volunteered for the same position as I had, but the competition came as no surprise. We were a generation of warriors who had watched the Twin Towers fall and the Pentagon smolder as impressionable schoolchildren. We were conscripted by the memories of our loved ones, our shared fear, our desire for retribution, and the shame of missing the chance to be worthy of our heroes from wars throughout American history. Simply joining the ranks was not enough: we sought a combat deployment to validate not just the investments we made in training, but also our very willingness to serve. For Americans who idolized the heroism of the Greatest Generation, this was our chance to prove that we, too, could take up the mantle to support the free world and defend our country. We honestly believed, as we desperately wanted to, that the war in Afghanistan was our generation's righteous battle against evil. We also believed that this view was shared by our civilian neighbors, who elected our policymakers and bankrolled the war with their tax dollars, and that was our mistake.

*　*　*

One Friday morning in March 2012, the entire battalion assembled to hike over the giant ridge west of Camp San Mateo and around through some flat fields known as the Tomato Patch. I rinsed off the sweat and dust in a quick shower and put on a fresh uniform to check in with the battalion executive officer ahead of my shift on duty that night. When I did, he delivered some encouraging news: "We decided to send you forward." I did my best to maintain a professional demeanor, replying calmly that I appreciated the battalion for sending me, but on the inside it was Christmas morning. With all the other volunteers from the battalion, I felt like I had won the lottery, but I would not let myself celebrate: it seemed too good to be true.

While I stood watch that night, a Sangin veteran suffering from post-traumatic stress disorder and chronic pain overdosed on his prescribed benzodiazepines and oxycodone; he was found shoeless, covered in mud, and incoherent, lying on the sidewalk with a rock in his mouth. I did what I could to organize a medical response team and get the Marine transported to the local hospital. Then, at just about the time when I could have taken my four-hour nap and turned the post over to the staff sergeant on duty with me, the military police called to inform me of a

Marine they had arrested for beating his wife. I needed to take him into custody. The busy night full of tragic reminders of the war's enduring burdens tempered my elation at the prospect of deploying.

About two weeks later, on the morning I learned I was "definitely going," three NATO members were killed by Afghan security forces in two separate instances. With thirty-four coalition members killed at the hands of our Afghan partners in 2011, and sixteen already killed thus far in the first twelve weeks of 2012, it was clear that the trend was accelerating. When I logged into the single computer shared by the four platoon commanders in my company office, a news article about the spate of these "green-on-blue" incidents popped up on my browser's homepage, prompting one of them to joke about how screwed I was in my new assignment. I enjoyed morbid humor as much as the next Marine, but I figured that when I got on the plane and watched America disappear out the window, no one would be laughing. (That assessment turned out to be very wrong; Lieutenant Sullivan and then-Lieutenant Quinn each took a sleeping pill before the flight and made a "slap bet," wagering a five-finger salute to the face of whoever fell asleep first.)

I put off telling my parents that their child was going to war until it was certain. I saw no need to get them worked up and anxious about a mere possibility. I also knew my mother would pray for me *not* to get the assignment if I told her while it was still undecided, and I didn't want her pleading voice in God's ears while He made His plans for me. After I learned that my orders were official in April, I called them and ruined a perfectly fine Sunday morning. My mother cursed for the only time I can recall; my father fell silent while she broke down and wept. "This is my worst nightmare," she reminded me.

I knew what I would put them through; I'd seen their nightmares come true in the lives of others. During a temporary stint on recruiting duty in Boston, I was invited to attend a Fallen Heroes of Massachusetts fundraising dinner with my friend and co-lieutenant Dave. All Marines were asked to wear their dress blue uniforms; so, with second lieutenant rank insignia and just one ribbon, it was clear to everyone that we were newly commissioned. We were seated at a table with three couples and a lone woman, all of whom had lost a family member in Iraq or Afghanistan. Dave and I had introduced ourselves to everyone when we sat down, and they each explained what service their sons had been in, and when they had died. The man I was sitting next to told me his son would have been twenty-two (my age at the time), and had passed three years prior. At the end of the ceremony he told me, as tears ran down his face, "Just keep your head down." The keynote speaker was General John F. Kelly, who had lost his own son, a second lieutenant in 3/5, to an IED blast in Sangin just one month earlier. There were a few other guest speakers who spoke of the tremendous honor and sanctity in the sacrifice of the loved ones we were gathered to commemorate. The eyes of every parent and one heartbroken fiancée at our table glistened throughout the event.

The guilt of what I was doing to my parents weighed heavily on me, so I told some white lies to make us all feel a little better. While I admitted that the deployment was what I wanted, I told them nothing of how I had volunteered or how persistent I'd been in pursuing it. I also concealed from them the fact that I would be isolated among the Afghans with only a few other Marines. And I neglected to share that I would conduct combat operations with the Afghans, who were increasingly turning their guns on their American advisors. Instead, I told them I was going to a large base that I would never leave, just training and advising the Afghans in a place of relative safety. This was the start of the *Don't Tell Mom* signature line I included at the end of all my emails to my brothers about my time in Afghanistan. My older brother printed the motto on beer-can koozies and distributed them to everyone at my bachelor party years later.

Telling my Marines was less nerve-racking. Like all new second lieutenants, I was entirely replaceable, and that absolved me of any guilt I might have felt for leaving them. I waited until my assignment was finalized before I told the three lance corporals I had chosen to serve as interim squad leaders; but by then the "Lance Corporal Underground," a wildly imaginative and occasionally accurate rumor mill, had beaten me to the punch. These young men understood my desire to get to the fight as well as anyone; we were cut from the same cloth. They expressed gratitude for my time with them and wished me luck. They knew I would need it.

Three

Sharpening Iron

The Taliban had given us the best gift an elusive enemy ever could: a pattern. Ever since the aerostat surveillance balloon above Taghaz came down for good with the closure of our outpost, the Taliban attacked the ABP in the wake of each Marine advisor visit, often within hours of our trucks' departure. Even on a local level, the Taliban seemed to send a consistent message: *we are lying in wait, ready to strike when the Americans leave.* The ABP were scared, and I wanted to deliver them a confidence-boosting win before we left and pulled up the ladder behind us. I also wanted to kick the Taliban in the teeth and disrupt their increasingly brazen attacks on the ABP each time the Marine convoys rolled out of town.

Borrowing a tactic used to insert sniper teams and observation posts in hostile territory, I devised a plan to exploit the Taliban's predictability ██████████████████████████████████████ ████████████████. We would drive our trucks to TCP 3 just like any other visit with 1st Tolai, conduct an overt foot patrol to spotlight our presence, and then our trucks would drive back to Taghaz Station. Only this time our trucks would be empty aside from skeleton crews to serve as drivers and turret gunners; my

Marines and I would remain with the ABP, ready to help repel any Taliban attack with the benefit of our night vision devices and thermal optics. As I did with any proposal for the boss, I first ran it by Captain Quinn.

Captain Quinn was Major Select's deputy, dual-hatting as the team's executive officer and operations officer. With a wiry frame and cauliflower ears from his days as a wrestler, Captain Quinn presented an easy demeanor but had an unmistakable insecurity about him. As he also came from 1/5, I had heard an enlightening story about him as a platoon commander; then-Lieutenant Quinn had made a big show of weighing down his pack with canned goods on a battalion hike, only to collapse along the way and end up in the medical truck. The shame of falling out of formation in front of the whole battalion probably weighed on him more heavily than the cans had. His failed stunt undoubtedly had a role in his subsequent reassignment when they deployed to Sangin; Quinn was sent from his platoon to join a team advising the Afghan National Army. It worked to our benefit, as his insights from that tour made him a valuable member of our team and bought him influence with Major Select.

Captain Quinn had spent the first four months of his advisor tour in Sangin without ever seeing or exchanging fire with the Taliban, so he empathized with my desire to trap and hunt after months of chasing ghosts. With such an empathetic ally, all getting his support took was a general explanation of my concept to bait the Taliban into attacking us. We talked through some of the details, and then Captain Quinn went to pitch it to Major Select. While I could call most of my own shots at the Tolai, Major Select was our overall mission commander and had to approve every operation outside the wire. I worried this might be a bit too aggressive for his risk tolerance; but, to my delight, Major Select approved.

* * *

Major Select was not yet a major, but since he was a captain selected for promotion the following year, the higher-ups signed off on his nomination to lead the team. As a former platoon commander in a reconnaissance battalion, Major Select had come to 1/5 with a solid reputation and then further cemented it in Sangin. Midway through that deployment, he stepped up to take command of Bravo Company after the original commander, while rushing to support the scene of a mass-casualty IED blast, was himself blown up by a secondary IED. Major Select was a steady hand at the helm of the unit in the most dangerous sector of the most violent district in the entire country. But whatever confidence Major Select's résumé inspired was immediately undermined by his appearance in a Kevlar helmet and ballistic plate carrier vest. Major Select was what Marines called a "gear bomb"—a mess of randomly organized pouches for his magazines, radio, grenade, compass, maps, tourniquets, antennas, zip ties, night vision optics, medical kit, and several others with no discernible purpose. Add to that a spiderweb of strings serving to "dummy-cord" each item directly to the vest in case they absconded from their respective pouches. He graced us with refreshing moments of comic relief whenever he got stuck popping into or dropping out of a truck's gun turret.

Like a good senior enlisted Marine, Gunnery Sergeant Jackson did his best to square away the gear of his officer-in-charge, but his powers were limited. Gunny Jackson looked to have fought in every American battle since Vietnam, and his experience nearly matched the appearance. His role as the Advisor Team Chief was to offer his sage counsel to Major Select and the Afghan unit's senior enlisted men, as well as to help sort out logistical and administrative issues for our team.

The rest of the team's headquarters section was a slew of lieutenants randomly plucked from different units across Camp Pendleton and sent to advise within their specialties and serve those same roles for the team. The original adjutant assigned to cover our administrative tasks suffered some side effects from his smallpox vaccine and lashed out at the corpsman who gave it to him in an unprofessional outburst. He was replaced just a month before we deployed with a more even-keeled colleague of mine from our early days in Quantico, Lieutenant Ramsey. After the initial few weeks when I was slated as the team's intelligence officer, a human intelligence unit eventually coughed up Lieutenant Ames, a thoughtful and newly wed redhead. Our burly and fun-loving logistics officer, Lieutenant Sullivan, brought his credo-turned-catchphrase "it's whatever" to many situations in dire need of radical acceptance. "Sully" led by example, graciously offering his cheek to then-Lieutenant Quinn after losing the Ambien slap-bet on the flight from Alaska to Kyrgyzstan. An artillery battery sent the amiable Lieutenant Teller to serve as the team's fire support officer, assistant operations officer, training advisor, 3rd Tolai advisor, and a handful of other random duties. We were also blessed with a joint terminal aircraft controller (JTAC), a baby-faced but serious professional who demanded the respect of always being addressed by his rank: Sergeant Polk.

The remaining Marines and corpsmen on the team were organized into two operational sections, Alpha and Bravo. Bravo Section was initially led by Captain Everett, a communications officer by trade. Before we deployed, he switched roles with our officially assigned "comm-o," Lieutenant Maynard, who felt more comfortable with responsibilities outside his pedigree. Backing up Lieutenant Maynard with years of leadership experience in the infantry was Bravo's Section Chief, Staff Sergeant Ortega. Another infantryman, Sergeant Diaz, joined as Bravo's driver/gunner midway through the workup after the original team member broke his ankle during training. The final addition to Bravo Section was Doc Matias, a cheerful corpsman who came with Doc O'Connor from the 1st Marine Regiment.

Relieved to drop my charade as the intelligence officer after delivering just a couple of briefs, I had the honor of leading Alpha Section. My right-hand man was Staff Sergeant Brian Pulst Jr., the very image of a Marine, complete with the linebacker build, deep voice, love of hard rock, and forearm tattoo of a black skull. As a combat engineer notching two prior deployments in Ramadi, Iraq, and a third in Helmand Province, Staff Sergeant Pulst brought a wealth of counter-IED knowledge and a seasoned non-commissioned officer's resourcefulness. Doc O'Connor was assigned to be my section's medic and medical advisor, and soon proved himself to be as good as an additional Marine when it came to tactics and combat skills. Major Select also assigned me the two Sangin veterans who volunteered from 1/5: Corporal Palacios and Lance Corporal Malone. While they were designated to serve as truck drivers and machine-gunners, I added "advisor" to both of their job descriptions in my official paperwork to acknowledge that their value to the mission extended beyond driving and shooting. As collateral duties, Corporal Palacios took charge of all our machine-gun maintenance, and Lance Corporal Malone became our vehicle maintenance supervisor. In time, I would realize how lucky I was to have these men in my corner.

* * *

We assembled for the first time in May 2012 at a collection of trailers perched on a hill in Camp Pendleton's Del Mar Beach area: Advisor Training Cell (ATC). Here, ad hoc teams of Marines and Navy corpsmen trained together before deploying as foreign forces advisor teams. The regular units we all came from were loath to lose competent personnel, but the orders to fill these positions trickled down all the same. The resulting teams drew from all military occupational specialties and ranks, which were often not an exact match for the job description, starting each group with a baseline of diversity in competencies and experiences. Part of this was intentional; since the teams were going to advise the Afghan equivalents of infantry battalions, each needed to have advisor corollaries for battalion-level functions of administration, intelligence, operations, logistics, and communications. The rest of the variance was simply a function of whoever units were willing and able to send. From such an amalgamation of talent, we had just five months to become a cohesive team.

The ATC curriculum was partially oriented toward preparing for officer-to-officer advising engagements and building the cultural and social skills to do so successfully. Subject matter experts and former advisors provided our instruction in counterinsurgency doctrine, Afghan culture, and Pashto language. These soft skills were vaguely familiar to a lot of the team members from prior deployments, but never carried as much importance. The bulk of the training, however, was to develop tactical, technical, and procedural competencies so we could function independently on dismounted foot patrols and armored truck convoys. We drilled in basic weapons skills; radio programming; searches of personnel and vehicles; and navigation by map/compass, GPS, and the computerized Blue Force Tracker system installed in every truck. We focused an entire week on learning about the IED threat environment, including classes on the components of homemade explosives and the ever-evolving trends in Taliban tactics.

Over the years of combat with coalition forces, iron truly sharpened iron. As one ATC instructor put it, every time Marines left the wire, they trained the Taliban. From observing thousands of Marine patrols, the Taliban learned the types of terrain Marines hid behind for cover when shot at, planted IEDs in those berms, treelines, and structures, and then fired on the patrols when they neared their prepared kill zone. The Taliban watched corpsmen and Marines rush to render first aid to IED-strike casualties, and buried secondary IEDs to blow up those first responders. They set up hoax devices or sent "informants" with phony tips to lure Marines into target areas where bombs lay waiting. They planted conspicuous explosives with anti-tamper devices and pressure-release switches to target explosive ordnance disposal (EOD) technicians or Afghan forces who tried to remove the obvious hazards. Marines used metal detectors to sweep a clear lane at the front of every foot patrol, and the Taliban offset the metallic batteries that powered the ignition switch or built devices with low metallic components. As we scanned the ground in front of each patrol, the Taliban encased the bombs in ceramic pots or plastic containers, and installed them aboveground in trees and walls. Marines equipped every mounted or dismounted patrol with electronic countermeasures to detect and jam incoming radio frequencies from remote-control devices, and the Taliban reverted to pull cords or victim-initiated switches like pressure plates. The lead truck in every convoy pushed a mine-roller to preemptively trigger any pressure plates, and the Taliban offset the explosive charge from the pressure plates by the exact distance to strike the vehicle, rather than the roller.

Despite the endless resources and ingenuity of the American military-industrial machine, there was no silver bullet to defeat the IED threat. So we did all we could to adapt. We upgraded our metal detectors from Vallons to CMD2s, which could also detect non-metallic IED components when properly calibrated to the soil density. We varied patrol routes and planned them to avoid the easily trod footpaths, often traveling through or across deep aqueducts that checkered the farming villages of the Helmand River Valley. Movement was slow and deliberate; the lead man in the patrol looked for signs of buried bombs and swept across the ground before him with the metal detector; the next Marine in line scanned for threats aboveground and marked the cleared path with dash-dotted lines of shaving cream. Medevac helicopters would only land once the Marines on the ground had swept the landing zone to ensure that it was free of IEDs. We exchanged our standard fatigues for special flame-retardant uniforms and gloves. And, to protect our virility, we tolerated the chafing of special ballistic underwear and donned a desert camouflage-patterned "blast diaper" as an outermost layer.

Even with every precaution, we still expected casualties. Since the teams going through ATC were small, everyone went through a two-week-long Combat Life Saving certification course. It was nowhere close to the training of a Navy corpsman or an Army medic, but it was a step above the Marine Corps's baseline, which essentially just told Marines where to find tourniquets and pressure bandages in their individual first-aid kits. After the classroom instruction, the practical application segments of the course were physically and psychologically intense. Veteran amputees volunteered to play realistic casualties who panicked and fought us as we attempted to fix tourniquets on them while slippery fake blood squirted all over our hands and gear. I failed my first attempt at the final test when one of the tourniquets I applied slid down my screaming, squirming casualty's slick "bloody" stump, and he "bled out." The standards were nearly as high as the stakes. Our follow-on Live Tissue course was scrapped after an animal rights protest group managed to track down and picket the location of the facility where Navy corpsmen drugged up and wounded pigs so Marines could get more realistic practice.

Not all the training was stressful. We spent two whole weeks driving all around the hills and canyons of Camp Pendleton, day and night, to complete licensing courses for the up-armored Humvee, Mine Resistant Ambush Protected (MRAP) truck, and MRAP All-Terrain Vehicle (MATV—a very Marine Corps acronym within an acronym). Then there was live-fire training for the machine guns we would mount in those trucks' turrets: the M240B 7.62mm medium machine gun, the M2 "ma deuce".50 caliber heavy machine gun, and the Mk-19 40mm automatic grenade launcher. Training, certification, and licensing courses like these were normally reserved for enlisted Marines and junior non-commissioned officers—the ranks that ordinarily led a four-person fire team, not a lieutenant who typically led a platoon of dozens. After being an officer-in-charge of several courses and ranges like these during my stint as a platoon commander, it was fun to become a participant again.

We filled our free time in the schedule by practicing our predetermined immediate actions or "battle drills" for various patrolling scenarios. We rehearsed calling for fire support from mortars or artillery over our handheld radios. We took turns scanning the ground with metal detectors where Staff Sergeant Pulst had planted various IED parts and components. Unless we had to report in early to draw our weapons out of the armory or hop on buses for transport to another training area, our days started at 0600 with physical training. On Mondays and Fridays, Major Select took the whole team for runs on the beach, stopping periodically for calisthenics. I led my section's workouts on Wednesdays and made it an opportunity for extra language drills by requiring everyone to count repetitions out loud in Pashto.

Language training had become my pet project. As soon as I found out the unit we would be advising was comprised of Afghans local to that area, where the prominent language was Pashto, I purchased a textbook and downloaded DOD resources to teach myself. I used my time commuting up and down the Five (Interstate Five) to listen to and practice along with Pimsleur audio lessons. Major Select eventually asked me to lead supplemental Pashto classes once our formal training block was over. In fact, the default plan for our language instruction was split between Pashto

and Dari; but having done my research on where we were going
and the composition of our Afghan unit, I requested in advance
that we spend both weeks on Pashto. I had to be *that guy* again
when the instructor began teaching the northern Pashto dialect.

"They'll understand what you say just fine," the instructor
offered to placate my concern.

"I think it might also help for us to understand what *they* say,"
I pressed.

Having studied some Modern Standard Arabic, Jordanian
dialect, Lebanese dialect, and Farsi in college, I knew enough to
understand how regional differences could be critical to effective
communication. The instructor did his best to hide his annoyance,
and relented. I like to think that it mattered.

The final segment of our pre-deployment workup was a month
at Advisor Training Group (ATG) in the Mojave Desert of
Twenty-Nine Palms, California. In addition to the oppressive
August heat, Twenty-Nine Palms offered Marines permissive and
expansive live-fire ranges, except when an endangered desert tor-
toise wandered in to shut down training. Thankfully, our shelled
friends allowed us all the live-fire training on the ATG schedule.
We practiced countering an ambush from our vehicles and learned
how to operate foreign weapons like Dragunov sniper rifles,
AK-47s, and Kalashnikov-style machine guns. On top of that,
we were supplied with extra ammunition and free time to train at
our discretion. There was some additional classroom instruction
on counterinsurgency theory, differences between advising police
versus military personnel, how to use an interpreter, and cultural
sensitivity. The instructors also recited a litany of facts to impress
the gravity of our everyday challenges upon us: we were up against
an 11 percent literacy rate, routine and public beatings of children
by their parents, and the lawful collection of "taxes" by Afghan

police, to name just a few. Ethical and practical complications abounded, and many were beyond the scope of our authority and ability to control. Setting appropriate expectations made good prophylaxis for headaches.

Ranges and classrooms were available on any base, but the reason units trained in Twenty-Nine Palms before deploying to Afghanistan was the similar environment. Not only did the desert approximate some of the terrain features we would encounter in Afghanistan, but the massive ensemble of Afghan actors who worked at the base created ideal simulations of our future engagements with the Afghan forces and population. These actors far surpassed the value offered by the traditional role players in Marine Corps training: Marines playing terrorist caricatures, shouting rudimentary Arabic phrases they'd picked up on previous deployments. ATG trainers observed, evaluated, and provided feedback to us from our scenario-based interactions with these role players. We learned to become diplomats and practiced parrying some of the common conversational maneuvers of our pretend partners: requests to promise some deliverable; noncommittal responses to advice; blatant lies; and subtle hostility.

We practiced our purpose-driven people-pleasing, but steeled ourselves for battle. Our teams assembled for pre-deployment training in 2012, a year when Afghan forces killed so many Americans, advisors and trainers in particular, that the term green-on-blue entered common parlance. In just one two-week period that August, there were eight such attacks that killed ten coalition servicemembers, one of whom was Corporal Palacios's forward-deployed roommate. The best we could do for Corporal Palacios was to give him an afternoon off from training to help the Marine's bereaved parents identify and sort through their son's belongings in the house they shared in Carlsbad. By the end of the year, green-on-blue attacks would account for 15 percent of all coalition deaths[10] and an unknown number of wounded—official

NATO reporting did not collect statistics on non-fatal attacks. We even worried that our whole deployment might be scrapped as a result of all the green-on-blue attacks that September, when the NATO mission commander issued an order to cease all partnered operations with the Afghans.[11] Around the same time, U.S. Special Operations Forces suspended their training program for about one thousand Afghan Local Police.[12] These changes turned out to be temporary, buying time to reassess security posture and vetting methods. They weren't meant to signal a conclusion that developing the ANSF was not worth risking American lives. But the question lingered: Why should Americans continue to stick their necks out for their increasingly hostile Afghan partners?

Ours was not to reason why. So, rather than stick our necks out, we turtled up. Conceding that we would have to spend 50 percent of our time acting as bodyguards for each other, we made it protocol to post Marines with a singular focus on the insider threat as "guardian angels" both outside and within the room, as discreetly as possible, during every engagement with the Afghans. The majority of insider attacks were not Taliban infiltrators, as much as their spokesmen liked to claim credit, nor were they part of a coordinated strategy to sabotage the working relationship between coalition and Afghan forces (though they did have that effect). The way the trends looked, most of the green-on-blue attacks resulted from personal grievances against specific coalition servicemembers, often stemming from a cultural faux pas and damaged honor. And so our emphasis on cultural competence and developing rapport had an ulterior motive: staying alive.

While we hoped that building good relationships would save us, we prepared for the worst. In addition to our tactical training for patrols, vehicle convoys, and other combat operations, we practiced killing our Afghan partners. Retired special operators working for the military contractor Blue Canopy put on a pseudo-scientific training session on how to recognize insider threats by reading facial microexpressions. The class was followed by more violent sessions in which we were confronted with an Afghan gunman during a meeting. We trained these scenarios with live rounds, drawing our M9 Beretta pistols from behind a desk and shooting at paper targets that represented an Afghan soldier or policeman. We would never be unarmed around the Afghans, and always had at least one rifle and radio in the room. We would never sit with our backs to the door or even across from one another, since that created a risk of friendly fire. As these practices undoubtedly created an atmosphere of distrust and undermined our efforts to build rapport, we worried that it could be a self-fulfilling prophecy.

The ATG instructors who'd been following us around with clipboards, checklists, and color-coded spreadsheets for the better part of a month finally signed off on our team's "readiness" to deploy. Not that there was anyone else more "ready" to send if we had failed to meet their standards, but the Marine Corps wanted some metrics to tell us what we already knew: we were going. So with some parting wisdom—don't chew or spit tobacco during meetings with your Afghan counterparts—we returned to Camp Pendleton in early September to square ourselves away administratively. This meant a trip over to the base legal services office, where we added the names of family members to boilerplate forms to execute our last wills and powers of attorney.

Then the only thing standing between us and a block of pre-deployment leave was a comprehensive inventory of everyone's pack list. We met in a covered parking lot where everyone in my section dumped their gear on tarps so I could inspect each item on the list and note delinquencies to reinspect when we returned from leave. When we finished, Staff Sergeant Pulst produced a bag of Saint Michael the Archangel medallions in honor of the patron saint of the Marine Corps, which the priest had blessed for him on the day of his wedding. We all graciously accepted the talismans, and I added mine to the inside of my ballistic plate carrier vest, where I already had affixed an amulet of Saint Christopher, protector of travelers. Not that we were a particularly superstitious group, but there sure weren't any atheists in our foxholes.

At the end of September we had two weeks of pre-deployment leave to make final arrangements and soak in as much as we could of what we loved and were leaving behind. Parents moved in to help wives with childcare, or, like Doc O'Connor's family, wives and children moved back in with parents. Bachelors like myself had packed our lives into storage units, leaving a key with a family member or friend on the facility access list. Corporal Palacios finalized a divorce from "the first woman who smiled at [him]" when he got back from Afghanistan in 2008. They had gotten married four months later, then she left him in 2010 while he was deployed on the 31st MEU. On the other side of the spectrum, Lance Corporal Malone married his high school sweetheart in the weeks before we left. And because junior Marines' nuptials on the eve of a deployment too often resulted in empty bank accounts and a Dear John letter, Staff Sergeant Pulst formally counseled Malone to ensure it was the real deal. It was.

I flew back East to visit friends and family in New York and Massachusetts. Knowing it all was fleeting, possibly forever, everything felt more poignant and so appeared more beautiful. I recalled the words of Dostoevsky's *Idiot*, marveling "what beautiful things there are at every step, that even the most hopeless man must feel to be beautiful! Look at a child! Look at God's sunrise! Look at the grass, how it grows! Look at the eyes that gaze at you."[13] A serene nap on the floor with my family's Bernese mountain dog in Syracuse; blasting Mumford & Sons' "Below My Feet" while I drove through the rain to visit friends in Boston; the warm tingle of the Jameson shots I didn't need but that those friends bought for me anyway; the prophetic kiss on my cheek from a girl I hadn't seen since college but would eventually marry—death's haunting of these moments only made them more cherished. Yet, the joy and gratitude these experiences delivered came with a bone-deep sorrow at their impermanence, blending into a bittersweet sense of peaceful resignation.

Wives, children, parents, siblings, and girlfriends who lived locally or traveled for the occasion met us at a brick building where a Family Readiness Officer put together a farewell reception. I said my goodbyes back East and asked my family not to come; I thought dealing with their emotions would be a distraction while I was on the clock and with my Marines. I spent the majority of the time alone, sitting outside in the dark, sending texts and making calls while my phone still had service. I had never been a smoker, but in my left shoulder pocket next to a laminated casualty card I carried a pack of "rapport-builders"—just one per day, I told myself—and drew a cigarette to mark the occasion. The nicotine helped relieve the pressure I felt watching my Marines' final moments with their families.

By this—their fourth farewell—it had almost become a ritual for Staff Sergeant Pulst's wife to drop him off with all his bags and "rip off the Band-Aid" by skipping the reception. Only this time, Staff Sergeant Pulst's three-year-old son understood what was happening, and the Band-Aid was that much stickier. Doc O'Connor had said goodbye before his previous deployment on the 13th MEU, but that seemed easy compared to this, leaving his wife with their little blond toddler and weeks-old infant to go into battle. As if to impress my responsibility upon me, Corporal Palacios introduced me to his parents and little brother, who had come to see him off. Not much was said, and it didn't need to be. His father, who had fled El Salvador's civil war in the 1980s, shook my hand firmly and looked me in the eye with a trusting, glassy-eyed gaze. *Take care of my son, and yourself.* If saying

goodbye became easier for military families at successive deployments, I saw no sign of it.

We quietly boarded a white school bus and rumbled along in
the dead of night from Camp Pendleton to Ontario International
Airport outside Los Angeles. After several hours sitting around
doing nothing, we boarded a commercial aircraft not unlike any
other civilian flight, except we all carried weapons. All of our serialized weapons and optics came with us into the aircraft cabin so I
could lay eyes on each item at every juncture. In the early hours of
the morning, we landed in Anchorage, Alaska, for a short layover,
and then we made the longest leg of the trip to Manas, Kyrgyzstan.
We spent three days eating and working out in the old Soviet satellite state, then packed into a C-17 cargo plane and spiraled down
to the largest base in Afghanistan's Helmand Province.

Adjoined by Camp Bastion airfield and the Afghan National
Army's Camp Shorabak, Camp Leatherneck sprawled over forty
square miles of tents, air-conditioned trailers, shipping containers, and Hesco barriers—stacks of giant wire-framed canvas bags
packed with dirt. The base functioned like a city, complete with
indoor plumbing, gyms, shooting ranges, a Pizza Hut, a bazaar,
and its own transportation system with multiple bus routes. We
spent six days living on cots in a giant tent while we marched
through a series of in-processing briefs, then loaded up on a
CH-53 "Shitter"—a helicopter not obviously nicknamed for the
appearance of pooping Marines down the exit ramp in the rear,
but for the tendency of its internal components to spew grease on
its occupants while in flight—and attempted to fly down to where
our work would begin. A mechanical issue in the Shitter's hydrau-
lic system turned us around mid-flight and grounded us back at
Bastion airfield, which had been overrun by Taliban raiders three
weeks earlier.

One night during our Bastion interlude, I struck up a conversation with a Marine sitting next to me on the bench of the bus

stop. He had witnessed the Taliban raid firsthand and described the utter chaos that unfolded that night to the soundtrack of explosions, gunfire, and the Troops-in-Contact alarm; how panic had spread across the airfield as they saw fighter-jet fuel bladders erupting in fireballs. Fifteen Taliban disguised in U.S. Army uniforms had crept up a wadi—a dry creek bed—on the eastern side of the base's twenty-five-mile perimeter near an unmanned guard tower. They breached a thirty-foot chain-link fence and single-strand concertina wire, split into three teams, and launched simultaneous attacks on the airfield with machine guns, rockets, and grenades. While flight crews and pilots slipped into flak jackets, grabbed rifles, and battled it out like infantrymen, a standby team of helicopter pilots scrambled to get airborne and provided close air support until a British quick reaction force rounded up the remaining insurgents. By the time fourteen of the infiltrators were killed and the remaining fighter was captured, two Marines were dead and another seventeen coalition members wounded. Six American fighter jets were completely destroyed, with several other aircraft, vehicles, and facilities severely damaged, amounting to hundreds of millions of dollars in financial loss.[14]

The improvements to security posture that were implemented in the immediate aftermath gave me comfort that I would never be more safe at Bastion than I was in the wake of that battle. Especially since, at that time, Prince Harry of Wales was stationed at Bastion as a Cobra attack helicopter pilot for the United Kingdom, and his security detail alone was a force to be reckoned with. However, these changes demonstrated to investigators that no lack of resources could excuse the responsible officers. The resulting investigation forced the retirement of a pair of Marine two-star generals for failing to employ adequate security measures at the base. Some of the blame was misdirected: despite the generals' request for more troops months earlier, the Pentagon stuck to the scheduled reduction of forces in the region from seventeen thousand down to seven thousand in the six months prior to the attack; and guard-tower duty on Camp Leatherneck's perimeter had been delegated to a small contingent of the Tonga Defense Services. Nevertheless, the generals' decision to cut the staffing of the Marine unit conducting security patrols outside the wire fell squarely on their shoulders. And so as these top generals struggled to manage their mission with fewer personnel, the enemy was able to exploit the drawdown in forces to strike at a key asset: American aircraft.

The Taliban held American air power in much higher regard than my team did, at least on first impression. It took several days to source us a functional Shitter. While we stood by for our lift, we squatted in a building used as a pre-flight staging area and relished our remaining days with ready access to a contractor-run chow hall that exceeded the quality and menu diversity of most college cafeterias. By the time our ride was ready, the sheer boredom of our week between Leatherneck and Bastion had doubled my daily ration of rapport-builders from one to two. I bore witness to what the reluctant smoker Eugene Sledge had observed of his time as an infantry Marine in World War II: "War is mostly waiting."[15] Whatever else my war would be, when our long-awaited Shitter finally dumped us into a whirling cloud of dust outside the gates of COP Taghaz, I was raring to go find out.

Chapter Four

Command Dynamics

19 JAN 2013

Major Select's approval of my stay-behind ambush was promising, but he was not the ultimate authority. Such was the inherent challenge of being an advisor as opposed to a unit commander: instead of giving an order, we had to influence the Afghans' decision-making. The team had adopted the title of a popular Christopher Nolan film to describe how we hoped to get the Afghans to do what we wanted by convincing them it was their own idea. So now my job, as I saw it, was to *Inception* the 1st Tolai commander into endorsing my plan. But I knew that getting him to do anything would be a challenge, from both my personal experience and the reputation that preceded him. The Marine I replaced had warned me.

* * *

Following our initial intelligence brief at COP Taghaz on October 22, 2012, a Marine lieutenant wearing dirty cammies and a crushed boonie cover plopped on his head introduced himself as "Tim" with the drawl of a native Texan. Tim was an aviation maintenance officer, originally stationed in Yuma, Arizona, where he led a team that kept an ancient fleet of Harrier jets in the air. It was a far cry from advising the ABP on ground combat operations; but, like every Marine officer—even JAGs and pilots—Tim had six months of technical and tactical training at the Basic Officer Course in Quantico to fall back on. Advanced infantry training was important, but there was no better teacher than experience. Tim was the authority on 1st Tolai after seven months with them, and I had just three days to learn all I could from him. As we chatted, Tim handed me a turnover binder. He'd typed up the pages inside to document several significant events in the Tolai's short and unfortunate history.

1st Tolai's original mission was to provide security at an airfield in Lashkar Gah. Aside from the occasional rotation down to a patrol base in Khan Neshin District, the ABP of the 1st Tolai did not patrol or conduct large operations. They lived in a large city, went home to their families at the end of each day, and had access to running water, medical care, air-conditioned facilities, cell-phone reception, alcohol, drugs, and (relatively) free-spirited women.

In the early winter months of 2012, hundreds of Marines swept through Khan Neshin District and established patrol bases in the area. Then the ABP 6th Zone commander sent 1st Kandak down the river in force. 1st Tolai planted their flag at Patrol Base (PB) Paygel, a remote and austere outpost. Their mission there was to interdict contraband traffic moving across the Helmand River at the nearby Dishu ferry, where drugs, guns, explosives, and fighters flowed into Khan Neshin and farther north. It was a drastic overnight transformation of their living conditions, and the ABP of 1st Tolai were beyond displeased. They were so hostile toward their new station that most patrolmen threatened to desert on a weekly basis.

Leading the Tolai in these challenging times was Haji Samad, a commander admired and respected by the ABP and Marine advisors alike. The IED blast that killed him in April 2012 sent shock waves through the unit, and it never recovered. When it came to the succession of command, the edicts of Pashtun culture had stronger, deeper roots than a Western-style military rank hierarchy. So most of the ABP, who were related to Haji Samad in some way, believed Haji Samad's youthful and ambitious nephew, Farid Khan, was the rightful heir to the command despite the fact that he was not a commissioned officer. When the Afghan Ministry of Interior appointed Baddar Gul as the new commander of 1st Tolai, Farid Khan did everything he could to undermine his new boss, who many observed to be corrupt, lazy, and self-serving. Farid Khan's petitions to the Kandak and Zone commanders fell on deaf ears, so the two rivals reached an agreement on their own: Farid Khan would remain in command of eight patrolmen, and Baddar Gul would command the rest. Before long, Farid Khan absconded with his eight loyalists to 2nd Tolai's patrol base in Sre Kala.

Under Baddar Gul's command, the men of 1st Tolai languished. The local Marine commander at the time required every patrol to have a dozen or so Marines and a handful of Afghans. The Marines led the patrols, excluded the ABP from the planning process, and treated them as little more than a tool for patting down the local Afghans they encountered. Paygel was not a populated area, and the patrols encountered the same individuals every day. The ABP left the patrol base on their own four to five times per day, usually to make purchases at the one shop in the village, fill jugs of water from the river, extort the locals, or abuse narcotics. The ABP referred to each of these outings as a "patrol" and insisted they were doing police work, but Marine observational skills easily pierced the thin veneer of those cover stories. Over the course of these months, the harsh living conditions at PB Paygel combined with Baddar Gul's incompetent leadership to chip away at the roster of forty-three ABP in the Tolai. By the time Paygel was leveled and the Tolai moved northeast to Gherdai, there were only twenty-one ABP remaining.

At PB Gherdai, the Tolai was responsible for patrolling a strip of small villages along about ten kilometers of the Helmand River stretching southwest from Taghaz Station. At night, they shone spotlights from Hesco watchtowers and took turns standing watch in two-hour shifts. Spread between the three fixed posts at the newly constructed PB Gherdai, the two posts at TCP 3, and whatever patrols they could muster, the men of 1st Tolai were hanging on by a thread.

In early July 2012, Baddar Gul disappeared from the Tolai without any explanation or advance notice. The acting Kandak commander tagged Farid Khan to return as the interim leader of the Tolai. Around this time, the advisors and Marines pulled back from PB Gherdai to consolidate at COP Taghaz, and the Tolai's self-sufficiency improved dramatically. Tim and his team continued to make weekly visits to Gherdai, but Farid Khan asked for little assistance and the Tolai's roster grew. About once per month the Tolai encountered small arms fire, found IEDs, located weapons caches, and seized drug stashes, each time while operating without any Marines. And aside from Haji Samad, neither the Taliban nor ABP suffered any casualties.

Tim documented one example of their proficiency in August 2012, when a patrol was engaged by two or three Taliban, returned fire, called for a Quick Reaction Force (QRF) from the patrol base, and promptly reported the engagement to the Kandak at Taghaz Station. At the Kandak's request, the Marines called in a fighter jet to do a low flyover as a show of force. By Tim's assessment, none of this would have been possible when the Tolai first deployed to Paygel in April, or at any time during Baddar Gul's command. Tim was beginning to feel hopeful.

Then Baddar Gul showed up out of the blue in late September 2012 and the acting Kandak commander reinstated his command.

Farid Khan led a mutiny in protest and left with twenty-five ABP
to petition the 6th Zone commander in Lashkar Gah for redress.
The ploy backfired; not only did the 6th Zone commander deny
Farid Khan's request, he also placed Farid Khan and his crew
under house arrest. After a week on home confinement, the Zone
commander sent them back to Taghaz for the Kandak commander
to deal with however he saw fit. As the fate of the mutineers was
still up in the air when my team took over from Tim's, he counseled against any intervention.

"Whatever happens needs to be an Afghan solution to a most
definite Afghan problem." Tim understood the war better than
any of us.

When I took over from Tim in October 2012, 1st Tolai had
around twenty bodies—far fewer than the eighty-nine each
Tolai rated on paper. The vast majority of the patrolmen were
recent transfers from 3rd Tolai who were sent to backfill the
rebelling Farid Khan loyalists. All but four of the ABP were
illiterate and none could read a map, much less navigate by one.
Simple arithmetic was a scarcity; and for many, an inability to
count frustrated the most simple tasks. They had no medic at
the Tolai and no explosive ordnance disposal capability, even at
the Kandak level. Besides a designated leader and some specific
patrolmen assigned to TCP 3, there was no internal organization
or chain of command, just the Tolai commander sitting above a
few sergeants and the patrolmen.

Despite all this, Tim's assessment of the Tolai, having observed
them actually function for a few months under Farid Khan, read
optimistic:

> Bottom line: The ABP in 1st Tolai have the required
> skill sets to operate as a viable police force. However,

how they execute their duties will be a direct reflection
of whatever Tolai Commander is in place.

Enter Baddar Gul. He looked like he was in his sixties, so
accounting for the unkind Helmand sun and perennial state of
warfare, I figured him for somewhere around forty-five. He stood
six feet or so, but his lankiness gave him the appearance of being
taller; save for the modest gut, I would have called him skinny.
When I met him, he was cleanly shaven (Tim pointed out to me
that this was for the special occasion) except for the mustache
that drooped far around the corners of his lips. Narrow-set eyes,
within the frame of his mustache, and an easygoing smile gave
him a goofy expression. The poorly mended damage to the skin
below his chin and the deformed, almost collapsed, ear with
crusting pus oozing from the center told the story of how he'd
survived an IED blast without a word. His mangled ear earned
him the nickname "Nemo" among the Marines on Tim's team,
after the fish with the "lucky" malformed fin in the animated
Pixar movie. His uniform seemed a size too small, leaving a
few inches between his cuffs and his wrists, which were bare—
Afghans loved to repeat the adage "you have the watch, we
have the time." Rank insignia of a lieutenant was scratched on
his uniform with a blue ball-point pen. With a home, wife, four
daughters, and a one-year-old son back in Lashkar Gah, Baddar
Gul had some higher priorities than the security of a few villages
out in no-man's-land.

Eventually I received a roster of the 1st Tolai ABP, and then
gradually learned who was worth their salt, who was just collecting a paycheck, who was a possible insider threat, and who was
a "ghost soldier," existing only on paper for the sole purpose of
having their wages sent to the unit's commander. As far as the
Tolai dynamics, Tim wrote up his summary:

If interactions with the Tolai and between the ABP seems like Afghan "Days of Our Lives" it is because that's how it is. Rather than operate on an agreed upon/understood set of rules and regulations . . . or even simple logic, the ABP make emotion-based decisions. They will get mad and act as if the world is going to end if "X" does or doesn't happen. However, if the relationship with the advisors is good they will get over it quickly.

They recognize and respect rank but that is about as far as it goes. A lot of how leave gets granted, jobs get assigned, and tasks are divided up is based on family or friendship.

The average member of 1st Tolai has a 2nd or 3rd grade *Afghan* education, if they have any education at all. Try to remember this when interacting with them. How would you react to circumstance "X" if you had little education and grew up in a third world country? How would you react if you had grown up in a world with constant war? It will be frustrating. At times you will feel like you are arguing with or trying to logic with a 3rd grader, because you are.

It is important to remember that their system might not be the most efficient or fair in your opinion but it is THEIR system. Some of the ABP have been fighting their whole lives and have a great baseline of what is normal. Others, not so much. As long as they make THEIR system work and meet Commander's intent, that is what counts. Their system or plan, no matter how "flawed," is better than a system or plan you come up with and shove down their throats.

While brutally condescending, Tim's attitude was not born of arrogance or bigotry; it was clear that Tim granted the Afghans a handicap out of empathy. His intent was not to demean, but to set realistic expectations that might obviate frustration and encourage patience.

But how could we be patient when we were running out of time? Troop numbers were back down to pre-2010 surge levels by the time my team had even landed in Taghaz, with a full withdrawal on schedule to conclude at the end of the combat mission in 2014. Base closures were fixed on the calendar, which left us only two months before COP Taghaz would be reduced to just a berm-enclosed "Annex" where we could park our trucks and sleep under the stars on our subsequent visits. With the drawdown in forces likewise set in stone, we were explicitly told there were no replacements coming to relieve our team.

That left three possible outcomes for our mission and the ABP of 1st Kandak: we did our jobs so well that the Kandak was truly independent by the time we departed; we left them despite assessing that they were not ready to sustain the fight on their own; or we reported them as "independent" without advisors—because they had to be—and gave ourselves a pass on an honest accounting. As the officer-in-charge of our team, Major Select was responsible for completing and reporting periodic assessments of the Kandak's performance. Since there were no Tolai-level evaluation metrics, I was never consulted and never knew exactly what our team submitted. All I knew was that there was more work to be done.

The approaching deadlines lit a fire under our team's collective ass. Of course I didn't expect the ABP to operate with the same proficiency as my platoon of Marines back in Camp Pendleton—hell, I couldn't even expect that of a regular U.S. Army unit. But I did feel a sense of urgency to help in every way I could to prepare them to take on the Taliban alone. We owed them that much, at least.

*   *   *

I made my stay-behind pitch to Baddar Gul on our next visit to
Taghaz. Between standing post in the Annex and serving as a
guardian angel for our headquarters Marines' advising engagements, I found time to call over the Kandak's radios to set up a
meeting. True to form, Baddar Gul forgot about the meeting and
showed up an hour late only after I asked the radio operator at
the Kandak headquarters to send a gentle reminder.

Over cigarettes and tea, we got down to business. First, I
pulled out my notes and hand-drawn map from my debrief of Nur
Muhammad to go over the most recent Taliban attack. Baddar
Gul confirmed everything and added that the Taliban also shot at
them from a machine-gun position on the roof of the clinic—an
abandoned compound we had raided two months earlier. I raised
an eyebrow.

"That's really far." I figured the distance to be around eight
hundred meters.

"No, no, with an AK-47 it's no problem."

This assessment explained some of the hopeless weaponeering I observed of the ABP throughout our time with them. Even
on single-fire mode with a calm, expert shooter, the maximum
effective range of an AK-47 was three hundred meters. Sure, the
bullets would travel farther, but not with any reliable trajectory.
Lance Corporal Malone had the great idea of organizing a live-fire
training to demonstrate the points we tried to make about basic
marksmanship. We just never had the time. Rather than debate
ballistics with Baddar Gul, I moved on.

Baddar Gul shared our alarm at the escalating attacks and
so took little convincing that something needed to be done. I
explained my idea of how he could exploit the Taliban's recent

pattern, and how the ABP could conduct similar operations after visiting certain compounds or shops during patrols in the village. He liked the idea of using more deceptive tactics, even suggesting that the ABP might dress in civilian clothes to disguise their presence from Taliban lookouts. While his lackluster leadership thus far made me doubt he would ever do anything so aggressive, I at least appreciated the display of enthusiasm.

We shook hands and finalized the plan. Bravo Section would set up a radio retransmission site inside TCP 3 and off-load our gear from the trucks, while I took Alpha Section on a short patrol with the ABP to investigate some possible IEDs that Baddar Gul had heard about through a local informant. We figured this was a good opportunity to assess the Tolai's counter-IED tactics, techniques, and procedures, which had been unimpressive to date. Of course, our ulterior motive for the patrol was to skyline the Marine presence, turning heads toward our position, heads that would then watch our trucks drive away at the end of the day. Baddar Gul promised to keep the advisors' presence at TCP 3 a secret, even from the rest of 1st Tolai at PB Gherdai. He was completely on board.

"I would be very happy if the enemy attacked while you were there with us."

"Us too," I assured him.

We returned to COP Castle for another interlude between missions. I wrapped up an ongoing series of instruction on mission planning and the operational orders process for my Marines. They had gained plenty of secondhand experience observing me and others over their many deployments, and now they were learning all the work required behind the scenes. I was preparing them to lead their own convoy, and now they were ready. For this next mission, Staff Sergeant Pulst would be the convoy commander and Corporal Palacios the assistant convoy commander. Staff Sergeant Pulst and I then spent hours working out the details of the stay-behind mission, where I would reassume the lead once we hit the ground. Corporal Palacios submitted our mission request up through 3/9's chain of command for final approvals.

At 1500 on January 22, the team assembled in our office around two maps, where Staff Sergeant Pulst went over the convoy and I briefed our plan for the foot patrol. Alpha Section would drive to TCP 3 in Gherdai, with Bravo Section in support. Headquarters Section would peel off to be on standby as QRF at the Taghaz Annex with a squad of Carnage Marines and three EOD technicians in support. I would remain at TCP 3 with Alpha Section after the foot patrol while Bravo drove the trucks away, luring the local Taliban cell right into the crosshairs of our thermal and ambient light-boosting optics. My intent for the mission, as I briefed, was to assess ABP counter-IED capabilities, bolster their confidence, and improve their public image in the village. A victory would give the ABP some talking points to use on their next patrols in the area to highlight their strength and disparage the Taliban.

We were covering the administrative and logistical details toward the end of the brief when Major Select, who was in a meeting with Bobo-6 and Wake-6 at the time, called Captain Quinn out of the room over the Motorola. A few minutes later, Captain Quinn burst back through the door.

"Stand down."

The whole tent groaned. *Dammit,* I thought, *it was too good to be true.*

The team dispersed while I awaited the details of how we expected Bobo-6 and Wake-6 to micromanage my operation. Ten minutes later, Captain Quinn came back with even worse news than we had imagined: Bobo-6 had just denied us permission to conduct the stay-behind mission.

"You're advisors, not warfighters," Bobo-6 had told Major Select.

It was a brazen insult to all of us and defied our organizational ethos that called every Marine a rifleman. He was wrong, of course: we were both. But I had failed to factor his risk aversion into my planning. Who could have foreseen that we would need to *Inception* our own command into letting us be Marines? Now there would be no stay-behind ambush, and Bobo-6 further mandated that Carnage and EOD would escort us to PB Gherdai as a QRF for our foot patrol. We grumbled our complaints, and I got to reworking the plan.

"It's whatever," Sully reminded us.

It sure was. An hour later, Major Select informed us that Bobo now wanted Carnage and EOD to join our Headquarters Section at Taghaz, and Bravo would join us at Gherdai, as I had originally planned. All the eyes rolled, and I tampered with the plan again. Semper Gumby. Always flexible.

After another round of revisions, I finalized the most aggressive plan Bobo would allow—a mere foot patrol in Gherdai with an overnight in the Taghaz Annex. It was 2200 by the time we finished planning, but I had too much negative energy pent up to go to sleep after fourteen hours of frustrating revisions and re-revisions. So I grabbed my iPod and hit the decrepit treadmill in the COP Castle exercise tent. The endorphins kicked in with full force during the middle of the song "Around the World" by the Red Hot Chili Peppers and turned my night around. Half an hour of treadmill catharsis later, I was buzzing with a runner's high and an artificial sense of accomplishment. All that effort just to end up back where I had started.

Chapter Five

Down the River

January 23, 2013, was a typical winter day in the Helmand River Valley, cold with clear skies. Lance Corporal Malone said it was the day I became a man. I think he may have been right, just not in the way he meant.

With no further interference from Bobo, we mounted the machine guns in our truck turrets, checked all our radios, went through our final pre-combat checklists, and rolled out of COP Castle into the desert. With Staff Sergeant Pulst riding shotgun as the convoy commander, I drove the lead truck with the mine-roller while Lance Corporal Malone kept a watchful eye behind the .50-cal in our turret. Two trucks of our headquarters advisors, two trucks of Carnage Marines, a truck containing Bravo Section, and another truck for our EOD team formed the train between us and our convoy caboose where Corporal Palacios brought up the rear with Doc O'Connor.

The most direct route to Taghaz from COP Castle, named Route Uniform, was twenty miles due west, but it was off limits: it was so heavily mined with Taliban IEDs that it was actually faster to drive a circuitous northern route that took four hours.

We had learned that the hard way. As a result, someone far above us decided that those bombs, while still a risk to local traffic, were not worth our time. We took the long way around and approached Taghaz from the north.

The comforting sight of the aerostat blimp had been gone for a full month by that point. Its absence was an invitation to the Taliban, who had never missed such an opportunity to exploit the gap in our aerial surveillance to plant IEDs. Now that our eye in the sky had gone permanently blind, it made our early fears over the short-term breaks in coverage seem silly. The perceived risk of Taliban activity had been so great that it had often grounded missions to a halt whenever high winds or other weather conditions forced the contractors to temporarily reel in the big white blimp.

*   *   *

The blimp in Taghaz was down for sixteen hours on October 23, 2012. That meant sixteen hours for the Taliban to run wild before our first patrol. We took those hours to settle into our home and start acclimating to the omnipresent musk of combusting trash and JP-8 kerosene fuel arising out of the open-air burn pit. On the western side, a double-stacked Hesco barrier separated the Marines at COP Taghaz from the ABP in Taghaz Station. Marines stood watch behind machine guns every hundred meters along the berm perimeter, with an interior ring of Hesco barriers enclosing the living quarters, mess tent, and Combat Operations Center (COC). A trailer full of cameras and recording equipment provided an anchor for the balloon and a home for the contractors that operated it.

My section occupied a portable tent on a plywood platform in the COP's inner maze of Hesco hallways. Our quarters came with a few wooden shelves fashioned out of recycled wooden pallets, an aluminum-and-canvas cot for each occupant, and some extension cords that ran back to the COP's generator. We strung up parachute cord in the ceiling and clipped on bedsheets and poncho liners to wall off semi-private eight-by-eight-foot rooms. We hung flytraps near the door and set mousetraps along the seams. Our latrines were mesh-covered PVC "piss tubes" that ran into a ventilated trench beneath the ground and a plywood shack where we hung "wag bags" beneath a plastic toilet seat. Another wooden hut with a drainage system stood separately for shaving and dental hygiene. These areas were frequently trafficked by combat Crocs, the footwear of choice for off-duty Marines. Around the corner from our tent, a camouflage canopy provided shade for a "prison gym" containing all the essential equipment, albeit rusted. We would have plenty of time to familiarize ourselves with all these amenities of outpost living, but I was eager to get the lay of the land beyond the Hesco walls.

October 24 brought calm winds, so, with the balloon floating above us, we got the green light for our first patrol. The outgoing advisor team was going to show us around the neighborhood before they returned home. Tim, the patrol leader, briefed a quick operations order and spelled out the plan.

I was assigned the back seat of the lead truck pushing the mine-roller attachment out front. Lance Corporal Malone would be in the turret, with Tim riding shotgun and his corporal behind the wheel. The movement would start with a short leg of a few hundred meters north from COP Taghaz to the Desert of Death. On the steep incline twenty meters up from the river valley onto "the Shelf," as we called it, there would be a blind hill and only one path to climb it that could accommodate the clunky mine-roller. In my head I "turned the map around" to view things from the Taliban's perspective: this was a highly trafficked choke point between two positions—the first place I would bury IEDs to target convoys between Taghaz and PB Gherdai. Here, I was to dismount with a metal detector and sweep for any IEDs in the vehicle tracks.

My body tensed when Tim gave me the task, but the trained automaton within grunted something affirmative. Tim assured me that his corporal had checked the metal detector to make sure it was operational, but I went over to their truck anyway to double-check the machine that could save my life. They were using Vallons, an older variant that could not detect the carbon rods that the Taliban had recently learned to employ. Throughout our training workup, we primarily practiced with CMD2s, the newer variant that could.

Well, I consoled myself, *at least I'll have my blast diaper.*

I powered-on the Vallon to calibrate it to the soil compensation, but it gave me some low beeping sounds—irregular. I conferred with Lance Corporal Malone, who had used a Vallon at the front of over one hundred patrols in Sangin and knew the device like his life depended on it (because it had). His expert verdict: the batteries were dead. So much for the corporal's function check. I swapped out the batteries, and once the rest of our pre-combat checks were complete, the gate at COP Taghaz lifted and our trucks rolled through the Hesco serpentine toward the Shelf.

When I stepped down from the MATV and into the sand, I confirmed with Tim that he wanted me to literally sweep along the tire tracks where the truck would climb up to the Shelf.

Affirmative.

Reservations repressed, I stepped forward.

"This poor sonnuva bitch gon' lose his legs on his first patrol!" Gunny Jackson thought as he watched me in apprehension.

I let my training take over. With my right arm extended to clutch the metal detector and my left hand pinning my rifle to my body, I gently swept the sensor head in overlapping arcs, parallel to the ground and about an inch above it, stepping slowly forward into the cleared lane. Tim followed a few paces behind me, eyes up but darting down to make sure he stepped in my bootprints. The metal detector chirped a few short beeps as I swept, but there were no physical indicators, so I bypassed those spots, careful to place my feet around them. Once I crested the hill and pushed forward enough for Tim to follow, we cleared the tire tracks in the blind spot and followed our bootprints back down to the truck.

I would have preferred to risk the mine-roller rather than my legs or life, but at that point Tim's team was still driving the bus—we were just along for the ride. Since the mine-rollers were mission-essential equipment, and the Taliban calibrated some pressure-plate detonators only to be triggered by thousands of pounds of weight to target Marine trucks rather than civilian vehicles, I could understand the decision to walk up there and scope it out first. Of course, an observant enemy would learn this technique, and place toe-popper secondaries to target dismounted Marines, but risks like this were part of the job. I also thought it was an early opportunity for me to show the team, and my subordinates in particular, that I was willing to share the risks and the hardships traditionally passed down to the lower ranks. At least Gunny Jackson took note.

The convoy chugged along through the open desert steppe, devoid of any signs of life but for the wandering shepherd in search of his flock, or an occasional vehicle driving in the direction to or from Lashkar Gah. After about ten minutes we arrived at PB Gherdai, where a smiling ABP patrolman came down from the watchtower at Post 1 and lifted the gate to welcome us inside.

PB Gherdai loomed over the village from its perch on the edge of the Shelf. A tall berm formed its triangular perimeter, with concertina wire fixed along the top between the three Hesco watchtowers. An inner grid of Hescos and plywood roofing made for 1st Tolai's rudimentary offices, storage rooms, and living quarters. There, on a good day, you could smell fresh bread baking in the oven of the outdoor kitchen along the eastern wall. On a bad day, you could also catch the repulsive odor wafting over from the plywood-covered pit they called latrines on its northern edge. Between the kitchen and Post 2 was the area where they parked their vehicles, of which many sat collecting dust with dead batteries and flat tires. On the south side, Post 3 offered a panorama of the fields, canals, and compounds below, with a direct line of sight to TCP 3 across a frequently flooded sandy bog we came to know all too well.

This trip was my first opportunity to observe Baddar Gul in his element. Confirming Tim's description, he declined to accompany us on the patrol, so Tim and his Marines took us out with just a couple of 1st Tolai patrolmen. As we started toward town on Route Mexico and filed into two columns, my Marines and I exchanged glances. Having developed our patrol tactics based on my battalion's previous tour in Sangin, where Major Select, Corporal Palacios, Captain Quinn, and Lance Corporal Malone all experienced heavy fighting, we were shocked by the lax posture. We trained to patrol in single file through fields and canals where the point man swept with a metal detector and number two covered him, marking the trail with shaving cream. But as the intelligence reports suggested, we saw that Taghaz was no Sangin.

One reason for the difference was that the enemy—*dushman* in the local parlance—wanted to avoid drawing Marines' attention to the border area, which they needed to be relatively open for trafficking money, drugs, guns, explosives, and fighters. Another was our timing. We were avoiding the brunt of the Taliban's fighting season, which spanned the spring poppy harvest through the autumn planting. The winter months brought foul weather and poor road conditions, which put a damper on Taliban movements across the mountainous border from Pakistan. We were thankful for both factors.

The patrol was short, just enough to show us the main roads and a few landmarks. We got a good look at the village, and I wrote my initial impressions in my journal: *fucking stone age*. To be fair, it was far more advanced than I gave it credit for; it was medieval. Gray mudbrick compounds and pine groves clustered around the dirt roads cutting through expansive grids of farmland. Livestock roaming through streets and fields gave the impression that shepherding was a part-time gig. Water had to be drawn from wells and canals—the same ones that drained away waste. The incidental motorcycle, bongo truck, white Toyota hatchback, or rusted-out sedan were the only signs that we had not traveled back in time.

The one nineteenth-century amenity was the Public Call Office. The PCO, at the intersection of Route Mexico and Route Virginia, consisted of a couple of shops sharing a common roof, organized by the offerings: food, agricultural hardware, and miscellaneous goods. True to its name, the PCO also had a pay phone for use by locals, ABP, and Taliban alike. Until a few months before we arrived, there had never been any cell-phone reception in the area. We saw a few regulars hanging around outside the shops, drinking tea, smoking, and gossiping. The ABP seemed familiar with the locals at the PCO, and I noted the friendly atmospherics with optimism.

The next day was Bravo Section's turn to get familiar with 3rd Tolai's area, and I went along to assist. Parking our trucks at TCP 4, we strolled along the northern bank of the Helmand through a village called Kerum, a relatively affluent area with a history of Taliban activity. In Taghaz, "affluent" meant that the dirt floors in the compounds were covered with rugs, and some of the windows even had glass.

Even though it was only a three-hour patrol covering less than five miles over flat terrain on a mild October day, Sergeant Diaz ran out of water and had to sit down. His brain was literally being microwaved the entire time, because he was humping one of the two THOR units. Every patrol was required to carry two of these backpack-portable, battery-powered, electronic counter-IED devices that would detect and jam radio transmissions in the vicinity, plus extra batteries. The bottle of water I gave Sergeant Diaz did little to help, but he was a proud Marine and shouldered his pack to keep moving after just a short break. We walked back to the TCP 4 along the same route—a major patrolling faux pas—cursing the outgoing team's tactics and waiting for the *dushman* to ambush us; but soon enough, we were all once again bullshitting over cups of tea, safely behind the Hescos of TCP 4.

The most immediate and recurring danger in 3rd Tolai's area of operations was a narrow bridge between TCP 1 and TCP 2, where more than once the Marines' wide-based and heavy armored trucks had slid off the edge, despite dismounting Marines to guide the trucks on foot and inching across slowly. We decided that a quick operation to reinforce the bridge might help prevent injuries from vehicle rollovers, obviate annoying vehicle recovery missions, and maybe even purchase us some goodwill with the locals.

It was Bravo Section's area; but we had the resident engineer, Staff Sergeant Pulst, so my section was tasked with the little project. We drove over to the bridge, dipped into TCP 1 to grab a few ABP patrolmen that could give the project an Afghan face, and went to work with a trailer full of sandbags and Hesco materials. Staff Sergeant Pulst jumped chest-deep into the canal to drive steel stakes into the metal Hesco webbing, creating pockets on the corners of the bridge, where we piled all the sandbags we had staged in the trailer. An old deaf man, who later identified himself as Haji Naseer, came out to the bridge with a few of his grandkids to supervise, provide his own engineering advice, and even help lift a few stakes and sandbags. The kids were friendly, and at the end of the day we were filled with the hope that maybe, just maybe, Haji Naseer would let us know the next time he heard of an IED or Taliban movement in the area. *At the very least*, we thought, *he might not shoot at us himself.*

On October 28, the ABP invited our team over for a feast to celebrate the Islamic holiday of *Eid al-Adha*, which commemorates Abraham's willingness to sacrifice Isaac at God's command. However, we received an intelligence report warning that a green-on-blue attack was planned that night at Taghaz Station. So, before the gathering commenced, I crossed over from COP Taghaz with three other Marines for a security sweep. Not that I had been there long enough to develop a reliable baseline; but aside from befriending a sheep mere moments before it was slaughtered in a ritual sacrifice, nothing seemed out of the ordinary. A few hours later, that sheep provided us with a delicious introduction to Afghan cuisine.

The next morning was my first mission. Major Select had tasked me to repeat Tim's guided tour so he could tag along with his counterpart, the recently appointed Kandak commander, Colonel Nasrullah. It didn't feel like a real mission, since I was just functioning as a tour guide of the place I had only seen once myself, but I still took it seriously and went by the book. Staff Sergeant Pulst ensured that all our vehicles, weapons, radios, and gear were ready while I scribbled my order down on some loose leaf, planning primary and alternate routes, vehicle load-outs, contingency plans, and the rest.

We woke up to find our lead vehicle with the mine-roller had a dead battery, and so we began all our pre-mission checks and inspections with a jump start. Then I briefed my order in front of a wall where some previous occupants had pasted a giant map of the area in grid-printed satellite imagery, with all the key routes and locations labeled. It took about forty minutes to cover all three parts of the movement, but I convinced myself that it stayed within everyone's attention span. Our link-up with the ABP from the Kandak was a little late, but they fell in line behind us as we departed friendly lines.

Our movement up to the Shelf began exactly as I briefed: the first two vehicles dismounted two Marines to sweep up either side about fifteen meters off the road to get eyes on over the blind hill to see if there was anything suspicious waiting for us in the choke point. It was my adaptation of Tim's less cautious approach. The ABP, however, dismounted from the truck behind me and decided to stroll up the center of the road parallel to us, defeating the purpose of our offset reconnaissance. There was a suspicious crater at the top that looked freshly dug, but the ABP just clawed through it with their fingers, stood up, and smiled at us.

"*Shi neeshta?*" I called out. *There's nothing?*

"*Ho, neeshta. Amniyat dai.*" *Yes, there is nothing. It's safe.*

We had just witnessed the quintessential ABP counter-IED technique. There was no denying that it was effective . . . that time.

With the choke point cleared, we mounted up, climbed onto the Shelf, and ten minutes later arrived at PB Gherdai. After a quick tour there, we drove down to TCP 3, a simple square of Hesco barriers with two watchtowers in opposite corners and a couple of solar panels for power. We couldn't park our vehicles inside the TCP due to its small size, so we parked them outside in a tight circle to "coil up" for 360 degrees of security. Since they were out in the open, we had to drop someone from the dismounted patrol to guard the guns and trucks. As anticipated, Major Select and the Kandak commander stole the show, and I found myself, the supposed patrol leader, in a turret behind an M2 .50-cal machine gun at a stationary position. I was bored, but kept busy by relaying messages between the patrol and COP Taghaz and staying active in the turret.

When the patrol returned, Staff Sergeant Pulst approached me. "Hey, sir, we just want you to know . . . that was pretty fucked up."

Staff Sergeant Pulst seemed uneasy speaking ill of our officer-in-charge. He had chatted with Malone and Palacios, who also felt outraged that Major Select essentially relieved me of command for that patrol. I told them I appreciated their loyalty but assured them that my dignity was intact. Major Select's breach of officer etiquette might have offended a more sensitive subordinate; but having worked with Major Select for the previous six months, I came to expect such power grabs and was glad I was not on the patrol itself, where his micromanaging would have only irritated me further.

Still, his assumption of control had a damaging effect on our advising mission: the ABP were insulted by Major Select's insistence on sweeping a cleared path with a metal detector, marked by the next man with shaving cream on the left side. It signaled to the ABP that he didn't trust their assessment of the IED threat environment. Again, this came as no surprise, but there wasn't much any of us could do about it. I just looked forward to the next patrol, where I could explain away the apparent mistrust by pointing to Major Select's previous deployment in Sangin, repair the relationship, and run things my own way.

*   *   *

When our relief-in-place and transfer of authority process was complete, we convoyed east to drop off the outgoing advisor team at FOB Payne where a Shitter was to fly them up to Leatherneck the next morning. We squatted in a transient tent overnight and took advantage of the amenities to do laundry, shower, and pig out at the contractor-run dining facility—the DFAC. I ran into Tim that night at the smokepit outside the hygiene trailers. We chatted more about 1st Tolai and I asked a nagging question: How did the ABP respond to getting advice from someone without any combat experience?

More than once, I had pondered the irony of my position advising a unit of men who'd been fighting for years, if not their entire lives. It was similar to what I felt back at 1/5 assuming command of a platoon of war veterans as a novice lieutenant fresh out of training. An ROTC instructor once assured me that Mustangs—officers who commission after serving in the enlisted ranks—were not categorically better officers in his view. It tracked with an ancient proverb that an old American Legionnaire had recited for me years earlier: "You don't have to fuck Marilyn Monroe to judge a beauty contest." Similarly, Tim reassured me that our status as Marine officers and the accompanying reputation earned by the aptitude of our predecessors gave us automatic credibility in the Afghans' eyes, regardless of any battlefield experience. If he could do it as an aircraft maintenance officer, I would have no problem with my infantry background.

As our orange embers faded into ash, I thanked Tim for his help during the turnover, and he offered some parting wisdom:

"Do your best with the Tolai, but don't risk the lives of your men." He looked me in the eye. "This war is a lost cause . . . ain't worth losing any more Marines."

I nodded, feigning a somber recognition; but deep down I was disappointed in Tim, who until that point hadn't seemed like such a cynical, defeatist POG.* How did he expect to be successful in his mission with that losing attitude? His outlook clashed with every tenet of Marine Corps leadership. But it wasn't long before I saw things his way.

---

* \'pōg\: a Person Other-than Grunt: a quasi-derogatory term used by infantrymen to describe Marines in other occupational specialties

Chapter Six

Government-Led Eradication

We arrived at PB Gherdai for what would be our final visit. It would be the final visit by any NATO coalition forces, though none of us knew that at the time. It began, like any other 1st Tolai advising engagement, with Alpha Section in the lead and Bravo in support. We backed two of our trucks up against the Hesco wall around the corner from 1st Tolai's living quarters, and pulled the third across the space between them to form a makeshift security enclosure in the shape of a horseshoe. Such was our home whenever we visited the patrol base. At all times, a minimum of two Marines stood watch at the trucks: one to provide physical security for the Marines in the enclosure, and the other to maintain radio communications on both internal Motorolas and an external line back to Taghaz. While I prepped Alpha Section for our patrol, Bravo set up the retransmission site to relay what we sent from our relatively weak handheld radios over the trucks' high-powered antennas to reach Headquarters Section at the Taghaz Annex, where Carnage stood by as our QRF. Just as Bobo-6 dictated.

I took Ahmed over to Baddar Gul's office/bedroom and brought Lance Corporal Malone as my guardian angel. I had some explaining to do, since the last time I spoke with Baddar Gul, we had still been on track for the stay-behind ambush. I expected disappointment, but Baddar Gul seemed to apply Sully's "it's whatever" philosophy to the change of plans. His mind seemed elsewhere as he hurried us to get moving on the patrol to inspect the possible IED. I still had questions:

"Do any 1st Tolai patrolmen have experience in disarming IEDs?"

"Yes, yes, some sergeants have been to a training course." Baddar Gul offered no specifics.

"Maybe Staff Sergeant Pulst can review some techniques with them before we leave?"

"Yes, yes, we can do that down at TCP 3."

Baddar Gul and a few other patrolmen rolled out of the gate in two of their green Ford Rangers—"Danger Rangers," as they were known for their lack of protection from blasts or bullets. We had to speed through our final pre-combat checks to avoid getting left behind. I managed to get a clear radio check with Staff Sergeant Ortega; and then Alpha Section, with Ahmed and our JTAC Sergeant Polk, walked down from PB Gherdai to link up with the ABP at TCP 3.

The marsh between the two positions seemed to have swelled in the weeks since our last visit, so I gave the nod to hop in the back of the ABP's Danger Rangers. This was strictly prohibited, but I was willing to accept the low risk that the Taliban had somehow managed to bury a functioning IED underwater in between the two ABP positions. True to the stereotype of my millennial generation, I could not resist the temptation to create photographic evidence of our transgression. On the other side of the ford, I hopped out of the truck bed and walked forward to the cabin.

"*Daira manana!*" I thanked Baddar Gul for the lift through the halfway-down window.

He grinned back at me. "I should charge you a toll for using the 'Gherdai Ferry'!" Ahmed delivered Baddar Gul's joke for us in English. At least, I decided that it was a joke.

Boots dry, we filtered into TCP 3, where we quickly surmised that nobody there had been to any course on handling IEDs. Staff Sergeant Pulst cracked a smile and shook his head. This was classic Baddar Gul. So was his next move: he immediately left the TCP to return up the hill to PB Gherdai, informing us, on his way out the gate, "Sher Ali will lead the patrol."

* * *

Sergeant Sher Ali was the one good thing to come out of Farid Khan's revolt. At the end of October 2012, the 6th Zone commander released Farid Khan and his twenty-five mutineers from house arrest and sent them back to Taghaz. In early November, Colonel Nasrullah made the prudent decision to redistribute the troublemakers between the three Tolais. As part of the reorganization, Colonel Nasrullah also reassigned a few of 2nd Tolai's competent patrolmen and sergeants to backfill 1st Tolai's loss of personnel.

From this lot came Sher Ali. He struck me as being in his late twenties: wise enough to know what he was doing, and young enough to still have the energy for it. He presented a relaxed smile within his thin goatee and sported a jet-black bowl cut, matted down under a sequined Kandahari skullcap. Staff Sergeant Pulst and I had set the goal early on to *Inception* Baddar Gul into appointing a competent subordinate to be his *mawin*—his deputy —like Staff Sergeant Pulst was mine. From just half an hour conversing with Sher Ali, Staff Sergeant Pulst and I knew he was just what the Tolai needed.

One of Colonel Nasrullah's top priorities for improving the Tolai's capabilities was training on vehicle maintenance and recovery. Since Lance Corporal Malone had the collateral duty of overseeing the maintenance of all our own armored trucks, I assigned him the task of teaching the drivers in 1st Tolai how to better maintain their fleet of Danger Rangers and Humvees. We marked it on our calendars for November 4.

When we drove our trucks to PB Gherdai for the scheduled training, Baddar Gul was absent. I was annoyed, because three days earlier, I had called over to him from the Kandak's radio to confirm the date of our visit. Instead we were greeted by Baddar Gul's brother, Sergeant Jan, who told us Baddar Gul was meeting with the Kandak commander back at Taghaz Station and had yet to return. Jan eased our irritation with tea, cigarettes, and easy conversation until Baddar Gul showed up just in time for lunch. Then it was time to work . . . for most of us, anyway. With the compelling excuse that he was "tired after lunch," Baddar Gul withdrew to his room to nap while his subordinates trained on the vehicles and stood watch along the perimeter. Such an unabashed dereliction of duty would have gotten me fired, so I left my counterpart to supervise the training by myself.

The six drivers that Baddar Gul sent over for training knew quite a bit about their vehicles. Lance Corporal Malone's initial approach was to ask them to identify the parts of the vehicle, and ask them how often they checked, cleaned, or swapped out those parts. After going over basic preventative maintenance for both their Danger Rangers and their Humvees, Malone taught a section on vehicle recovery techniques, to include power-braking, rigging for tow, and how to effectively use straps and chains. He then dismissed class for a quick break before a practical application portion.

We had picked out a steep, sandy slope right outside the berm of their position, but still within their outer concertina wire perimeter. The ABP, however, seemed to want to challenge the expertise of the young advisor teaching them. As a group, they complained that they wanted training in a high-trafficked area of the route into town where they always got their vehicles stuck: the sandy marsh between the PB Gherdai and TCP 3. I was familiar with the spot, as I had watched a few vehicles get trapped there while I was stuck in the turret the week before when Major Select took over my patrol.

The area was technically outside the wire and so I was supposed to get the mission preapproved by Bobo-6. But the ABP maintained continuous observation on that area (in theory) and it was only a few hundred meters away. I gave Malone the thumbs-up, and Alpha Section rolled out in two of our trucks to follow the ABP down the hill. I drove the front truck, with Staff Sergeant Pulst in the turret and Lance Corporal Malone riding shotgun, ready to dismount and provide instructions. In the rear vehicle, Doc O'Connor drove with Palacios up in the turret, and our linguist, Ahmed, in the back. Things rapidly devolved when we arrived on scene.

A bongo truck was already stuck in the sand, and the ABP were getting into position to recover it. Cargo was loaded up above the sidebars and a couple of children were perched on the top, about fifteen feet in the air. ABP were digging in front of the tires and laying down planks and brush, trying the conventional approach to liberate a stuck vehicle. Their Humvee tugged the bongo truck forward a few meters, and then it became stuck again. Malone instructed and advised as long as his patience would allow, until finally he had to try it himself. Even then, the bongo truck wouldn't budge.

Advisors were taught to let the Afghans fail, so they could learn from it and get used to what it would be like when we weren't around anymore to support them. With the civilian spectators gathered there, though, I feared the ABP would lose a lot of legitimacy in their eyes if we were unable to free that bongo truck. On the other hand, I worried that helping them might reinforce the appearance that the ABP were dependent on the Marines. Since that was 100 percent true, and since I also considered how it would reflect poorly on the Marine Corps to sit idly by, I decided to get more involved. As my vehicle had the cumbersome mine-roller, I called up Doc O'Connor's vehicle to move in and save the day. We made a little more progress, but the bongo truck was too heavy and the sand too soft for us to liberate it, even with all the high-tech functions that allowed us to deflate the tires for better traction on sand; lock the differentials; activate the designated tow-mode; and set the transfer case in low. Finally we got the locals to start off-loading the cargo from the bongo truck onto a tractor that had pulled up to marvel at the spectacle.

That was when Doc called over the radio to let me know they had about fifty bags of fertilizer in the truck, along with some other goods. Some fertilizers were illegal in Afghanistan due to their propensity for use in homemade explosives. Those were the fertilizers smuggled north out of Pakistan, and these goods were heading south from Lashkar Gah. The bags in the bongo truck were labeled urea nitrate, which was legal, but smugglers had been known to empty the legal bags and refill them with ammonium nitrate, an illegal look-alike.

Doc and Malone grabbed a handful of the white prills, dropped them into a half-empty water bottle, and swirled them around in an improvised chemistry experiment. As we had learned during counter-IED training back stateside, the illegal fertilizer would turn the water to a cloudy white as it dissolved, whereas adding the legal one caused the solution to remain clear. Doc and Malone's mixture was slightly murky and unable to assuage any concerns. Major Select, eavesdropping on the radio traffic between Doc and me, was getting antsy. He was about to launch a QRF from Taghaz with EOD, and told me to detain the guys transporting the goods.

"Stand by." I radioed back. It was time to handle the situation myself.

Ordinarily, Marines outside the wire always leave their drivers and gunners in the vehicles for security and mobility, but this was far from an ordinary situation, or an ordinary mission. I walked over and got the story from Malone and the ABP. The truck driver owned a store at the PCO and sold goods to a couple of other prominent shops in the village. The ABP claimed he was a good friend of theirs and they wanted to help him. I grabbed a small handful of the fertilizer and added it to a water bottle to test it myself. It was still inconclusive, but I had a good look at the bright white round prills, which looked to me more like urea nitrate, the legal fertilizer. I also did some quick math; one fifty-kilogram bag was enough to fertilize about three acres of farmland; and the amount seemed proportionate for its intended destination, since we knew the owner of the PCO to own 120 acres himself. We had the truck driver's name and location; the ABP had vouched for him; so I concluded that these guys were most likely clean and told the QRF to stand down. Our vehicles finally pulled their truck out and, after briefly getting my own truck stuck (the mine-roller complicated maneuvering on the swampy terrain), we made our way back uphill to the patrol base.

Lance Corporal Malone shared afterward that he felt disrespected by the ABP, who challenged and questioned him throughout the training. I could relate; it sounded like being a new platoon commander. I encouraged him not to take it personally, and explained how, like the immature and punchy Marines he knew quite a few of back at 1/5, these patrolmen would try to challenge the authority of any new instructor, especially one who is younger. *Think of it as a kind of "Lance Corporal karma."* I held back the jab, sensing that he was not in the joking mood. Malone was visibly frustrated, so I assured him that his contributions were meaningful, especially his lessons about maintenance scheduling and power-braking.

"Take the little victories," I told him. Those were the only ones available.

While we may have spent an afternoon literally bogged down and spinning our wheels, I focused on the little victory of my own. I had stood firm behind my own judgment in defiance of orders from above that would have made the situation worse. By sacrificing some of the goodwill in my relationship with Major Select, I avoided an embarrassing overreaction to fertilizer that could have eroded whatever goodwill was left in our relationship with the locals, our relationship with the ABP, and, most importantly, their relationship with each other. Despite our efforts, and in some ways because of them, the stress on these relationships was about to get a whole lot worse.

As we returned to PB Gherdai, happy to be done with the vehicle-recovery training, we passed Baddar Gul heading out to purchase (or possibly extort) some rations for our dinner that evening. So Staff Sergeant Pulst and I sat with Sher Ali and talked over a few ideas we had for improving the Tolai's daily operations, such as burning and relocating their unsanitary latrines; fortifying their observation posts with additional sandbags; standardizing the parking of vehicles backed-in; and recording and reporting personnel, weapons, and vehicle numbers. We also emphasized the importance of the *mawin* in enforcing standards, maintaining accountability of property, and taking care of the little things so the commander could focus on the big picture.

When Baddar Gul returned, we ate an oily chicken dish with rice, each of us polishing off three whole pomegranates for dessert, and then we discussed our work over tea and cigarettes.

"What did you and Colonel Nasrullah speak about earlier today over at Taghaz Station?" I probed.

He struggled to recall anything beyond the new personnel we had already met, so I told him about the security shura and the anti–poppy farming program about to be implemented across Khan Neshin District.

The day before the vehicle-training debacle, I had led a convoy across the desert from COP Taghaz to COP Castle so Major Select could attend a security shura—a meeting for all the local leaders. Located in the District Center of Khan Neshin, COP Castle was also home to the district headquarters of the Afghan National Police, of which the ABP was a component agency. As with COP Taghaz, a Hesco barrier down the middle of the base separated the Marines from the Afghans, with one convenient difference: where we had to exit COP Taghaz and walk outside the perimeter to enter Taghaz Station, Castle had a fortified gateway in between the two sides, under constant Marine guard.

Key leaders all packed into the COP Castle conference room, where the district chief of police issued a directive for all the Afghan police in Khan Neshin District: it was time to warn the local population in advance of a massive government-led eradication (GLE) effort against poppy farming. The chief instructed his subordinate commanders to spread the word that farmers growing poppy would be arrested, without exception. Patrolmen were not only to seize narcotics and destroy poppy fields, but also, as the current time of year right then was planting season, confiscate seeds and even the farmers' tractors.

The issue had long been a huge source of tension between farmers and the U.S.-backed Afghan government representatives in Helmand and was bound to be exacerbated by the adoption of such a hard-line approach. While GLE was more merciful in practice than what the official messaging conveyed—Afghan police often collected unofficial "fines" for their personal coffers in lieu of imposing harsher consequences—it was a tricky political issue for government representatives to navigate without disaffecting the local farmers.

Past eradication campaigns in Helmand had backfired spectacularly, alienating the population. Numerous diplomats and military officers specifically blamed Operation River Dance in 2006 for delivering the Taliban a strategic victory by inspiring poor, disgruntled farmers to join, or at least welcome, an armed insurgency against the occupiers who destroyed their livelihoods.[16] Other alternatives likewise foundered. Staff Sergeant Pulst recalled to me how, during his deployment to Nawa District in 2009, the government was giving out corn and wheat seeds to any farmers who promised not to grow poppy; but too many of those farmers were caught with the contraband anyway. The Afghan government ended that incentive program, which relied on the goodwill of the farmers, and was once again pushing GLE.

Baddar Gul claimed to have heard nothing about the shura. Apparently, Colonel Nasrullah failed to pass the message along to 1st Tolai, whether out of neglect or discretion, I couldn't say. In any event, Baddar Gul assured me that he had always been a proud proponent of GLE.

"Yes, yes, my men and I always spread the message in Gherdai that farming poppy is against Islam and against the law."

He told me he regularly threatened villagers with imprisonment if they were caught with poppy in their fields. I suspected this might have been lip service, especially since Baddar Gul had been known to dabble in the substances himself, but I gave him the benefit of the doubt. I had nothing to prove the rumor, and nothing to gain by confronting him anyway.

Exploring his relationship with the locals, I asked about his role in providing services in the village.

"Did locals ever come up to ABP on patrol, or at the patrol base, to ask for help?"

Baddar Gul offered a couple of anecdotes about smuggling some villagers back to the base in his Danger Ranger to get them medical aid, but he said that the locals were all afraid of Taliban retribution if they were seen collaborating with the ABP.

"One hundred percent of the time, if a civilian is seen collaborating with the ABP, the *dushman* will come for them."

The Taliban's murder and intimidation campaigns were effectively dividing the population from the ABP, and the villagers of Gherdai did not trust 1st Tolai to keep them safe. The lack of trust between them did not bode well for the counterinsurgency strategy, but I saw an opportunity to exploit on the tactical level.

"If the *dushman* come 100 percent of the time to punish collaborators, why not get there first and wait for them?"

Baddar Gul tilted his head. I paired my suggestion with an analogy I thought he might understand.

"Like a fisherman, we can help a local villager in public view and then cast them out as bait for the big Taliban fish. We hide, wait for the fish to bite, and then hook them when they come."

I explained how this would demonstrate to the villagers that 1st Tolai controls the area and take the initiative from the Taliban. Baddar Gul seemed more amused by the concept than convinced, but I was happy to get those gears turning.

One deceptive tactic Baddar Gul told me he already employed was pretending to arrest his informants so they would not appear to be collaborating with him. He claimed that, in this fashion, he could rely on the locals to tip him off to IEDs and enemy activity. Setting aside how easily that tactic could backfire when the Taliban wondered why the informant had been released, I wanted to learn more about his sources and intelligence operations. "Who in the village gives you information?"

Baddar Gul swore me to secrecy and told me about two of them. I wrote the names down in my book and kept the information to give to our team's intelligence officer, Lieutenant Ames.

The conversation turned to planning a patrol for the following day. I requested to revisit the PCO to talk to the man whose vehicle we pulled out and to meet the elder Haji Siddiq Khan. Baddar Gul came up with a plan to stop at three of the shops and then have tea with the elder. We would cover mostly the same ground as previous patrols, but I was excited by the idea of reconnoitering the human terrain—uncharted territory for my team.

Staff Sergeant Pulst and I stood the final two hours of watch together early the next morning to update the encryption keys in all our radios at the appointed hour and ensure that the scheduled "crypto-rollover" went smoothly. After we finished packing up our sleeping bags and shaved, Staff Sergeant Pulst and I went over to Baddar Gul's room to find him wrapped up in a blanket on the floor. He said he would send someone to get us in an hour and we would have tea before the patrol, so we waited back in our vehicle enclosure to get ready. An hour and forty-five minutes went by before Staff Sergeant Pulst, Ahmed, and I went back to check on Baddar Gul.

"We will patrol after I talk to the Kandak at 0700," he told us, gesturing toward the radio.

"What time is it?" he asked Ahmed.

"0815, *Sahib*."

Baddar Gul jolted up and ran outside with his radio. I made a note to get the man a watch. What good was having all the time if he couldn't tell what it was?

Chapter Seven

Key Leader Engagements

23 JAN 2013
1449 AFT (UTC + 4.5)

"Our bosses won't let us stay here and fight with you tonight."

Baddar Gul had departed without informing Sher Ali of the change in plans, so I was left to break it to him. Sher Ali looked disappointed—he had been excited about the stay-behind mission like the rest of us—but spoke with his characteristic positivity.

"No problem—maybe next time!"

There would be no next time.

We reviewed the plan to inspect the possible IED, and I reminded Sher Ali of a discussion we'd previously had about how to avoid getting ambushed again from the jungle of meadow fox-tails and salt cedar bushes near the bridge. He recalled our idea to send an advanced party to reconnoiter the danger area from a wide angle before the main patrol advanced into town. Sher Ali then gathered his men around him and briefed a quick order, dragging his boot across lines in the dirt to illustrate the clearing maneuver. We checked our metal detectors one last time to ensure that they were operational and calibrated to the soil density. Then I called up to Staff Sergeant Ortega at our retransmission site to report our departure, and we stepped out from the TCP around 1500.

Eight ABP swept a wide arc in advance of our patrol, where Sher Ali, a few ABP patrolmen, and the advisors slowly made our way down Route Mexico. The ABP executed the tactic well, securing the area around the choke point that was the main bridge into the village. Sher Ali pointed out to me the exact positions from the most recent ambush as we made our way up to the bridge. They still had a long way to go, but these tactics were light-years beyond what I had seen on my first and only patrol with Baddar Gul.

* * *

In every training environment from Officer Candidate School onward, Marine officers are taught to lead from the front. Baddar Gul took this to the extreme. Armed with only a radio and a patrol belt that holstered a Leatherman multitool (which I guessed was a gift from Tim or some other past advisor), Baddar Gul walked the point on our November 5 patrol. Traditionally, the point man is one of the lowest-ranking members of the squad, or a particularly savvy specialist—Lance Corporal Malone in Sangin, for example. In many combat environments, Marine Corps doctrine prescribes the point man to carry a shotgun as a quick way to amass firepower at a short range. On an IED-laden battlefield, the point man is most likely to trip any victim-initiated switches, like the common pressure plate. It was the most dangerous position in the formation, but there was Baddar Gul, marching at the front for the duration of the patrol, unarmed.

What's his plan for contact with the enemy? I wondered. *Unfold the three-inch blade from the Leatherman and charge?*

No, he wasn't insane—just lazy. He would simply demand the gun from one of his subordinates or run away. Probably both. To do my job and advise Baddar Gul, I had to walk beside him and cover point myself, eyes up and scanning but ever mindful of my step, with Ahmed trailing close behind to supplement my rudimentary Pashto. With the rest of the patrol falling in behind, Baddar Gul led us down Route Mexico and across the bridge to the PCO.

A group of men was standing around outside the PCO, and it seemed like the usual crew at the usual hangout. One of the village elders, Haji Musa, dominated the crowd, about half a foot taller than the others.

"This guy here, he says he is the tallest Pashtun man in Helmand," Ahmed translated a patrolman's commentary.

I laughed at the claim. There wasn't exactly a census in these parts.

Staff Sergeant Pulst and I took off our sunglasses and helmets to show respect while Corporal Palacios and Lance Corporal Malone provided security with Doc O'Connor and the ABP around the PCO. Baddar Gul introduced me to Haji Musa. I stripped off a flame-resistant glove to shake his hand.

"*Pe leedo mo khoshhal shwam,*" I told him. *Pleased to meet you.*

We met the other shopkeepers as well, and everyone seemed very friendly. Malone helped stimulate the local economy by purchasing a carton of cigarettes. But when I introduced myself to the owner of the truck we had recovered the day before, I caught a flash of disgust upon his face as he shook my hand. I was unsure how scientific the training we received in facial threat recognition was, but I was never more certain of a sign than that one. He expressed no gratitude when I confirmed with him that it was his truck we'd helped recover. I found it very curious, since the ABP had insisted he was a friend. He and Baddar Gul seemed to avoid each other while we were there, and I sensed there was some unspoken history between the two.

Baddar Gul spent most of his time at the PCO pushing the anti-poppy talking points, and made a good show of it for me. Ahmed narrated the exchange in which Haji Musa pushed back, criticizing the government for enforcing rules without giving a solution. Then the elder tried negotiating.

"Fine. I will stop selling poppy if you give me a barrel of fuel to cover my losses from growing a less profitable crop. If I harvest only corn and wheat in those same fields, it would leave me at a loss of twenty-five thousand rupees." The local currency was that of Pakistan.

Baddar Gul offered no quarter and stayed consistently on-message, so Haji Musa turned to me. I reiterated what Baddar Gul had said and tried to reason with him.

"You might as well only grow corn and wheat, because when the ABP come to eradicate your poppy fields you will be left with nothing."

Finding no ally in me, Haji Musa decided the conversation was over.

"Fine. I will comply," he conceded and walked off, back up Route Mexico toward his compound.

We pushed on east up Route Virginia, home to the main residential and commercial strip of the village. At this point, a pair of helicopters came on station and decided to fly at low altitude right above us, alerting everyone within two kilometers to our presence. The aerial show of force might have helped the higher-ups feel like the patrols were safer; but for a combat patrol in pursuit of an evasive enemy and needing to evaluate how the ABP operated in combat, I found them counterproductive. Staff Sergeant Pulst shared my annoyance and radioed our JTAC, Sergeant Polk, to call the birds off our backs. The cavalier maneuvering of the helicopter pilots irritated me so much, I decided not to schedule aircraft on any of our future patrols. I would come to regret that decision.

The patrol continued to the next shop. Men and children perched atop a bongo truck smiled and waved as we rounded the corner of the building to the rear entrance. They laughed when the bulky antenna from the THOR radio-frequency jammer on my back got caught on the head jamb as I ducked into the doorway of the shop. The shopkeeper's cool, courteous demeanor contrasted that of his companion, a deaf and mute man who seemed overly happy to see us. I asked the shopkeeper his name, and he started to produce his *tazkera*, or ID card, as if it were an interrogation. I insisted that it wasn't necessary, and he gave his name as Mohammed.

I introduced myself by name, sort of. The Afghans all omitted the "n" in my last name to call me *Breedman Izat*. It translated to "Lieutenant Honor"; when Ahmed told me that, I decided not to correct them. Mohammed scribbled my moniker on a sheet of paper, and I noticed him slip it into the cash register moments later. Baddar Gul regurgitated his anti-poppy message and declined Mohammed's offer to stay for tea, as we planned to have a few cups at our next stop.

At our third stop, a young shopkeeper manned the register and greeted us as we entered. His eyes darted around the room, and he fidgeted with his hands. Staff Sergeant Pulst commented on the shopkeeper's unease in our side conversation in English, and we hoped it was due to our presence, not Baddar Gul's. We ordered tea, which was brought out by an old man while Baddar Gul ran through the same anti-Taliban, anti-poppy script. The shopkeeper politely promised to spread the message, and stood attentively behind the register. I questioned my understanding of Pashtun culture; it seemed backward for the young man to be in charge behind the register while the gentleman twice his age served us. I also wondered if any of Baddar Gul's supposed "friends in town" ever joined him for tea or a cigarette, or if they stood behind the counter out of respect, fear, or disdain.

As we finished our tea, Baddar Gul barked an order: "Tell the Taliban this is an ABP shop, not a Taliban shop."

I cringed.

The shopkeeper somehow kept from rolling his eyes.

Here, Baddar Gul either demonstrated a fundamental misunderstanding of counterinsurgency tactics, or he was posturing under a mistaken belief that it was what I wanted to hear. If the ABP wanted to earn this shopkeeper's loyalty, insisting that he confront the Taliban on our behalf was not the way to do it. The ABP needed to be there to protect him and his family when the Taliban came. I made a note for my debrief. We smiled and thanked the shopkeeper, and with that, we were on our way.

The series of deep canals just north of Route Virginia complicated our plans, but the ABP knew where to cross. Unfortunately, they planned their crossing points for a 135-pound Afghan man, not a 185-pound Marine with another 80 pounds of equipment. They shimmied across tree branches laid over canals we couldn't see the bottom of, and laughed at our caution as we teetered along behind them. I made a note for our next patrol to bring a holly stick, a lightweight collapsible sickle usually used for probing possible IEDs. That way, we could test how deep the canals were, since a Marine in all that gear would have serious trouble staying afloat. We accepted a lot of battlefield hazards, but none of us was eager to take a plunge. Suffocating with lungs full of sewage water would be an awful way to go out, and it was a realistic possibility if we lost our balance or the branch gave way beneath one of us. We had no choice but to ford a few of them, but in some spots we were able to scurry across a car-tire culvert wedged atop a mud dam, or hop over an area where the canal narrowed.

A few sketchy canal crossings later, we found a dirt tractor path that led us to Haji Siddiq Khan Village, a large compound owned by the Ishokzai tribal elder of the same name. As we organized the patrol formation from what can only be described as an elongated clusterfuck down to a single file, we traced the edge of a field that a few men were plowing. As we rounded the corner, heading north into the compound, Baddar Gul pointed at one of the farmers and shouted:

"Arrest that man, bind his hands, and bring him to me."

I asked Ahmed who that man was and why Baddar Gul wanted to detain him, but Ahmed had no idea either. Baddar Gul was about twenty meters in front of me, and I thought about catching up to ask him directly, but I saw that the farmer complied willingly, faked like he was getting handcuffed, and walked over to Baddar Gul between two of the patrolmen. I watched the charade from a short distance; Baddar Gul brought the farmer behind a cluster of trees around the corner of the compound's exterior wall and emerged alone seconds later. The farmer disappeared as the elder approached our patrol, and Baddar Gul turned his attention to our host.

The elder Haji Siddiq Khan brought us through a courtyard into a large open room with glass windows and fine carpets. Alpha Section executed our bullshitting battle drill, with Staff Sergeant Pulst passing off reporting responsibilities to Corporal Palacios, who remained in the courtyard with Malone and Doc. Staff Sergeant Pulst and I removed our helmets, sunglasses, and gloves and we sat down in the room. While the elder left to go prepare the tea, Baddar Gul told me he had just received intelligence: a man I recognized as a code-named High Value Target was in Kerum, a nearby hamlet, just two days earlier. It was easy enough to piece together the theory that Baddar Gul had just had a brief encounter with one of his informants. I hastily copied down the intel and confirmed with him that I had it right, just before the elder came back with two of his grandchildren carrying a platter of teapots and glasses.

While Haji Siddiq Khan oversaw the attendance to his guests, I practiced my Pashto by making small talk with one of the little boys.

What's your name?

Fazal.
How many years are you?
Four.
Do you help farming?
No, I am studying.
He began to recite the alphabet: *"alif, baa, taa . . ."*
Can you write?
He shook his head. I tore a page out of my notebook and showed him how to write his name. Ahmed gave him an extra pen, and Fazal practiced, copying my script to write it himself beneath. We let him keep the pen and paper to keep practicing; and about that time, the elder came back inside. Staff Sergeant Pulst asked permission to offer the kids some gum, and the elder gave the okay. The boys took their gum, said thank you, and ran off to play outside. Pulst and I psychically high-fived over our campaign for those little hearts and minds.

Baddar Gul formally introduced me, and I introduced Staff Sergeant Pulst as my *mawin*. Baddar Gul mentioned that Haji Siddiq Khan was the brother of Haji Musa, who we had met just an hour or so earlier, and began to warn the elder of the upcoming GLE campaign in the district. To this, Haji Siddiq Khan did not respond favorably, and it shifted the whole tenor of our visit. He paused after each sentence just long enough for Ahmed to translate, but began speaking again before Baddar Gul could respond.

> I've lived here my whole life and I've been fighting here
> for thirty years. I know this area and I know how to
> provide for my family on this land. The government
> says to grow corn and wheat, but I would need to farm
> that in all my land, and you've seen my land, where
> your trucks get stuck in the sand. It would cost me fif-
> teen thousand rupees to make that land arable, another
> fifteen thousand for the tractor to make it so, and

another fifteen thousand to irrigate that land. Even if I
grow corn or wheat on all my land, it still wouldn't be
as profitable as with poppy. But still the District tells
me to farm my land at a deficit. And they do nothing
to help our economy. How long has the government
been here?

"Five years," Baddar Gul chirped at this first opening in the
conversation.

Excellent contribution, answered my sarcastic inner monologue.
Haji Siddiq Khan continued:

Five years, and they have done nothing to fix the road
between Gherdai and Taghaz, so instead I have to take
an expensive taxi up to the Shelf to go around. . . .

His rant continued for another few minutes about how the
Afghan government only brought problems and no solutions.

When the elder finally finished, Baddar Gul remained silent. I
looked at him expectantly, but he just flashed me a nervous smile
and averted his gaze. It was quite the awkward silence, but I let
it linger until it felt borderline disrespectful. Then, trying to be a
voice for the ABP, I began:

Sahib, you are undoubtedly the expert on your own
land. As you said, the government is relatively new
here, and it will take time to learn enough to find a
solution. That's why it is important for you to contrib-
ute your ideas and your expertise to solve the problem.
You need to bring your concerns and ideas to Baddar
Gul, he will bring them to the Kandak, and the Kandak will bring them to the District. You understand
why this is a slow process, but I am asking you to be

patient. Poppy may support your family, but it poisons your community and supports the Taliban.

Haji Siddiq Khan flatly rejected the idea that the government was capable of helping anyone in the area.

Baddar Gul maintained his steadfast non-participation.

I referenced our project improving the bridge in 3rd Tolai's area of operations, and suggested that if he brought a specific problem to the ABP's attention, they might be able to help in kind. Otherwise, the ABP would have no way of knowing what needed fixing.

The elder decided that our meeting had reached its end. "Well, what will you promise me as a gesture of goodwill to conclude our meeting?"

ATC had warned us about promises in Pashtun culture, so I had to tread lightly while still inspiring confidence in the capabilities of the Afghan government.

"My mission is to help the ABP help your community. I promise you that I will not fail my mission. But you need to work with us, *Sahib*, not against us."

"*Sha.*" *Good, we are finished.* Haji Siddiq Khan then produced a laminated card, which I saw had been issued by the Marine battalion in the area before 3/9. Printed in English and spelling his name wrong, the card listed the serial numbers and description of weapons he was licensed to have in his home: two AK-47s and one pistol. It disappointed, but did not surprise me, that he recognized me as the authority in Gherdai, not Baddar Gul. Unfortunately, previous Marine units and Baddar Gul's selective mutism during that meeting did little to dispense with that perception. In their defense, the transition from Marine-only, to partnered, to ABP-led operations was swift and recent, taking place over the course of just a few months.

I told Haji Siddiq Khan that there was no need to show me this license and that Baddar Gul was in charge, to which he seemed pleasantly surprised. "I have these weapons to fight the Taliban myself," he told me. Baddar Gul then slid out into the courtyard, eager to escape the confrontation. I was on my own.

"Let the ABP know the next time you see any Taliban. It is their job to fight the Taliban."

"No." The elder puffed up his chest. "If they are on my land, it's my business. I take care of my own business."

I wanted him to recognize that the ABP had responsibility for security. "Any problem of yours is a problem of ours and the ABP, and we take pleasure in fighting the *dushman*. I hope you call the ABP so we can come fight together."

"*Sha.*" *Good*, he said, and we shook hands.

"One last thing," he interjected. "Bring me twenty Hesco."

It was my turn to be noncommittal. "I'm just an advisor; Baddar Gul is in charge of all the Hesco."

My deflection was effective, since Baddar Gul had already left to start the last leg of the patrol without me. I hurried to catch up and waved the elder goodbye.

As Baddar Gul took off at what felt like an Olympic power walk, Sergeant Polk came over the net at our retransmission site to inform us that the helicopters had spotted five or six men unloading several boxes at a compound. This compound, according to the Carnage Marines monitoring our patrol in the Taghaz COC, was a suspected IED factory. I checked the compound number with the grid map I carried of the area.

What the fuck? I thought when I made the association. *Haji Musa's compound? Who the hell thinks the elder has an IED factory?* I filtered my thoughts into something I could pass over the radio. Sergeant Polk conveyed back Major Select's orders. "Talk to your counterpart and let him know about the IED factory, then let us know your COA."

Before deciding my Course of Action, I needed to confirm the intel.

"What activity besides unloading boxes is suspicious? And who exactly suspects this to be an IED factory?"

"Good questions, sir; stand by!" Sergeant Polk relayed the response moments later. "Carnage says the owner of that compound has been known to facilitate Taliban activity in the past."

I recalled an old intelligence report indicating that Haji Musa had once, several months earlier, been coerced into allowing some Taliban to stage in his compound before implanting IEDs. So because he was unloading boxes in broad daylight, I was supposed to suggest to Baddar Gul that we raid the compound of a village elder, a man I had spoken to only a few hours earlier, whose brother had just hosted us for tea?

"Yeahhh, Mobile from 1-Actual, my COA is RTB. Break." I paused in case any urgent transmission needed to interrupt me. "That's the elder Haji Musa's compound. Unloading boxes is not actionable intelligence, or really even suspicious activity."

"Roger!" Sergeant Polk sounded thrilled at the opportunity to tell Major Select to fuck off, and passed up my decision to Return to Base. Minutes later we arrived back at the TCP.

"Just so you know, sir, I also think hitting that compound was a stupid fucking idea," Sergeant Polk told me as soon as I got back to the trucks. Staff Sergeant Ortega chimed in his agreement. Twice in two days I had disregarded guidance from Major Select and 3/9, so it was comforting to hear that these experienced Marines found the proposition as ludicrous as I did. While I hadn't disobeyed any direct orders, I felt uneasy with the repeated necessity to swat away overreactions from my own command. Despite our occasional disagreements, I trusted Major Select and valued his trust in me. It was essential for our working relationship that I pick my battles when our views diverged, as with the suggestions to detain a truck driver and raid an elder's compound. Nobody, myself included, wanted a subordinate who questioned or defied orders. That trend worried me as much as did the torrent of bad ideas pouring down on me from above.

After a quick drive up the hill to PB Gherdai, I found Sher Ali sitting with Baddar Gul in his office/bedroom for our joint debrief. I nudged him to invite the others who had joined us for the patrol.

"We usually debrief together with everyone in the patrol to make sure everything of importance that anyone noticed makes its way into our report."

"Yes, yes, I already asked the patrolmen, and they didn't see anything."

I didn't know whether to doubt his honesty or question the patrolmen's observational skills, so I moved on. "Ready for lunch?" he asked when I reached the end of my notes. We all had worked up an appetite and welcomed the meal before we began our drive back to COP Taghaz.

Back at Taghaz, we cleared our weapons of the live rounds in the chambers, counted all our gear, and then funneled into our tent for an intelligence debrief and "hotwash"—an airing of grievances and discussion of learning points. We had a lot of information to pass on, and Lieutenant Ames was excited by how much we were able to collect through Baddar Gul. I was proud of my team's performance and considered our mission a success, particularly in how it illuminated the dilemma the Afghan government faced with poppy farming in Helmand Province. Another encouraging observation was that the ABP paid for the items they took from each shop along our route—something I did not take for granted.

However, after meeting with Baddar Gul several times and now completing our first patrol together, I was feeling pessimistic. It was obvious to me that Baddar Gul was unfit to lead the Tolai, and

I told Major Select that he needed to be replaced. On the upside, Baddar Gul's unreliability and incompetence helped me feel more comfortable giving advice to an experienced war veteran nearly twice my age. The next day, I wrote an email to one of my brothers lamenting how my inept counterpart wouldn't even carry a weapon on patrol. I described how, to succeed in my assignment, I felt I had to become a sorcerer, "like Jafar hypnotizing the Sultan in *Aladdin*." Success would take nothing short of Disney magic.

His concern cut through my whimsical bullshit: "I swear every week I read about another Helmand Province Green-on-Blue. . . . Those fuckers don't even deserve your training."

He was exaggerating, but not by much—such attacks had occurred in Helmand only every *other* week at that point in November 2012.[17] Yet, while the insider threats and incompetent leaders may not have deserved our efforts, I still believed there were Afghans who did.

Chapter Eight

Hidden Hazards

23 JAN 2013
1500 AFT (UTC +4.5)

Sher Ali gripped his machine gun by the barrel and balanced the drum of ammunition on his shoulder as we strolled down Route Mexico *shana pa shana*, shoulder to shoulder. We approached the bridge, where I talked him through how we typically handle a "danger area," and then showed him. A herd of goats that could only be described as hostile pushed between the patrol, isolating Corporal Palacios on the bridge in an awkward standoff. The goats were not the only hostiles we encountered. Passing a child on the side of the road, Doc waved with a friendly "*Salaam Alaikum!*" and received only an empty stare in reply.

"He probably doesn't like us . . . future Taliban," he commented to Sergeant Polk.

Meanwhile, the satellite squad of ABP patrolmen had pushed about two hundred meters farther south, so we could inspect the suspected IED locations on Route Virginia without interference from that direction. According to Baddar Gul, the ABP had seen a white sign between the PCO and the compound we called the clinic with a message warning of IEDs and disparaging the ABP and the Afghan government. Sher Ali chatted with the lone shopkeeper at the PCO and learned that, aside from a few pedestrians that morn-ing, there had been no traffic from that direction for the previous three days. Three of the four shops were shuttered. We noted the foreboding atmospherics; usually there were many civilians around that community center with all four shops open.

With just Sher Ali and a few patrolmen accompanying the advisor element of the patrol, and none of them having any counter-IED experience, the best I could do was talk with Sher Ali about how he would approach the reported hazard. He shrugged and told me they would just leave it be, or, if they had to, care-fully remove it by hand. I noted that we should revisit this in our training, and stepped up to show him our procedure. Counter-IED was Staff Sergeant Pulst's forte, and Lance Corporal Malone and Corporal Palacios both had a wealth of experience, but by that point in the deployment I felt confident in my own abilities up at the front of the patrol.

I grabbed the metal detector out of my pack and went to work. I pushed west from the PCO, clocking no visual indications or metallic hits on the road until about one hundred meters east of the clinic. There, clumps of dirt and rocks had been stacked up to form a line across Route Virginia. Tire tracks from local vehicles could be seen to have turned around near this marking on either side of it. About two feet off the road, I detected a strong metallic hit, just under a foot in diameter, where the earth had clearly been disturbed. I called this back to Staff Sergeant Pulst, repeated myself in Pashto to inform Sher Ali, and called in the grid coordinates from my GPS over the radio.

From where these indicators suggested a metallic power source, I swept in an arc around the possible IED to approach it from the south side of the road. Careful not to disturb the stacked rocks and mud, I maneuvered the metal detector's sensor head around the markings. Exactly where a tire would fall on the northern side of the road, I registered a high metallic hit running across it about a foot long. This was the pressure plate, I figured, and called up Staff Sergeant Pulst with the holly stick to rake through the dirt from a distance. Before he could interrogate the suspected device any further, we were called off on the radio. 3/9 denied us permission to take action.

"Mark and bypass."

"Just leave the IED . . . in the road?" I needed to hear it again.

"Affirmative, sir." Staff Sergeant Ortega relayed the order.

Why? So they can come roll over it with one of their trucks? I almost radioed back. That seemed to be 3/9's preferred method of route clearance.

*   *   *

3/9 had hit their first IED of many within days of their arrival in Taghaz. There was a security shura at COP Castle a few days later on November 9, and I was assigned to lead our convoy so Major Select could attend. I planned a circuitous route arcing almost twenty kilometers north through the desert, where the IED threat would be essentially nonexistent. This time I agreed with Major Select's guidance: better to let a specialized route-clearance convoy with engineers and EOD deal with the perils of Route Uniform. But my route had other hazards.

During one of several wadi crossings, the mine-roller on our lead truck sank into about three feet of loose sand. We managed to pull it out by attaching chains to another truck from the front and employing the power-braking technique that Lance Corporal Malone had taught the Afghans. Despite our long route and sandy pit stop, we got to COP Castle in two and a half hours. But our excellent timing came at a cost: my driver kept breaking 3/9's speed limit of twenty-five miles per hour in the open desert, despite multiple calls over the radio net from Major Select in the rear truck ordering us to slow down, and my repeated instructions to my driver to do so.

Chugging through the desert at a snail's pace was about safety. Slow speed meant better observation of natural and man-made hazards, and more time for drivers to react to what they or the other passengers saw. As the vehicle commander, I was responsible for our truck's speed; and, unlike pushing back on dumb ideas, violating the speed limit in defiance of Major Select's reminders was disobedience of a direct order. This infuriated Major Select to the point where he pulled me and the driver aside afterward and gave us the business. He went so far as to threaten me with a "NiPLOC"—Non-Punitive Letter of Caution—a toothless form of personal reprimand. Not wanting to throw my driver under the bus, I stood there and took it. In retrospect, I think it would have reflected worse on Major Select for being so petty as to NiPLOC an officer for going a few miles per hour over the speed limit, but I felt ashamed at being scolded like that, especially in front of a subordinate. The event took up half a page on my official counseling document two months later.

We were all looking forward to returning to COP Taghaz the next day on the Marine Corps Birthday. As part of the celebrations, we had been promised two beers each and a delivery of mail, along with a visit from the mobile Post Exchange (PX) truck with a disbursing agent for cash withdrawals. Beer, mail, a PX call, and money—what could be better for morale? It was a solid plan in theory.

In the morning, we woke up to news that the PX truck was already at Taghaz and scheduled to leave in the afternoon for FOB Payne. There was no way we would be back before it left, but we also learned that repairs had been completed on two of our trucks, which were ready for pickup at Payne. Not to miss our PX call, Major Select decided we would spend the night at Payne, get our vehicles, hit the PX, sip our beers, and convoy back to Taghaz the next day. It was a short drive to the FOB, and we arrived just after the commanding general choppered in for the birthday celebration. By a stroke of good luck, we arrived too late to stand in formation for the general's speech but still reaped the benefits of his visit with lobster and steak for lunch at the DFAC. It was shaping up to be a happy Marine Corps Birthday.

Things took a turn when we learned that our trucks were still waiting on repairs. Then things turned further—the PX truck hit an IED right after it left COP Taghaz. To cap it off, we found out our names were nowhere on FOB Payne's roster for receiving our promised birthday beer. Major Select called over to Taghaz, where we had also been left off the roster. That night as we all laughed about our misfortune, Major Select submitted our list of new call signs with "NoLove" at the top of the list.

Our fortunes improved somewhat the next day: the repaired PX truck made it to Payne and opened its doors for us, and Captain Quinn let us know that he'd salvaged one beer each for us back in Taghaz. Our mail was still lost somewhere, but the beer was a huge morale boost for everyone after consecutive days of disappointment. The celebrations were short-lived; we learned our team's call sign was now "Vampire." Aside from Captain Quinn, who submitted the idea, nobody was happy with the name that evoked the pop-culture fad favored by teenage girls. Ironically, NoLove seemed more appropriate than ever, but Bobo-6 seemed intent on disgruntling us further.

Shortly after assuming ownership of the mission in Southern Helmand Province, Bobo-6 issued what nobody could call a thoughtful or operationally necessary order: no mustaches. It was common for Marines to grow mustaches on deployment, an opportunity to experiment with facial hair and look ridiculous for a while even if we were governed by strict grooming standards that prohibited hair from touching or extending beyond the corners of the lips. As advisors, several of us indulged in the tradition, encouraged by the prospect of building rapport with Pashtun men who viewed facial hair as a symbol of masculine virtue. Although it gave me the appearance of a registered sex offender due to the other infantry tradition of shaving one's head at the start of the first combat deployment, I had grown fond of my whiskers. And after Baddar Gul had asked me, "Are you impotent?" when he found out I had yet to sire children, I was really banking on my mustache as the last crescent of manliness to buy me credibility with him. Major Select verified that the order to shave deployment mustaches extended to advisors as well, so we all grabbed our razors and, cursing Bobo-6, complied.

The only Americans exempt from the shave order were the two civilian Embedded Police Mentors (EPMs) attached to our team. Coming from decades-long careers in police departments from across the United States, EPMs joined Marine advisor teams assigned to Afghan police units to balance out our pure military roles with some law enforcement expertise. Our EPMs, Sonny and Chris, were at the tail end of their yearlong tours and brandishing the best mustaches they could grow.

*   *   *

Sonny joined my section for a memorable overnight and patrol with 1st Tolai on November 13. My original plan was for the ABP to practice searching vehicles and personnel so we could see what, if any, techniques they employed. But with Baddar Gul on leave and Sher Ali at Taghaz Station supervising truck repairs, there was really nobody in charge when we got to PB Gherdai. Sher Ali's brother, a patrolman named Omar, hosted us in the sergeant's room where we drank tea and played cards for a couple of hours.

One of the sergeants, Karim, took a truck down to TCP 3 to get vegetables and got stuck in the sand on his way back. Another truck from TCP 3, trying to recover the first, also sank into the loose, wet sand that offered no friction for the treads, immobilized. The ABP then took a Humvee out, and soon it, too, was just spinning its wheels. Just before sundown, the ABP asked us to bail them out. I had reservations about going outside the wire so close to dark, but I empathized with the ABP's anxiety about leaving several vehicles stuck in the mud overnight, and compassion prevailed. Staff Sergeant Pulst and I did our pre-combat checks to make sure we were prepared for night operations, and we pushed down the hill in two trucks. It was another goat rope that included one of our own trucks getting stuck at one point, but we eventually recovered all the vehicles and made it back to the patrol base within an hour of sundown. We talked about finding a long-term solution to this problem, either scouting another route or contracting a road-improvement project that could help the ABP and their community. When Sher Ali returned from Taghaz Station, I encouraged him to take the issue up his chain of command.

Dinner was rice with an oily dish of leafy greens called *sabzi*, similar to creamed spinach. Afterward, we charted a patrol for the next day over tea and cigarettes. The plan was very tentative, as Sher Ali was trying to get leave approved so he could visit two of his men that had been flown to Camp Bastion after being injured in a Humvee wreck. One of the men had no family except for Sher Ali and his brother Omar, and the three of them, with wives and children, shared a compound in Lashkar Gah. Sher Ali's concern for his friend was a real distraction that night—he kept pressing us to get more information over our superior radios. I felt frustrated, but I recognized that I would have felt the same concern had it been one of my Marines. By the morning, we had received the report and shared that all three were in stable condition. The news helped mollify Sher Ali to an extent, but did not change his plan to visit the Kandak headquarters to petition for leave to visit them. He set out for Taghaz Station in the morning and left one of his sergeants to take us on patrol.

What Sergeant Walid lacked in height and maturity he made up for in confidence. He only got a short brief from Sher Ali and then snapped into action, gathering seven other patrolmen and leading my section on a foot patrol along with Sonny and an interpreter, Mustafa. "Moose" was a laid-back Afghan-Canadian who Major Select usually retained to work with Headquarters Section, but we rotated him into the lineup to give Ahmed a break from patrols. We all shuffled down the Shelf from the patrol base, through the sandy swamp, and on to Route Mexico. They clearly had a routine of patrolling south down Mexico, across the bridge to the PCO, and then east down Virginia. This was the third consecutive time the ABP took advisors on that same route. I made a note to encourage them to vary their path before the Taliban could exploit their pattern.

After a quick stop at the PCO where Lance Corporal Malone overpaid for a pack of local cigarettes, Carnage radioed down to me from COP Taghaz that the aerostat blimp had spotted a few individuals who were digging next to the road and stopping everyone who walked near them. Two of the diggers departed, heading east in a white car, but a man in black stayed there beside a cornfield. I passed the report to Walid and, given a GPS grid from Carnage, talked Walid onto the exact location as we made our way east along Route Virginia.

"Two hundred meters ahead . . . now about one hundred meters ahead, that's the cornfield with the man in black clothes who was digging. . . ."

As we approached, carefully scanning the sides of the road, Walid called out to the man, "*Dalta rasha.*" *Come over here.*

When the man propped himself up on two crutches, it became clear why he had sat there all morning, and why he had what could have been mistaken for shovels. On the other side of Route Virginia, a shopkeeper showed the ABP patrolmen the new irrigation ditch he had dug that morning alongside the road.

As we pieced together the story, my guts twisted and burned with a feeling of biological urgency that I would soon come to know all too well. Soiling yourself on patrol was almost a rite of passage for deployed Marines, especially those who ventured to eat the local food. I accepted that my number had been called, and looked around in a panic for somewhere to relieve myself. Not seeing many options, I confided in Moose off to the side.

"Dude, I'm about to shit myself. Where should I go?!"

Moose surveyed the options. We were in the middle of the main residential and commercial strip of town, but there was some farmland to the south with a drainage ditch that came right up to the road.

"Just go in the ditch," Moose replied in a high pitch, like the answer was obvious.

"Seriously?" I was eyeing the privacy of some shrubbery by a windowless compound wall on the opposite side of the road, hoping to conceal my sin.

"Yeah, that's what they do." Moose lived in Vancouver, so the practice of open-air defecation was foreign to him as well.

With the green light of Moose's cultural expertise, I hopped into the ditch while everyone else was distracted talking to people and waited for that moment of certain humiliation, acutely aware that it would be recorded for modernity by the aerostat cameras zoomed in on my patrol. As I hit the pressure-release valve on my gastrointestinal distress, I looked up from the ditch and locked eyes with a nearby farmer, instantly compounding my panic with guilt. *Did I just create another Taliban? Did my diarrhea lose us the battle for hearts and minds? Was everyone watching the live feed at COP Taghaz laughing at me? Would Major Select threaten to NiPLOC me for this too?* The immediate physical relief was soon followed by a psychic calm, and I climbed back onto the road, relaxed but ashamed.

"Should I give something to the farmer, or try to clean up?"

Moose reassured me. "Nah, man, you could have even gone in the middle of the field if you needed to—I'm telling you, it's what they all do."

His explanation was enough to remove whatever doubt remained that the freshly harvested *sabzi* from the night before was the insider threat I never saw coming.

We continued down the road to where it ended with a group of buildings. An old man came out to greet us, next to bags of fertilizer and corn from his farmland.

"What are you growing?" Walid asked the man, introduced to me afterward as Haji Barak Khan.

"Poppy, mostly."

I watched to assess how Walid would handle it and see what guidance Baddar Gul had provided. Walid struck a tone of curiosity.

"Why do you grow poppy when you know it's illegal?"

"I make more money growing poppy than from growing the same amount of wheat."

Walid nodded to concede the point, and Haji Barak Khan invited us into his courtyard for tea. Around a dozen children, curious and friendly, slowly converged on us as we sat on the soft grass in his courtyard. Haji Barak Khan complained to Walid of a fever and achiness, so in a gesture of goodwill I broke out my single dosage of Tylenol from my first-aid kit and gave it to the grateful old man. When our glasses were empty, we thanked the old man and stepped off to the southeast on a path he pointed out for us to navigate around his farmland.

Our next objective was a cluster of buildings one kilometer away from the main strip of Gherdai. Nobody, including the ABP, knew the name of this small hamlet, and there had been no known coalition presence for a year. I had set a goal to visit the area ever since I'd observed it on my map in between the areas of responsibility assigned 1st Tolai and 3rd Tolai. The boundary, if detected by the Taliban, would have been a perfect gap for them to exploit to move weapons, drugs, and fighters through the lines.

As we approached the hamlet from the north, an old turbaned man came out to greet us with a smile on his face. I gave Walid space to talk with the man as Moose quietly interpreted their conversation for me. While they were talking, more and more young boys came out to watch and gathered around our group, while the rest of the patrol provided 360 degrees of security for our local engagement. The locals all squatted down around us as we stood. I asked the man, Haji Alim, if he would lead our patrol around the hamlet so we could become acquainted with the area. He declined.

"If the Taliban see me helping you or somebody tells them, they will come for me."

"There are Taliban here? Or you don't trust your neighbors?"

"No, there are no Taliban here, but they could be watching from the surrounding farmland."

This response fit in with Baddar Gul's description of the local villagers' level of cooperation with the ABP. Respecting the limits of his hospitality, we thanked him and guided ourselves on a quick tour of the hamlet before returning back toward the PB.

On the way back, we passed by Haji Siddiq Khan's compound. He came out to greet us for a short, friendly encounter.

"You promised me twenty Hesco!"

I chuckled to myself at his predictability.

"*Sahib*, I made no such promise. But we did inspect the road and bridge you told us about, and the ABP are going to see what they can do about it."

Gracious in defeat, Haji Siddiq Khan smiled as we said goodbye, and the patrol climbed up to the patrol base on the final leg of the journey. After a quick debrief and lunch with the ABP, we mounted up and drove back to COP Taghaz.

The next day, we learned another reason why Haji Alim had been squatting down while talking to us and refused to guide our patrol through the hamlet. In rural Afghanistan, the locals popped a squat on occasions when a Westerner might sit in a chair, a practice colloquially referred to by Marines as the "haji squat." But recent intelligence indicated it might also be a good survival technique around coalition forces. An informant in the area just south of that hamlet reported that the Taliban had been warning civilians not to hang around our patrols because they planned to start shooting at the ABP and Marines. Eager to confront the *dush-man* who had been hiding from us so far, the intelligence generated some excitement among the advisors. However, it was not good news for the counterinsurgency effort; the Taliban were effectively driving a wedge between the ABP and the local population. Unlike the Imodium I received from Doc O'Connor to avoid desecrating any more farmers' fields, there were no magic pills to assuage the locals' fear of the Taliban or skepticism of the ABP.

Chapter Nine

Escalation of Force

23_JAN_2013_
1531_AFT_(UTC_+_4.5)

Leaving the possible IED behind as 3/9 ordered, Staff Sergeant Pulst and I cleared the clinic compound with Sher Ali before pushing farther west. The rest of the advisors and ABP took a break at the clinic, except an ABP patrolman who we began to call "Old Boy." With silky black bangs protruding down from the knit beanie worn askance on his head and a thick black mustache on his neatly groomed face, Old Boy could have fit right in at a boutique Brooklyn coffee shop if not for the machine gun he carried and its attached drum of 7.62mm ammunition. He looked to have at least ten years on me, but carried himself with a youthful, unrefined enthusiasm. He and Ahmed trailed behind where Sher Ali and I walked *shana pa shana* in the field, with Route Virginia on our right and Staff Sergeant Pulst about ten meters to our left.

We were about seventy-five meters west of the clinic when the air burst around me with an earsplitting crack. I turned my head and saw Staff Sergeant Pulst looking back at me. We both dropped to the ground as our eyes met and Pulst called out, "We're taking fire!"

Instinct and training automated my response. I felt the butt stock of my rifle press into my shoulder as the rest of my body slammed into the ground; then I clambered a few meters to conceal myself behind a thornbush along the road. I peered around the bush and scanned the horizon for targets, but, finding none, the only thing I could fire off was a short contact report on my radio.

Bullets continued to impact all around us and against the walls of the clinic every few seconds. An urgent cacophony of "Where's it comin' from?!" resounded from the Marines going firm at the clinic.

"I dunno, but they can see me!" Malone answered with a maniacal laugh. He and Doc O'Connor, both on the north side of the clinic, ducked into an alcove just as a bullet impacted the wall next to Malone's head. He recognized the sound of the Dragunov sniper rifle from his days in Sangin.

"Hey, that shit was close, Doc!" Malone came around the corner into the alcove, cackling. "They were aimin' for us."

"Yeah, I fuckin' caught that." Doc was not amused.

Malone chuckled. "Yeah, one a' those . . . one a' those rounds 'bout three foot from me."

He was grinning ear to ear. "Hey, Doc, how you like gettin' shot at?" This was Doc's first combat deployment, and Malone was demonstrating his proficiency in combat small talk.

"I don't give two fucks about that!"

"I'm just tryin'a ease the . . . calm the situation down on you, Doc."

"Well, I'd feel a hell of a lot fuckin' better if I knew where this fucker was at and I could shoot at that!"

A burst of machine-gun fire spat up dirt inside the courtyard of the compound, which opened to the west, sending Sergeant Polk and Corporal Palacios behind a caved-in wall for cover. Palacios loaded a 40mm explosive round into the breach of his M203 and scanned for a suitable target. From my patch of dirt behind the thornbush, I assessed a rough enemy position to the west and called it up to our retransmission site, where Staff Sergeant Ortega manned the hooks as "Vampire Mobile" and relayed the news over to the rest of our team at the Taghaz Annex.

In those initial moments, it didn't even occur to me that Sher Ali had disappeared from the space between me and Staff Sergeant Pulst, where he had stood moments earlier. Nor did I have any clue that he had been shot.

*   *   *

Why was it that Baddar Gul could march at the front of patrols unarmed, while every effective Afghan leader—each a potential rival of his—fell victim to the Taliban? Maybe competence put a target on their backs. Maybe the Taliban calculated that they were better off with Baddar Gul alive and inept than dead and replaced by someone more effective. But I couldn't shake my suspicion that something more sinister was afoot. What urgent business had called Baddar Gul back up the hill that day? The pattern had started with the killing of Baddar Gul's predecessor in command of 1st Tolai, Haji Samad, and it hadn't ended there.

On November 7, 2012, Lieutenant Yaqub and Lieutenant Zarif, the commanders of 2nd and 3rd Tolais respectively, had set out from Taghaz Station to spend a few days of leave with their families in Lashkar Gah. Out on a desert road, they came upon a truck that seemed to be riding low—too low for the five bags of onions bouncing around in the bed. When they pulled the truck over and searched it, they discovered eleven hundred pounds of opium and four bags of refined heroin stashed beneath a false bottom in the bed. They arrested the driver and brought the contraband back to Taghaz Station, where they were celebrated as heroes. Lieutenant Zarif, Hollywood-handsome with a thick black mustache, secured his place of celebrity among the ABP and

Marines in Taghaz. Lieutenant Yaqub, round-faced and balding, received some praise too.

One of the bags went missing amid the revelry, prompting one of our team's linguists to remark aloud in Pashto that the Marines could review video footage from their aerostat balloon to track it down. The odds that one of the balloon's roving cameras happened to be recording inside Taghaz Station at that very moment was quite low. But regardless of whether or not we had the footage, raising the possibility was enough to scare the errant bag back into ABP custody. Major Select put me on standby to run a convoy to the District Center the next day as an additional armed escort for the ABP transporting the prisoner and evidence. Instead, Colonel Nasrullah decided to personally bring both the prisoner and contraband up to the Zone Headquarters in Lashkar Gah, where the triumphant Tolai commanders also made the journey and spent some well-earned time at home.

Three weeks later, once everyone was back from Lashkar Gah, we heard the sound of sporadic gunfire to the south of Taghaz Station. I was the guardian angel posted outside Colonel Nasrullah's quarters where he was meeting with Major Select about an upcoming operation. Per our protocols, we had chambered rounds in our pistols and in our rifles to make them battle-ready before we walked over to visit with the Afghans, and we took Motorolas to maintain communications with the COC in COP Taghaz. After the burst of gunfire, my radio crackled.

"Post 2, we hear shots fired about one thousand meters south of our position."

At the same time, one of the ABP radios came to life and Moose translated for us.

"These guys say they were test-firing a weapon after cleaning it at TCP 2."

That was a plausible explanation, until we heard some more shots fired and the Afghan radios picked up with an urgent tone.

The first report was that Lieutenant Zarif's truck had been hit. In the chaos of a combat engagement, the first reports are always incomplete, if not inaccurate, and this was no exception. Subsequent transmissions indicated that Lieutenant Zarif himself had been shot. As the interpreters translated the radio traffic and the panicked exchanges of the ABP who were present, we watched the ABP strap on their chest-rigged magazine pouch carriers, grab their AK-47s, and dart into the closest vehicles. Five Danger Rangers peeled out of the gate by the time we got a clear report over the radios.

Colonel Nasrullah stepped away from the men around him and looked up at me as a frantic voice on the radio broke through the static. His usual soft, fatherly expression seemed to drain of all vitality. Moose didn't need to whisper the translation for me to know what had happened to the 3rd Tolai commander. The look in the colonel's eyes announced that his protégé, the rising star of the Kandak, Lieutenant Zarif, was dead. Two other ABP patrolmen had also been killed. The colonel shook his head, and as he walked past me, I muttered a weak, "*Commandan, Sahib . . .*" and trailed off, unable to offer condolences in that moment of shock. Major Select sent me and a few others back to the Marine side of the outpost to prepare to source a QRF.

We walked back into COP Taghaz knowing that we weren't going out to the ambush site. The fighting was all over. Instead we grabbed Doc O'Connor, Doc Matias, Lieutenant Maynard, and the other 3rd Tolai advisors to go back and help with the arrival of the casualties. Meanwhile, I listened on our internal radio as more information trickled in over the wire. One of the bodies had been shot more than twenty times. That detail, combined with the first report we'd received about a weapons test fire, had everyone speculating about whether this ambush could have been an insider attack. When the responding ABP reported back from their rage-fueled manhunt, where the aerostat balloon observed them shooting across the Helmand River into berms, the picture became more clear.

In a Baluchi settlement just east of the Taghaz Bazaar that everyone called Cluster Town, Taliban fighters had taken positions behind the walls of a compound whose owner had been away in Lashkar Gah for the previous three days. When Lieutenant Zarif drove past in his Danger Ranger, they opened fire with an initial barrage from the rear of the truck, then closed in on the cabin to empty their magazines. Once they were certain the ABP were dead, they fled on motorcycles to the river, forded across on foot, and escaped on the other side in a white Toyota hatchback—the exact color, make, and model of the local taxis. Our aerostat cameras missed them, since its operators had followed the initial reports from the ABP radios and interpreters that placed all the action in the Bazaar. Eventually the cameras panned out from the Bazaar, searching for the *dushman*, but only in time to see the ABP running through fields, firing wildly across the river at ghosts.

One of the first ABP on the scene was Amir, known to the Marines as Holy Moley after the giant mole on his nose. Holy Moley and Abdul, a patrolman from 1st Tolai, were buying Moose some pomegranates from the Bazaar. Hearing the gunfire, Holy Moley and Abdul were first on the scene to discover the bodies in the truck, riddled with bullet holes. They gave chase and shot at the vanishing shadows of the Taliban, but they were too late. They did, however, recover the motorcycles the Taliban abandoned at the river, which were Iranian-manufactured and bore Iranian license plates. They also found a hand grenade, which they disabled with a "hard det"—pulling the pin to blast it on-site. This was the ABP's preferred method of rendering explosives safe.

We returned to Taghaz Station later that night to talk about coordinating a casualty evacuation. Holy Moley joined us with the rest of the ABP who had responded to the firefight, but his characteristic smile and enthusiasm were strikingly absent. We expressed our condolences but had little else to offer as advisors, so we stood around burning cigarettes together in somber silence. I'd already smoked my daily allowance, but, given the exceptional circumstances, I rationalized a fourth. Bobo-6 initially denied our request for a helicopter to transport the bodies to Lashkar Gah, and instead suggested that the Kandak call the Afghan Air Force. Major Select made phone calls into the early morning, and finally got approval for an American helicopter to fly them out that next day.

Every member of Border Advisor Team 1, plus our linguists and embedded police mentors, stood in line as the ABP ambulance ferried the casualties out the gates of Taghaz Station to the landing zone. Gunny Jackson called us to attention and gave the command for a hand salute. We raised our hands slowly in unison, counting to five seconds before reaching the peak of the salute and remaining in position while the three bodies passed before us. Lieutenant Maynard and Doc Matias helped the ABP escorts load the three body bags onto the bird, and it took off into the orange morning sky, leaving only a whirl of dust in the wake of the rotors.

The Taliban hit Major Select the next day.

It was Thanksgiving. Major Select was invited to a meeting that afternoon and a security shura two days later at COP Castle, so we developed a morale-boosting plan: two nights at FOB Payne with showers, real toilets, and DFAC—just a hop, skip, and jump away from Castle. Major Select tasked me with planning and leading all three days of the convoy operations.

My mission brief included an intelligence update. In the previous few weeks, several IEDs had been found or struck by convoys driving on the highly trafficked Route Uniform, which ran parallel to the river a few kilometers to its north, just below the Shelf. The Taliban were emplacing pressure-plate IEDs with secondary devices to catch overly hasty or adrenaline-influenced responders to the first blast. Some reports indicated that the cell operated out of the town of Khyrebad, where the ABP used to have a patrol base. Recently, the Taliban had started moving their IEDs northward into a large wadi with steep slopes on either side, creeping slowly up the latitudinal lines on our map to the 86 northing.

As I briefed, the mine-roller restricted our trucks to only a few known crossing points, and part of every mission was to recon other places to get in and out of the wadi. Our route would be along the 88 northing—Route 88 was our creative name for it—two kilometers away from the most recent IED. This route balanced out the risk of enemy activity with speed, as Route 96—guess where that was—added an hour or two to the trip but had virtually no threats.

Our mission was delayed by a visit from the commanding general, who flew down from Leatherneck to demonstrate his care for us on Thanksgiving. After a little formation and a short speech, the general took off, leaving us to go to work.

We zigged and zagged out the serpentine entry point of COP Taghaz around 1120 and waited outside the wire to link up with two ABP vehicles, which folded into the rear of our convoy. Sitting next to me behind the wheel of the lead vehicle—"Vic 1" in Marine-speak—Corporal Palacios took us slow and steady up to the Shelf, and then to the east as we approached the wadi north of Khyrebad. At the wadi, we cut farther north to avoid the crossing point that would bring us down to Route Uniform and pushed up to Route 88. As we approached the wadi north of Khyrebad, I spotted a promising entry point and marked it on my dashboard's computerized Blue Force Tracker.

"Vics 3 and 4—hold at the crest while we find a crossing point on the far side," I radioed to the others as we dropped into the wadi with Vic 2 behind us.

The wadi floor was about one kilometer across, filled with loose-packed sand, a peppering of shrubbery, and some tracks from previous convoys and civilian vehicles. We scouted for a route up the other side and attempted to climb out in two different sets of tracks, but the earth was too soft for us and the mine-roller sank in both times. We backed down to the solid ground and ran straight north, looking for other options. Finding none, we arrived at a location we'd used twice before.

The climb was steep, and there was a sketchy dip in soft sand at the top where, just for a moment, we would teeter on three wheels, but we knew it was trafficable for our trucks and hoped it would be for the ABP. Corporal Palacios put the truck in neutral to lock up the differentials, climbed up the first step to where it leveled out, and then shouted up to Malone in the turret.

"Hold on!"

Corporal Palacios accelerated before the second slope up to the top. We almost had enough momentum to make it, but stalled where the mine-roller sank in at the crest. We backed halfway down to where it leveled out and tried again, Corporal Palacios slamming the pedal to the metal. The mine-roller pushed through the sand and we bounced around inside as the truck got the job done for us this time. Pulling ahead onto the open desert about 125 meters to allow room for Vic 2 to set up behind us, I called back for Vics 3 and 4 to break down their overwatch and follow our tracks through the wadi.

Thanks to the four pots of coffee we'd drained while we stood by for the general's speech that morning, I took advantage of our momentary pause to release my five-point seat belt with the flick of a wrist and dismount from the truck to relieve myself. I went through the layers (patrol belt, blast diaper, flame-retardant trousers, and blast panties), did what I had to do, and then layered back up. I climbed back up the two running boards and into my seat, closed the armored door, and cranked down the lever of the steel combat lock. I was straining to pull shoulder straps from behind my neck to buckle up when we were rocked by a thunderous blast to our rear. Shrapnel whizzed past my window, where seconds before I had been standing with my treasures exposed, as a dark brown plume billowed upward behind us.

Fuck, they have mortars!

My initial thought was instantly corrected by Malone's shout from the turret:

"IED! IED! IED!"

I leaned forward to see Vic 3 come into view through the explosion in my side-view mirror. Mortars had come to mind since Vic 3 was in the same tracks where the mine-roller, both sets of our vehicle tires, and both sets of Vic 2's tires had already rolled over any buried pressure plate. But an IED was still the more likely culprit, and I was thankful that the enemy had not suddenly developed the capability to shell us with such accuracy.

While we all waited what seemed like an hour for someone in Vic 3 to get on the radio, I directed Corporal Palacios to pull our vehicle around to the south and drive up to the edge of the wadi ██ and provide security for Vic 3. Staff Sergeant Ortega in Vic 2 radioed back to COP Taghaz that we had hit an IED, since he had heard my unacknowledged attempt to transmit the report moments earlier. He pulled his vehicle forward to take our previous position ██.

That's when I finally heard Major Select's voice.

"[static] . . . Vic 3 . . . [static]."

I was about to call back to ask about casualties when I saw the contingency signal flare shoot up from their turret and out of sight. An eternity later, the pyrotechnic burst in the air and Malone reported the color down to us in the cabin: green. No casualties, thank God. I took a deep breath and got to work coordinating our recovery.

While I worked the radio and Blue Force Tracker, Staff Sergeant
Pulst dismounted from Vic 4 with the metal detector and swept
a lane up to ███
███████████ assess the damage. The left rear tire was blown to
shreds. The whole rear panel was missing on the left side. The
CVRJ, a vehicle-mounted equivalent of the THOR radio frequency jammer (and a Russian doll of acronyms) was blasted
beyond repair. The Marines' packs that had been strapped down
in the truck bed were launched away and scattered across the
wadi. There was no way we could recover the vehicle; this was a
mobility kill.

Doc O'Connor followed the cleared path up to Vic 3 and ran
Captain Everett, Gunny Jackson, and Major Select through initial
assessments to screen for signs of traumatic brain injury (TBI).
The blast had lifted Major Select and Gunny Jackson up into
their five-point seat belt restraints instead of the ceiling, while
the gunner's harness had kept Captain Everett from launching
into the air—or, perhaps worse, into the steel turret cover. They
were rattled, but all passed Doc's initial TBI assessments. Next,
the five of them started sanitizing the truck, taking down the gun,
disassembling the radios from their mounts, and grabbing all other
serialized gear out of the vehicle. By then, the dust trails on the
horizon had materialized into the four trucks from the Carnage
QRF.

Our dreams of showers, shitters, and Thanksgiving feast at the
DFAC had blown up with the truck. Since we were still closer to
Taghaz where the QRF originated, that's where we would return.
Ever thankful, we found some hot turkey and mashed potatoes
saved for us back at the COP Taghaz chow tent. Best meal of the
deployment, hands down.

The EOD team gave us their post-blast analysis based on their
survey of the scene and some component parts they recovered,
including a barcode on some packaging. The IED was composed

of aluminum powder and about forty pounds of ammonium nitrate—the chemical we had tested for in the fertilizer of the truck stuck in the sand near TCP 3. Its trigger was a simple victim-initiated pressure-plate switch built with bracketed wood planks and wire. The force of the mine-roller, two tires from Vic 1, two tires from Vic 2, and a front tire from Vic 3 all compacted the wooden planks into the loose sand, so that the rear left tire of Vic 3 was the straw that broke the explosive camel's back. The pressure collapsed the space between the two planks, connecting the wires to form a circuit and spark the fuse. ███████████
██
███████████████████████████████.

Given how the mine-roller had failed to detonate the pressure-plate and restricted us to a single crossing point coming out of that wadi on Route 88, I saw two options for adapting to the Taliban's northward-creeping IED threat: drop the mine-rollers so we could utilize our All-Terrain Vehicles as designed to avoid choke points in wadi crossings; or allow the Taliban to deny us an area of operations by charting our routes even farther north into the Desert of Death. Citing how the mine-rollers restricted our mobility into predictable patterns and the Taliban knew how to defeat them, I made a futile request for permission to deviate from our standard operating procedures (SOPs) and ditch the mine-rollers. Bobo-6's risk tolerance being what it was, we convoyed to FOB Payne the next day on Route 96, mine-roller leading the way.

* * *

When it was Bravo Section's turn to lead the convoys, I often demoted myself into the role of a truck driver or a turret gunner. As it had been for Captain Everett, Lieutenant Maynard, and Captain Quinn on our Thanksgiving convoy, it was a treat for an officer to simply cover a sector with a machine gun for a few hours. Only it wasn't always simple.

One morning as we chugged along through the desert, I was up in the turret behind an M240B medium machine gun. I shouted down to Corporal Palacios to relay over the radio to the other three trucks in our convoy that a lone blue sedan, weighed down with luggage strapped to the roof, was speeding across the desert directly toward our trucks from our nine o'clock. That was my assigned sector. We had trained specifically for this possible vehicle-borne IED scenario, but my heart rate skyrocketed and I felt my muscles tense nonetheless. I raised my rifle to observe more closely through the optic; but at our speed on the rough terrain, I couldn't make out the driver or passengers clearly.

Following ISAF SOP 373 (Escalation of Force) I fired a pen-flare in the direction of the suspicious car, but it maintained its rapid advance, undeterred. Next were disabling shots—the flare was their warning. I flicked off the safety lever of my rifle and aimed for the car, now only a couple of hundred meters away at my eleven o'clock as it closed in on the trucks in front of me. As I rotated my body to aim for the hood, my muzzle hit the side of the steel turret cover. The turret was already broken, unable to rotate mechanically; the purpose of that convoy was to drop the truck off to the mechanics at FOB Payne for repairs. I twisted and lunged, but in the time it took to switch my rifle to my left shoulder to get a better angle, it was too late. At the exact moment I had to take the shot, I physically could not. I shouted a curse as a surge of anxiety, guilt, and fear washed over me, terrified that I had let a hostile vehicle reach my convoy. But as the car sped through the seventy-five-meter gap between the two vehicles in front of me, Corporal Palacios relayed up the message that it was merely a cavalier driver with his family, not an insurgent on a suicide mission with a car bomb.

While I was unable to open fire on that family, I had tried to. And I know that, by policy, I should have. With imperfect information and apparently threatening behavior, all I could do was follow our SOP, which could have easily caused the death of an innocent family. We all had just gotten lucky. My panic eventually subsided into relief, but I was furious at that driver for endangering his family. NATO coalition military convoys had been cruising around Helmand for over a decade at that point; what fool thought speeding right through the middle of one was a good idea? How many more tragedies would it take before they learned to keep their distance? At the time, I felt justified in my anger. But in retrospect, blaming the Afghans only masked the more troubling possibility: that we, too, were failing to learn from history.

A view of the Helmand River Valley from Patrol Base Gherdai. (AUTHOR'S COLLECTION)

Lance Corporal Cory Malone (left) teaching vehicle maintenance to the Afghan Border Police with Corporal Alfonso "Fonz" Palacios (right). (AUTHOR'S COLLECTION)

Two Marines check the crest of a blind hill on "the Shelf" with a metal detector. (BRIAN PULST JR.)

ABP Lieutenant Baddar Gul in his office/bedroom. ("AHMED")

Staff Sergeant Brian Pulst Jr. having lunch with the ABP. (AUTHOR'S COLLECTION)

The author (left) brings up the rear of the patrol after a helicopter insertion on Operation Steel Dawn. ("MUSTAFA")

Lance Corporal Malone provides overwatch for the Aerial Interdiction Force on Operation Steel Dawn. (AUTHOR'S COLLECTION)

Farid Khan lounges in the overwatch position during Operation Steel Dawn. (AUTHOR'S COLLECTION)

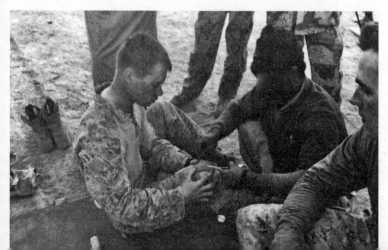

Zach "Doc" O'Connor (left) teaches Old Boy (center), other ABP patrolmen, and author (right) how to sew sutures. ("AHMED")

Sergeant Max salutes at Patrol Base Gherdai. (AUTHOR'S COLLECTION)

Alpha Section advisors stay dry in the back of a Danger Ranger. (AUTHOR'S COLLECTION)

Author (left) and Sergeant Sher Ali (right) discuss an ABP satellite patrol. ("AHMED")

Corporal Palacios confronts a herd of goats on patrol. (AUTHOR'S COLLECTION)

Doc O'Connor (left, sitting) prepares an injection for Sher Ali (right, standing) while Lance Corporal Malone (center, standing) takes a smoke break. Sergeant Polk (far left, standing behind the corner) and an ABP patrolman (far right, holding a brick) find work. ("AHMED")

Sergeant Karim tries to establish radio contact with Patrol Base Gherdai along Route Virginia. (AUTHOR'S COLLECTION)

Staff Sergeant Pulst provides security on patrol. (AUTHOR'S COLLECTION)

Border Advisor Team 1, Alpha Section. From left to right: Ahmed, Staff Sergeant Pulst, Lance Corporal Malone, author, Sergeant Polk, Doc O'Connor, and Corporal Palacios. ("KARIM")

The two mawins, *Staff Sergeant Pulst (left) with Sher Ali (right) at our last meeting.* (AUTHOR'S COLLECTION)

Sergeant Max cuddles up with Lance Corporal Malone at Patrol Base Gherdai. (AUTHOR'S COLLECTION)

Corporal Palacios watches an approaching sandstorm from a parapet at Combat Outpost Castle. (BRIAN PULST JR.)

Marines of Border Advisor Team 1 kill time in the Taghaz Annex during our final visit with the ABP. (AUTHOR'S COLLECTION)

Meme circulating in early 2013.

The author in an unguarded moment on the day of his homecoming with his uncle JGI II in the background. (KELLY WILLARDSON)

Chapter Ten

In the Dark

I saw Staff Sergeant Pulst pinned down in the open field without so much as a shrub to hide behind.

"Bound back to the clinic! I'll cover you!"

"Roger!" he bellowed back and grabbed Ahmed to move with him.

I popped my rifle sights over my beloved thornbush to scan for targets, but, unable to discern where the Taliban position was, all I could do was search and assess. The incoming rounds seemed to come from the west, but I also heard gunfire to our south, beyond the compound where our ABP satellite patrol took cover. The liberal spraying of automatic gunfire over my shoulder confirmed that Old Boy was still with me, and that he also thought the Taliban were to our west. I heard Staff Sergeant Pulst holler that they were set, rogered up with a shout of my own, and then yelled to Old Boy.

"Dzoo! Dzoo!" Let's go! Let's go!

As I turned and started my first bound back to cover, my peripheral vision registered Staff Sergeant Pulst and Ahmed behind walls of the clinic's courtyard, which surprised me. Not coming from an infantry background, Staff Sergeant Pulst was spared from having the rhythmic ditty *I'm up—they see me—I'm down* seared into his brain. It served to remind runners in the open to limit their movement to the amount of time it took to recite it. I meant for us to alternate our movement back to the clinic. Instead, since there was no cover in the open field, Staff Sergeant Pulst had taken Ahmed all the way back to the clinic in a single sprint. Pulst's first thought behind the thick mud wall was, *I wonder if the PCO is still open.* We were on our last packs of cigarettes, and resupply was an unofficial, tertiary goal of our patrol. His second thought was relief that he and Ahmed had both made it to cover unscathed.

Sher Ali was almost as lucky. He had caught a round from the opening salvo as he walked between me and Staff Sergeant Pulst. It grazed his right leg below the knee, splitting open the skin across his shin but with no more serious damage visible. He managed to book it back to the clinic on his own and ran around the corner into the alcove where Doc and Malone were conveniently posted. This nook, with solid mud walls that ran up to the roof on three sides and a fourth side that opened north, became our casualty collection point (CCP), and Doc O'Connor got right to work. Sher Ali took off his boot, rolled up his pant leg for Doc to bandage, and gave a thumbs-up with his favorite English phrase: "No problem! Ha ha ha!"

Bursts of automatic fire riddled the ground and the walls of the clinic before us as Old Boy and I darted back to take cover. Doc was still patching up Sher Ali when we rounded the corner and joined them in the alcove. We all figured the Taliban were shooting from the west, but we still needed to get eyes on targets. I tossed my pack and the metal detector on the ground next to Doc and told them I was heading around the east side of the clinic to get a position where I could gain some situational awareness, either over the top of the courtyard's crumbling five-foot mud walls or up on the roof. Malone offered to join me, but I didn't want to leave Doc O'Connor isolated from the rest of us.

"Do we have any security here for Doc?"

"Sher Ali can hold security with me," Doc interjected as he finished wrapping the wound with a pressure bandage.

"You sure, Doc? You want me here?" Malone gave Doc the out.

"No, I got it, it's good. You just fuckin' secure this shit and get this fucker figured out."

If it had been any other Afghan, there was no way on earth I would have let that fly. But I trusted Sher Ali, as did Doc, and we were as shorthanded as ever.

"Good to go." I peeled around the corner with Malone and Old Boy, leaving Doc alone with Sher Ali at the CCP.

I found the rest of my Marines in the courtyard behind various broken walls, all trying to pin down the exact location of the enemy positions. We observed that the ABP to our south were firing toward the southwest, at a compound about five hundred meters from where we were at the clinic. Old Boy fired at some movement behind a berm to the west, about four hundred meters away, but I couldn't positively identify any targets. As the sun sank in the clear sky, it backlit the Taliban positions and obscured our views with glare in our optics. Sergeant Polk gave a voice to our frustration.

"God damn! I can't see shit in that thick-ass fuckin' treeline over there with the stupid sun right where it's at; can't make out anything!"

I kept relaying information up to higher command as the fog of war lifted and we tried to pin down the exact Taliban positions, which seemed to be shifting. I saw a figure moving behind a berm some four hundred to five hundred meters to our west, and an ABP machine-gunner got a burst off at him before he ducked down out of view.

I called it in and realized that a few minutes had gone by without getting any response back from Vampire Mobile.

"Vampire Mobile, this is Vampire-1 Actual, radio check."

No response.

I pulled out my radio and saw the battery was almost empty. My spare was on the other side of the compound, in my pack with Doc.

"Shit. Who has a 152 battery?"

Sergeant Polk tossed me the green cube, which I swapped out as smoothly as I could change out an empty rifle magazine—this was a well-rehearsed battle drill for any infantry officer. After a solid radio check, my first transmission requested air support, "preferably fixed-wing or ISR."

Sergeant Polk advised me afterward it was best to let the JTAC do the weaponeering, so I explained to him my reasoning: we were not pinned down under heavy fire; helicopters could be heard from farther away than their optics could see; and I still wanted an Afghan face on this fight, not a "Marines come in to save the day" message ringing loud and clear. Imagery, surveillance, and reconnaissance platforms (ISR) or a jet's optical "pods" could provide support for us without giving away the Marine crutch. Only after the gunfire abated did an unarmed ISR platform ███ ███████ come on station overhead. I directed it west to look at the Taliban positions we'd spotted, but never heard anything back about what they saw.

Meanwhile, as our THOR systems jammed any incoming radio frequencies that could trigger a buried IED, they were also jamming the ABP's handheld radios.

"*Karwan—Polad—Karwan.*"

Sher Ali spoke into his Motorola, framing his call sign with Baddar Gul's to call back to PB Gherdai. Since our THORs were blocking the transmission, I asked Vampire Mobile to inform the ABP at Gherdai that Sher Ali was shot and asked them to send a medevac truck with reinforcements.

"You want us to send *our* QRF?" Staff Sergeant Ortega asked.

"Negative. Carnage QRF cannot reach this point." The bridge to the PCO was too narrow for our trucks. "It would be another half hour on foot from the QRF link-up point. ABP is primary QRF."

I felt confident we could handle the situation without Marine reinforcements, since I had a working radio, a full team of Marines, an aircraft controller, the two THOR systems, a corpsman, another hour of daylight, and an interpreter. During my first ambush at the clinic two months earlier, I'd had none of those.

*   *   *

We were acting on a tip from one of Colonel Nasrullah's informants about a possible IED-making facility in Gherdai. I was in the middle of a meeting with Sher Ali at Taghaz Station on November 28 when the colonel dropped in to share the preliminary report. He pledged to get a few more details from his source, a local villager whose cousin was a 2nd Tolai patrolman, and asked me to come back in the morning to discuss it. In the meantime, Sher Ali and I planned a patrol for the next day, when we would drive out to spend the night with 1st Tolai. We hoped to be able to act on the new intelligence.

With the planning complete, Sher Ali entertained us by recounting about an hour's worth of shit-talking he and the Taliban had exchanged over their unsecured radios a few nights earlier. It sounded like a serious debate about which side was actually helping Afghanistan, with Sher Ali attempting to persuade the Taliban to support the government and the Taliban arguing that the ABP should surrender. In addition to some offensive and hilarious insults, Sher Ali articulated a strong ideological argument and laughed about inviting the Taliban to come to PB Gherdai for tea. He was a happy warrior, certain in the justice of his cause.

We wrapped up our meeting by covering a few administrative issues. First, Sher Ali agreed to regulate Bazaar runs to control how often and how many ABP traveled down Route Mexico, where they were vulnerable to ambush. We also discussed the need to winterize the ABP's living quarters. It had rained so hard the night before, Sher Ali told us, that the water soaked through their plywood roofs. He was worried about his men getting sick. The Kandak had passed his request for materials up to the Zone level, and we promised that we would push it up the parallel advisor chain of command as well. At least, I told him, the weather should stay dry for us tomorrow night while we were there. Sher Ali laughed at the idea of a weather forecast.

"How do you know? Are you God? Ha ha!"

He was poking fun at the predominant view in rural Afghanistan, where most Afghans lacked access to technology that could predict something as random as weather. I laughed with him, and conceded that our weather experts are often wrong too. Only God knows, we agreed, and wrapped up our meeting.

That night, Captain Quinn burst into my hooch just as I was falling asleep.

"Izant, you know Arabic, right?"

"More like I *used* to know Arabic. What's up?"

He went on to tell me that a Carnage interpreter had heard some traffic on his radio ███████████████████████ ████████████████████████████████████. The 'terp said the voices were speaking in Arabic, but he didn't know Arabic.

"Shit, man, I dunno how much use I'll be at this point . . ." I offered.

"Dammit, Izant, you're worthless." Captain Quinn scowled as he walked out of my tent.

We both knew what a huge deal it would be if there were previously unknown Arab fighters now in our area of operations. I slipped into my combat Crocs, grabbed my Beretta, and wound through the maze of Hesco to the COC. By the time I got there, the radio traffic had died out. Ahmed talked with the Carnage interpreter to try to figure out if it was actually Arabic. Ahmed suggested it could have been Punjabi, which would sound foreign to a native Dari speaker like the Carnage linguist. I hung around with Ahmed for a little while to see if the traffic would pick up again; but, after half an hour and no further chatter, we called it a night. There was good news, though—3/9's intelligence analyst at COP Taghaz had managed to capture a directional bearing from his "Wolfhound" signal interceptor that showed the mysterious transmission came from the Gherdai area. I doubted there were Arab fighters in Gherdai, but this signals intelligence seemed to corroborate the reporting from the colonel's informant.

In the morning, I briefed Major Select on the signals and human-source intelligence that both indicated Taliban activity in Gherdai—a possible IED-manufacturing site, no less. As Major Select had been on the receiving end of a Taliban IED blast just one week earlier, I had his full attention. I suggested he join me at my meeting with the Kandak commander since Colonel Nasrullah was his counterpart, after all. We grabbed Mustafa and another interpreter and rolled over to the ABP station with Staff Sergeant Pulst and our communications officer, Captain Everett. Those two went to find the ABP communications officer, and the rest of us accepted an invitation into the colonel's private building for some tea and discussion of the ABP's intelligence reporting. He gave us the rundown:

Ibrahim, an ABP patrolman in 2nd Tolai, had heard from his cousin in Gherdai that the Taliban were using a compound near the PCO as a headquarters and IED-making facility. The compound had been home to a doctor with an in-house clinic, but the Taliban had kicked him out and took over the building. Recently, an old man who was just walking by was snatched up, beaten by the Taliban, and warned to stay away from the old clinic. Ibrahim's cousin reported that this clinic was five hundred to six hundred meters west of the PCO, behind some other homes.

We asked permission to walk back around the plywood wall that divided the colonel's living quarters from his office so we could see his map and try to pin down the exact location. Colonel Nasrullah called for Ibrahim to join us so there would be no mistake. From what Ibrahim's cousin described, there were two possible compounds: one right along Route Virginia, and another two hundred meters to the southwest, separated by a few acres of farmland. The four of us all agreed that the clinic was mostly likely the compound next to the road.

The colonel wanted to hit the clinic as soon as possible. Major Select deferred to me on the tactical advising; I would be the ground commander for the Marine side, since my Tolai was conducting the mission. The colonel's map had a very small scale, and the imagery was poor. More familiar with the area than the colonel, who had only assumed command a couple of weeks before our team arrived, I painted the ground-level picture for him. The bridge across the canal near the PCO, for example, was a dangerous choke point that the Taliban had recently exploited.

"Is there any other way to cross to the south side of the canal where the enemy wouldn't expect us or receive any warnings from their spotters?" The colonel stroked his neatly cropped beard, dyed black to hide the grays.

"*Sahib*, I think we could swing out west and then ford the canal to take positions in the jungle across the road from the clinic."

"*Dair sha.*" Very good.

Colonel Nasrullah labeled that the "ambush" team. He wanted the ambush team to set in on the northwest side of the compound to stake it out, while the main force pushed down Route Mexico.

"This way, the ambush team can shoot anyone who runs away once the main unit starts closing in."

The colonel's plan was exactly what I'd had in mind when I pointed out the choke point. The *Inception* was working.

"When should we go?" Colonel Nasrullah asked Major Select and me.

We reflected the question back to him, but he clearly wanted our input.

"You are my advisors," he pressed us. "When do you think we should go?"

"*Commandan, Sahib,*" I began in Pashto before burdening Moose with the translation, "the *dushman* can see our patrols coming from far away during the day, and their spotters let them know to depart before we get there. But, if we go after sundown when it is dark, we can have the element of surprise and a better chance at catching them."

I continued, having done my astronomical data research the day before as a part of my mission preparation.

"Tonight, a full moon rises just after the sun sets, and will provide excellent illumination for the operation all the way until sunrise."

"*Dair sha!*" The colonel instantly praised the idea and decided on the night raid. "We go tonight."

The colonel talked through the timing and sequencing of events: "The ambush must set in secretly before the main force comes, so they can stop the enemy from escaping. They need at least ten men. Then the main force will come with at least twenty men. How many Marines can we have on each team?"

Bravo Section was out with 3rd Tolai at the time, and Headquarters Section was conducting a convoy to the security shura the day after, so I knew it would fall to my section alone. Lieutenant Teller had also volunteered to join us, but, beyond that, advisors were spread thin.

"We can put two advisors with the ambush, and four with the main force."

The colonel frowned. "You don't have more Marines than that?"

I apologized that we did not, but submitted that the fewer Marines, the more likely we would maintain the element of surprise.

"*Dair sha*, then the ambush team can leave after sundown at 1800, and at 1900 or 2000 the main force can come. This is a good idea?" He looked to us to confirm.

"In my view, later in the night would be better, *Sahib*. If we find explosives we'll have to guard them until morning when EOD could come to support us."

Colonel Nasrullah paused to consider it for a moment, but waved it away. "We need to strike before the *dushman* can get away."

We finished the plan: At 1700, the colonel would bring some reinforcements from 2nd Tolai to Gherdai and brief Sher Ali on the mission (Baddar Gul was still on leave at the time). We would link up with our trucks outside Taghaz Station and convoy over to PB Gherdai together.

We walked back to COP Taghaz to prepare. Major Select got on the hooks to talk to the Wake-6 about the operation to request air support and EOD on standby. I used the aerostat balloon's surveillance camera and some imagery on our classified computer systems to study the area, then briefed the Carnage platoon commander and a few EOD technicians who would stand by as our QRF. We loaded up the trucks, conducted our final checks, and, driving the lead truck with the mine-roller myself, departed friendly lines right on time.

We reached PB Gherdai just as the sun dipped below the horizon. The colonel brought all the key leaders up to Post 3, which overlooked the village, to orient everyone to the area and review the plan one last time. Lieutenant Yaqub from 2nd Tolai would lead the ambush team and take Ibrahim as a guide. Sher Ali would be in charge of the overall operation on the ground, and he would lead the raid force. The colonel ended his brief with twenty minutes left for our final preparations. Right at 1800 when the ambush team was about to depart, the colonel invited Major Select and me to have dinner with him. I had to decline, since I was going on the ambush.

"But don't let Major Select eat all the food—I'll be hungry when I get back!"

The colonel laughed, embraced me, and shook my hand.

"Good luck, Lieutenant."

We filed into the night through a narrow gap in the concertina wire near Post 3 to avoid any Taliban spotters with eyes on the gate. The ambush team was just eight ABP, Corporal Palacios, and me. I strapped on an extra medical bag, but we had no corpsman. We had no THORs. We had no interpreter either. Between the two available for the mission, I had to leave one with Major Select and the colonel, and the other for Staff Sergeant Pulst with Sher Ali in the raid force. Our mission depended on my Pashto language proficiency and ability to navigate with my GPS at night in an area known only by aerial imagery. And I depended on Corporal Palacios to guard the two of us against whatever threats might emerge from the dark.

Our SOPs stated otherwise, but the illumination was so good that I gave the okay for Corporal Palacios and me to flip up our helmet-mounted night vision optics during movement. On security halts, we pulled them down over our non-dominant eyes to peer into the sharply cast moon-shadows. The ABP had no trouble moving in the moonlight either. At the marsh between PB Gherdai and TCP 3, Corporal Palacios and I hopped in the back of the

Danger Rangers with the rest of the ABP to be ferried across. It was a cold night, below freezing, and getting wet on the way out was a sure way to catch hypothermia. We were making so many exceptions to the rules, I figured we might as well bend another one to stay dry.

As we made our way past the first civilian compound, at least three dogs detected our presence and alerted everyone in a two-kilometer radius that something was afoot. We continued southwest into open farmland next to Route Mexico. I felt uneasy being that exposed and would have preferred to skirt a treeline to stay in the shadows, but this was the Afghans' patrol, not mine.

We were in the middle of a field when I noticed light splashing the trees along Route Mexico and heard the rumble of a motor.

"*Keshata shey!*" I whisper-shouted. *Get down*!

Ahmed told me afterward that the phrase I used was more like telling someone to come downstairs or dismount a horse . . . but it got the point across. We all dropped into the muddy farmland while the vehicle passed just fifty meters to our rear and continued down Mexico without slowing down or stopping. As soon as the car was out of sight, we picked ourselves up and continued on our way.

The patrol proceeded into the next acre, which was flooded to the point where the ABP could tread atop the mud without much trouble, but Corporal Palacios and myself sank down to our knees under the weight of our ballistic plates and the rest of our gear. The mud suctioned our feet into the ground with such strength that we had to pull hard to free our boots, which in turn put us off balance. We staggered through the field, struggling not to fall with each step. At the edge of that field we intercepted a pair of farmers walking to the compound of the elder Haji Musa. Yaqub must have received some directions from them, because we cut abruptly to the south about seventy-five meters and found an east–west-running trail.

Yaqub called a short halt when we got there to consult with me for directions. He sent Ibrahim down the line of patrolmen to verify that we still had everyone. I hit the power button once on my wrist GPS to turn on the low orange backlight and check our grid coordinates. I called a short position report up to the retransmission site at PB Gherdai, which they sent up to COP Taghaz, who sent it up to FOB Payne, and then FOB Geronimo, which was Bobo-6's operations center. I had also arranged for the aerostat balloon at COP Taghaz to track our patrol with its thermal optics. And I managed to bring a Predator drone on station to orbit our patrol and watch for threats it could take out with its Hellfire missile at my command.

"How much farther?" Yaqub asked me, eager to get into position.

In my best Pashto, I told him it was a few hundred meters to our southwest, through the jungle and across the canal. But, I cautioned, if we go straight there we will have to ford the canal. Or we could go to a bridge fifteen hundred meters west and then cut back, warm and dry. During my mission planning earlier that day, I had located the bridge crossing point on aerial imagery and marked down the grid. Yaqub agreed it was better to stay dry on such a frigid night, so we picked up and pushed west down the trail, threading a tall berm on our right and the thick jungle on our left.

That was about the time I lost communications with the retransmission site at PB Gherdai. I could still hear them, but my whispered transmissions were only coming in static. Per our "no comms" contingency plan, COP Taghaz continued to track us by using the lasers on the aerostat balloon to pull an estimated grid. They would relay the grid to me over the radio and I would confirm by keying the handset three times. Even that stopped working after half an hour and we were completely in the dark. Just eight Afghan patrolmen who had no idea where we were and two Marines who barely spoke the same language. We made it work.

My GPS told me we were close to the crossing point, but none was in sight. Up ahead seventy-five meters was a mudbrick house with lights on inside. After some deliberation, we began to approach the house to inquire about the bridge. Just before one of the patrolmen got to the door, Yaqub spotted the bridge to the south of the house and waved him back. We pattered along the footbridge, traced the edge of some farmland, and came to another canal crossing. Panic struck; I had memorized the map as well as I could, but did not remember another canal. At this point we were surrounded by darkened compounds and farmland. I wouldn't dare take out my map and use a light. We had no radio communications to request the aerostat balloon or drone operators to talk me on to my planned route. I tried to get a sense of our general bearings and gestured toward the direction of the target house, and Yaqub got the idea. *We have to find a way.* Eventually we hopped through a shallow ford, skirted across a wide canal along a large culvert, and found our way onto Route Virginia, over one kilometer west of the target.

Yaqub took my advice and led us eastward toward the clinic through the jungle between the road and the canal. I used my GPS to keep Yaqub updated with how far away we were, and Ibrahim spotted the target compound from about three hundred meters away. The jungle north of the road disappeared, and we found ourselves out in the open. We hustled down the road and hopped down into some recessed farmland. The field had a north–south-running berm, about four feet high and five feet thick, that ran from the road all the way down to the next compound, two hundred meters south. The ABP and I proned out on the western side of the berm in the defilade while Corporal Palacios leaned back on the berm facing west to cover our rear. Setting my sights on the clinic, I scanned for heat signatures through the thermal attachment I had fixed in front of my scope. Nothing. Feeling my way around the buttons in the dark, I switched the polarity from black-hot to white-hot, but still detected no warm bodies.

And sill no comms. I desperately tried to troubleshoot my radio and alternated between calling for the retransmission site and flashing my infrared-laser rifle attachment at the aerostat balloon I could see hovering over COP Taghaz six kilometers away. At last I heard Major Select come over the net to get a radio check with Staff Sergeant Pulst.

"Vampire 1 Bravo, this is Vampire 6, radio check, over."

I interrupted to make contact. "Break-break, this is 1 Actual, can you read me?"

"Roger, Vampire 1 Actual, uhhh, break. . . . We got your POS from the aerostat, uhhh, break. . . . Can you send your GPS to confirm?"

I passed our grid, rounding to the nearest ten meters.

"Roger, Vampire 1, looks like you guys are in perfect position, uhhh, break. . . . We'll establish a restrictive fire line along that road and make sure 1 Bravo passes your POS to his ABP before they head out."

Relieved to have mitigated the risk of friendly fire by reestablishing contact, I relaxed a little. The ABP relaxed a lot. Corporal Palacios first alerted me to the unmistakable stench of marijuana, wafting over from where the ABP were sitting behind the berm, backs to the target. I smelled it myself a second later. Normally we would refuse to operate with ABP on drugs—that was "no-go criteria"—but we were past the point of no return. What else could we do? The two of us leave the ambush to try and make it back on our own, while we left a group of high Afghan patrolmen to shoot at whatever moves? Realistically, we had to turn a blind eye. I made a mental note to inform Lieutenant Teller, who had the job (in addition to a dozen other responsibilities) of advising Lieutenant Yaqub and 2nd Tolai.

Lying flat in the dirt in sweaty cammies for over half an hour by then, Corporal Palacios and I were getting cold. The ABP had beanies and winter jackets, but they were starting to freeze as well. As if Corporal Palacios and I had no idea, we were reminded "it's very cold" almost constantly in Pashto whispers. The waning of their focus accelerated with every minute out in the frigid night air.

"Where is 1st Tolai? When will they be here?"

I felt like a sitcom dad on a road trip with a station wagon full of kids whining, *Are we there yet?* Instead of relaying Staff Sergeant Pulst's current position, I told them they were "almost" at the next major landmark, trying to inspire a little more hope through ambiguity.

When the raid force left PB Gherdai, I knew it would be at least an hour before link-up, so I did what any Marine in a night ambush would do: I broke out my chewing tobacco. I stuffed a fat wad of Redman Gold into my cheek and passed the envelope to Corporal Palacios, who gratefully partook. Next, I offered my American tobacco to the ABP. *Naswar ghwarey? Amrikayi naswar dai.* The pack was passed down the line and came back to me almost empty. At some point in the next hour, we were surrounded by howling coyotes, which made the stoned ABP giggle. I kept my mind busy tracking the movement of Staff Sergeant Pulst, who was with Malone, Doc, and Lieutenant Teller, as they moved south to TCP 3, then the PCO, and began heading west toward the target compound.

In our hasty preparations and concern with the ABP's planning, I had forgotten to do a little of our own. I had a red star parachute loaded in the breach of my M203 and briefed this pyrotechnic signal for "cease fire" to the ABP; but as far as a marking plan and near/far recognition signals, I dropped the ball. Instead, Staff Sergeant Pulst and I had to coordinate over the radio.

"Doc's up front with an IR strobe." Pulst relayed the impromptu mark for lead-trace—the visual indicator of the front of the patrol.

"Roger, flash three times. I can't see you."

I saw the infrared beacon flash in my night vision optic. "Got you. Let me know when you cross south of the compound to complete the cordon so we don't think you're Taliban in egress."

Our lack of detailed planning meant we were sending a lot of unnecessary radio traffic on a night mission where we wanted to maintain noise discipline. It was no help that Major Select was using the same net to talk to the retransmission site from Post 3. Every time he came on the radio it was loud as all hell, forcing Staff Sergeant Pulst and me to turn our volumes down. Consequently, almost every transmission needed to be repeated because we had to turn our volumes back up to hear each other's whispers.

As soon as the cordon was complete and Yaqub and I linked up with the ABP from 1st Tolai on the southwest corner, noise discipline went out the window. At our ambush position, ABP started playing music on their phones, stood up, and smoked cigarettes. Corporal Palacios and I still focused on security, but figured two more orange dots for the enemy would make little difference against the eight already burning, and each lit one.

Then through my thermals I saw a man on the roof. In a moment of nervous alarm, I stuttered out on the radio, "On the roof—there's a guy!"

Staff Sergeant Pulst heard the panic in my voice and undoubtedly knew my thumb was pressing my rifle's safety lever. He broke in:

"Friendly! Friendly! ABP are on the roof. We just made entry."

I flicked the lever back on safe and gave a heavy sigh. In the debrief afterward, I learned that Sher Ali announced himself loudly to potential occupants of the compound and then entered faster than Moose could interpret. An Afghan patrolman climbed up to the roof before Pulst even realized what was happening. It was a close call, and I was glad I had shown the patience necessary to avoid killing one of our own.

Pulst followed Sher Ali inside, using a flashlight to investigate the clinic's interior rooms. The ABP tore down doors that were wired shut to check every nook and cranny, and it appeared that the clinic was deserted. All they could find were pills, vitamin powder, syringes, and other medical supplies, some of which had been burned. Our findings corroborated at least part of our intelligence, that this had been a medical clinic and the doctor looked to have been forcibly removed. Frustrated with the dry hole, the search party began to approach the compound two hundred meters south to look for more answers, but Colonel Nasrullah called them off and gave orders to return to PB Gherdai.

When news of that order reached the ABP, they cheered in celebration and took off down the road in groups of four to eight. Once I confirmed that we had all the Marines, our corpsman, and our interpreter, we followed with a few straggling ABP and Sher Ali himself. As we approached the PCO, we saw a fire fan up about four hundred meters to our south. The aerostat balloon relayed that it was only a shepherd with his flock. To assert the ABP and Marine presence in the area and signal our location to PB Gherdai, Staff Sergeant Pulst let Sher Ali fire off a white star parachute out of his M203.

Sher Ali smiled as he launched the lumination round into the air, happy with the relative success of his mission. We'd failed to find any Taliban, but we had executed the plan without a hitch, at least in the ABP's eyes. After a quick ferry ride across the marsh in the bed of the Danger Rangers, we climbed up the edge of the Shelf to the patrol base, just the six of us from the advisor side and one remaining ABP guide. I counted our group in, checked all our serialized gear, and gave the word to Major Select that I had full accountability. Before I could get my hands on any of the leftover food, we mounted back up and convoyed back to COP Taghaz at around 0100. Major Select had a flight to Lashkar Gah in the morning for a planning meeting with Zone.

I woke to see my dusty rifle with the thermal sight still attached lying next to my bed, shaming me to get up and start my day by cleaning it after just a few hours of sleep. By the time we arrived at Taghaz, got final accountability of all our gear, and off-loaded everything from the trucks, it was close to 0200, so I had allowed my guys, and myself, to rack out without performing maintenance on our weapons and gear. Not that any of it was too dirty to function, but it broke the cardinal rule of "weapon before gear, gear before self." I swore not to violate that critical infantryman's commandment again.

I think I'd grown a little too comfortable deviating from our SOPs over the course of the mission that night. Corporal Palacios and I were outside the wire on our own, without a corpsman or the required THOR counter-IED radio jammers; we rode in the Danger Rangers instead of our armored trucks; and we partnered up Afghans who had consumed mind-altering substances. Major Select could have easily shot down the plan for deviating from Bobo-6's directives, or scrapped it when I lost communications, but instead he gave me the freedom to do my job as I saw it.

The exceptions to the rules and the additional risks contributed to the thrill of that mission. But what really excited me was the empowerment that came from shedding some of the cumbersome restrictions that made Marine patrols slow-moving targets for Taliban. It was liberating. Instead of being watched, hunted, or evaded on the occasional daytime patrol, that night we were the hunters. If only we had something to show for it.

Chapter Eleven

The Better Part of Valor

23 JAN 2013
1620 AFT (UTC + 4.5)

Sher Ali limped around the corner with Doc into the clinic's inner
rooms where Ahmed was hunkered down. Spotting them, I ran
across the courtyard to propose a course of action.

"I think we need to link up with Sergeant Karim to coordinate
a maneuver on the *dushman*."

Sher Ali held up his radio and shrugged. With our THORs acti-
vated to detect and jam radio signals, he couldn't get comms with
Karim, who was in charge of the ABP satellite patrol to our south.
In previous situations like this, we would momentarily deactivate
our jammers to allow the ABP transmissions to go through. But
we were in a compound that was twice now linked to Taliban IED
activity, and the compound would be obvious cover for anyone
under fire in that area. I was not about to let the Taliban bait us
into a remote-control IED attack, so I kept our THORs running.

"You'll have to send a runner," I told Sher Ali through Ahmed,
"just like the good old days."

It seemed that the fire had let up at that point and we needed
to make a move. I thought of a simple and effective plan.

"All right," I began, "drop both THORs here." I wanted to keep jamming signals at the clinic and free ourselves to maneuver more easily. Corporal Palacios would set up a hasty support-by-fire position on the roof with Sergeant Polk. Staff Sergeant Pulst and Doc would guard their rear at the bottom of the stairs inside the clinic. Sher Ali agreed to send a runner south with orders for Sergeant Karim and his men to cease fire so we could maneuver. I finished briefing my plan, which Ahmed interpreted, called it up to the retransmission site at Gherdai, and didn't wait for a reply. "Questions?" I asked. None. "All right, Malone and Old Boy—on me." Peeling around the northeast corner of the clinic, we darted across Route Virginia and jumped down behind the berm between the road and canal to its north. Using the berm to screen our movement, we crept west until we heard an unmistakable AK-47 burst ring out to our south. It was close—within a hundred meters. I nodded back to Malone; he popped the cap off the thin silver canister I had handed him at the clinic and reattached it to the bottom. When he looked up, I raised my left hand, palm out toward him: *Ready?* He curled his fist around the bottom of the signal flare and located a sturdy, flat surface to rest to strike it. He nodded back to me. Crawling up to the thin concealment offered by some salt cedar bushes, I peeked over the crest of the berm to see a black-clad fighter with an AK-47 crouching low, looking south toward a second fighter. I rolled to my back, ducking down from my reconnaissance to hold up two gloved fingers to Malone and Old Boy. I could feel the adrenaline surging in my blood and took a deep breath. My fingers scooped a 40mm explosive round off my belt and placed it into the breach of my M203, sliding the barrel down slowly, gently, quietly to lock it in place. I flipped the leaf sight up on the top rail of my carbine's barrel guards. Another deep breath. I rolled back to prone and shimmied back up the berm, muzzle first, to a gap between two bushes. Gripping the rifle magazine with my left hand and my finger flush with the M203's trigger, I exhaled and lined up my target at just shy of 150 meters. One more deep breath. There was a full second between the unmistakable clunk of the grenade launching from the tube and the concussive *WHOMP!* of its report at the far Talib's feet. During this eternity I thumbed the selector switch of my M4 to semi and released a controlled pair of 5.56mm through the near Talib's hips and chest as his colleague was blasted backward in a puff of dark brown. Malone slammed the canister down and the flare rocketed upward to burst into a cluster of bright green incandescence. "Go!" I shouted down my sights to Malone, who tapped Old Boy on the shoulder and led him in a bound across Route Virginia and down into the tilled farmland. Once I saw them set along the east side of the berm, I crossed over myself. Both Talibs were down, but Malone and Old Boy spotted the nearer man start crawling for his dropped AK-47 and fed him rounds until he was still. The three of us bounded through the Talibans' position, Old Boy kicking each of the bodies for a "dead-check" as we passed them to make sure they weren't faking it. . . .

That's what I wanted to do. That's what I was trained to do as a Marine, as an infantryman, and as a small unit leader. But that's not what I was meant to do as an advisor. Back at the clinic, this fantasy of combat leadership cycled in my imagination as I pondered what could have been and replayed it in the hours and days that followed. As loudly as my gut shouted *fire and maneuver* and my mind ran through variations of what I would do on a patrol of Marines, I knew that indulging in my infantryman's impulse would achieve little, and could needlessly endanger my Marines to both enemy and friendly fire. If we had been pinned down or had taken any American casualties, concern for our own safety would have outweighed the advising angle and I would have had no qualms seizing the reins. But this encounter, though still unclear and developing, appeared to fall squarely within the parameters of the combat advising mission. That mission was to get the Afghans to do the maneuvering, so I forced myself to abide by the advisor

tenet "never show them your camelback," and pushed Sher Ali to
decide on a course of action.

*   *   *

Not every advisor was quite as intentional about our role.
Certainly not the Zone-level advisors, who, in search of some
impressive-sounding bullet point to list among their accomplish-
ments, planned the series of misadventures known as Operation
Steel Dawn. Every local farmer, Talib, criminal, and ferry operator on the Helmand would hear, if not see, a helicopter-borne
aerial-interdiction operation coming from miles away. But this
obvious reality must not have dawned on the Marine advisors to
the Zone commander when they devised Phase One of Operation
Steel Dawn. There was no specific intelligence driving the operation on November 26, 2012; we would merely post a temporary
checkpoint on the north side of the Dishu ferry crossing for a few
hours to see if anyone nefarious stumbled into our nets. If there
was any way this advanced the mission of building ABP competence and confidence, it was lost on me. The ABP didn't have
helicopters. They could barely keep their trucks running and out
of the sand pits. But as the assistant patrol leader for the Marine
contingent, supporting Major Select in the lead, into the Shitter
and off I flew with a few dozen ABP.

At daybreak, we landed on the edge of the Shelf some twenty
kilometers southwest of Taghaz, overlooking the Helmand River
Valley and the Dishu ferry crossing point. Planning for contin-
gencies like "red air," when no medevac helicopters would fly due
to unsafe weather conditions, we had to pack two days' worth
of water and food plus all the gear in our standard loadout. I
was tasked to set up an overwatch position with Lance Corporal
Malone, while Major Select went with the main interdiction force
to set up a checkpoint closer to the ferry crossing. Mostly for

the use of its powerful optic since neither of us had any live-fire training with it, Lance Corporal Malone and I took out a Barrett M82A1 .50 caliber Special Applications Scoped Rifle. We carried it disassembled in two pieces, and each took a cartridge of ammunition to spread-load its heavy weight. While tactically questionable but convenient for us, we only had to lumber one kilometer from the helo insert point to our overwatch position, where we settled in with a sweeping view over the farming village below.

In theory, this was still an ABP operation, so two Afghans—a young patrolman and the notorious Farid Khan—tagged along with Lance Corporal Malone, Moose, and me to the overwatch position. For all his infamy and insubordination, Farid Khan seemed like an agreeable guy on first impression. He was smaller than I had pictured and maintained a casual, friendly demeanor throughout the operation. Unlike Baddar Gul, he carried a weapon with him and even wore a watch, as if to signal his embrace of modern warfare. From our brief interaction, I could see how, as Tim described, the Tolai functioned better with Farid Khan as a leader. But alas, he lacked Baddar Gul's pull with the Ministry of Interior.

As expected, the day was uneventful, especially for the five of us in overwatch just glassing everything that moved in the fields below. We noticed a truck speed away from a small compound when we landed, but nothing else of note. Not to call the operation a total bust, the ABP called in an Aerial Interdiction Force, which flew out from FOB Payne in helicopters to raid that compound. The ABP might have lined their pockets as they "secured" the surrounding fields of marijuana, but there was nothing else of interest. We called the Shitters to take us back home.

*   *   *

The second phase of Operation Steel Dawn was an improvement in theory, since a ground-based clearing operation was something we could reasonably expect the Afghans to execute on their own. But the only thing that was actually made clear was that "Operation Steel Dawn" was just a fanciful label the Zone advisors applied whenever 1st and 2nd Kandaks worked together. Except for those left behind to defend their patrol bases and TCPs, all the ABP in the Kandak took part in Phase Two that December, supported by nearly all the advisors and a trio of EOD technicians in tow.

My section was tasked the day prior with a convoy to FOB Payne and back to pick up Major Select, who had flown to Lashkar Gah for the planning conference, and grab some other logistical supplies for the operation. Since we were going out for a full week, we loaded up a seven-ton cargo truck with an extra fuel tank, water, and chow. We had only learned that we were going along with the ABP on the operation the night before, when a furious Captain Quinn threw the handset at the classified phone line to hang up on the Zone advisors. Orders were orders.

It was a mess from the start. On paper, we were to begin the clear on December 5, 2012, starting seventy kilometers southwest of Taghaz, and gradually work our way up to an end point at the village of Paygel. From COP Taghaz, we plotted a 107-kilometer route across open desert, well north of the Helmand to avoid having to cross through wadis. It was slow going even before the seven-ton broke down on Day 1. Falling behind at the outset, we had to spend the night in the open desert to wait for a logistics convoy from FOB Payne to bring us a functional seven-ton.

Day 2 was another failure. In the morning, the ABP left us behind with the disabled seven-ton to go start the operation without us. We got the replacement truck and were about to return to Taghaz instead of chasing the ABP around the desert when three dust trails appeared on the horizon. Colonel Nasrullah with his detail had come to guide us to their location. We brought our vehicles out onto the edge of the Shelf to provide overwatch for the ABP down below, "clearing" (i.e., parading through) the villages on the northern bank of the Helmand. Second Kandak was operating independently on the southern side of the river, having also abandoned their advisors out in the desert. Border Advisor Team 2 (BAT-2) ended up returning to their quarters at FOB Payne after a day and a half with no sight of or contact from their ABP counterparts.

First Kandak had cleared the first village in the morning before we showed up, and the rest of the day was spent waiting for 2nd Kandak to catch up on their side of the river. Days 3 through 5 were about the same as Day 2. We would push northwest to the next overwatch position, as the ABP would "clear" each successive little village, and return to their trucks at the end of each day.

Up on the Shelf, we were bored, frustrated, and restless. We took turns up in the turret, maintaining visual contact with our ABP or 2nd Kandak when we could, while the rest of us lifted some weights we brought out, played music on our iPods, smoked cigarettes, brewed coffee in Doc O'Connor's percolator, bullshitted with the ABP who were left in overwatch with us, stacked rocks in competitions to see who could create the tallest structure, or simply tossed rocks at other rocks. Captain Quinn took great pride in the textbook fighting holes he dug in the sand at each successive overwatch position. Sully looked so content in his folding camp chair, you'd have thought he was on vacation.

At night we set up a watch rotation of two-hour shifts, keeping our minds busy by alternating between thermal sights and our night vision optics, between looking out toward the villages and in toward the ABP camp one hundred meters away. On the third night I discovered that the rolled-up fire blanket stowed under the front passenger seat of our truck made for the perfect pillow on the desert floor where we slept.

In the dead of night I woke up to panicked screams.

"Help! Please, help! I can't get out!"

It disturbed but did not startle me. The night terrors were routine. I unzipped my bag and leaned over to soothe Lance Corporal Malone, still asleep on the desert floor next to me.

"You're good, buddy. It's all right, you can get out."

Without waking, Malone settled back into silent slumber. His Sangin demons visited so frequently over our time working and living together that everyone in Alpha Section knew to expect—and how to pacify—these outbursts. It happened again the very next night. I responded the same, this time unzipping the bug-net cover of his sleeping bag, just in case it might help for him to feel like he really could get out of wherever his subconscious was trapped.

Every morning out in the desert, Chef-Doctor-Barber O'Connor would plug his electric skillet into our truck's electrical outlet and cook up some eggs from the Bazaar, scrambled with dried onions and bacon bits that someone had ordered on Amazon. I survived off Doc's cooking and the snacks I accumulated from all the care packages I received from friends, family, and strangers. I'd made it a personal goal not to eat a Meal-Ready-to-Eat the whole deployment, and this weeklong operation was a challenging test, especially since the ABP chow was off the table. With the intent to force the ABP to rely on their own logistics, we had orders not to share any of our water or food with them, which they asked for constantly. Someone would saunter up to our trucks and run through the spiel of "How are you? Operation is good? You aren't too cold at night?" before eventually coming straight out to ask for water. We knew it would have been unfair if we ate their food and did not reciprocate.

Our apparent indifference to the ABP's pleas for water and declining invitations to eat together had noticeably damaged our rapport with them. About midway through the op, Major Select ordered my section to join 1st Kandak's clearing operation down in a random village in order to strengthen his relationship with the

Kandak commander. I had to protest. I was bored out of my mind and desperate for something to do, but this was just reckless. Our mission on Operation Steel Dawn Phase Two was to assist the ABP from the Shelf by screening north of their clearing operation and provide limited medical, QRF, and EOD support. As far as our own backup, 3/9 had an aerial QRF on standby at FOB Payne, but from our remote position the closest medevac would be outside the "golden hour" of transport time for getting lifesaving care. Furthermore, not only had there been no coalition presence in the village for over a year, but we had no intelligence at all about enemy activity in the area. We didn't even have a map. In my tactical judgment, this was an unacceptable risk, especially since the purpose was merely for Major Select to regain some rapport. After voicing all of these concerns to Major Select, he asked me one question:

"Is that all?"

We'd worked together long enough by that point for me to recognize that this was his code for "shut the fuck up, Lieutenant."

Despite the code of officer conduct prescribing that junior officers take ownership in commands from above, I made little effort to veil my frustration when I informed my section of our task. I wanted them to know I had gone to bat for them, and lost. No part of me enjoyed arguing with Major Select, but it was far more important to me, anyway, for these Marines and corpsmen with whom I shared meals, trucks, tents, batteries, tobacco, and ammunition to have faith in my judgment than for me to be a yes-man for my commanding officer. I gave them a bare-bones frag-O and began performing pre-combat checks as we threw on our gear.

Just then, Captain Quinn came over to my section's horseshoe of trucks and asked what we were doing.

"Are you serious?" he asked when I told him.

"Well, those are my orders." I flashed a flat, tight-lipped smile, inviting him to read my mind.

"Stay right here." Captain Quinn went off to talk sense into Major Select. The accumulation of the many tactical disagreements between me and Major Select had left me at a disadvantage, diluting my credibility in his eyes. Without this handicap, Captain Quinn was able to more effectively persuade Major Select, and he came back to tell us to stand down. We dropped our gear, relieved to be bored once again.

The ABP requests for water continued, and on the final night of the op we relented. Staff Sergeant Pulst and I gave Sher Ali a case of water and accepted an invitation to eat with 1st Tolai. At that point, we reasoned, we could spare the supplies since we were going home the next day, and they had clearly demonstrated an ability to sustain themselves for days on end, if not by their own logistics then at least through "tactical acquisition" of supplies from the local villages. It also bothered me that we really hadn't had any interaction with our Afghan counterparts over the course of the operation.

Sher Ali and his go-to, Sergeant Karim, set up a bonfire and brewed some tea they purchased in the Bazaar during the day's clear. They offered us sugar for our tea, which we accepted. One of the ABP clicked his tongue at us, warning that sugar was not just "no good," but "double no good" due to its effects on the teeth and their lack of toothbrushes. Staff Sergeant Pulst and I promised to bring them a couple extra toothbrushes so they could enjoy their tea sweetened.

The ABP chow truck rolled up shortly after dark with some bread and a hot stew of undercooked potatoes and chickpeas. As they passed out the pita discs and the trays of stew, Karim bashed their logistics officer for this substandard meal, getting everyone to laugh. It appeared that bitching about your chow, no matter how good or fresh, was not unique to Marines. After our meal, Sher Ali's brother Omar offered Staff Sergeant Pulst and me some of the Afghan tobacco, or *naswar*, which was finely ground and mixed with "other things," as we were told. Pulst and I each scraped out a pinch and placed it under our tongues. A strong menthol aroma tingled my mouth and I started salivating like crazy. The ABP and our linguist were amused and promised us we would soon be dizzy. We both had to spit frequently from how much saliva the *naswar* stimulated, and I got a solid nicotine buzz, but for Marines accustomed to straight-leaf chewing tobacco like Staff Sergeant Pulst and myself, the effects were short of dizzying.

One development I did not anticipate was the ABP's fascination with showing us pornography on their cell phones, which both Marines and ABP found hilarious for different reasons. The Afghans got a kick out of showing off this novelty to the Marines in a breach of our professional relationship; we thought it was funny that the Afghans thought it was funny. No doubt their heads would explode if one of them ever got access to the material on a deployed Marine's hard drive.

The recent technological advances that brought cellular reception to Khan Neshin District had gone a long way toward bolstering the ABP's morale, but it was constantly under threat. One of them explained to me why the Taliban often attacked cell towers: Good Muslims built the towers to please God so He would carry messages and images to and from their phones. The Taliban wanted to destroy God's beloved towers so He would become angry and stop carrying the transmissions. It was a phenomenal theory and only marginally less sophisticated than my own understanding of cellular technology at the time.

As we finished our third cup of chai, Karim reminded me to bring him some toothbrushes next time we came out to Gherdai. We parted ways so I could go stand watch, having lucked out with the early shift for the final night of the op after standing graveyard posts at either midnight or 0200 all previous nights. The prospect of six hours of uninterrupted sleep excited me nearly as much as the plan to return to COP Taghaz the next day.

* * *

We were nearly home when a spontaneous decision by the Kandak commander pitched us into an overwatch position at Gherdai for a few hours while the ABP paraded through the village, down to Kerum and back. They achieved no contact with the enemy or any other discernible effect—a fitting end to the week. We rolled into the gate at COP Taghaz just before sundown and made efficient work of our post-mission debrief and weapons cleaning, gleeful in anticipation of a decent night's sleep on our canvas cots.

Major Select woke me at 0200 on December 12 with a warning order. While we were out in the desert, the ABP had worked their informant networks to get a lead on a High Value Target suspected of taking part in the assassination of Lieutenant Zarif the previous month. Carnage set the aerostat balloon to focus on the target compound, where it captured footage of some men loading up possible weapons or drugs from underground caches. The ABP had set out to raid the compound immediately—we were too slow to make that mission. Instead, Major Select tasked my section to assist in the search if the ABP were unable to uncover the caches on their own. I roused the team into motion, planned out an operation, and staged vehicles to roll out of the COP with five minutes' notice. The ABP crossed the river and moved to the cache site with ease, uncovering multiple white bags filled with marijuana. They collected some for evidence, probably some to consume or sell themselves, and then burned the remainder. By then the detainee was on his way to Lashkar Gah, where the National Directorate of Security would take him into custody.

We got the word to stand down, and, shortly after that, to come collect our mail. Between shipments that arrived while we were cruising around the desert and another haul that morning, I had received over a dozen care packages. Most were Christmas presents from my family, friends, and future wife, so even though it was two weeks early I decided it was close enough to celebrate. After the second pot of coffee in the Alpha Section tent, I ran four miles' worth of laps around the inner perimeter of the COP; and as I finished, the bomb-sniffing canine was out with her handler at the smokepit. With the handler's permission and for the first time in two months—a personal record—I pet a dog. She was an affectionate black Lab named Misty. When I tore myself away from that calming dose of oxytocin, I felt like I was leaving home for the war all over again. Then, after seventeen days without a shower—another personal record—I took out two Nalgene bottles I had filled with tap water in San Diego before we left, heated them with an electric pitcher, and showered myself in the warm, cleansing waters of America. I threw on a clean pair of cammies and some new wool hiking socks I'd received in a box from my uncle, and felt like a new man.

When I walked into the COC to toss the return addresses from my packages into the burn box to be discarded with other sensitive documents, I was overwhelmed with the smell of mission success. I recognized the skunky sweet stink drifting over the wall from Taghaz Station, where I imagined a substantial crowd of ABP patrolmen were gathered "to supervise the evidence destruction" from a position downwind of the flaming pile of contraband. Maybe it was a coincidence, but I soon felt very hungry and went over to our chow tent for a hearty dinner of freshly grilled chicken kabobs with mashed potatoes and corn. It was the best meal COP Taghaz served up during my time there, second only to the post-IED strike Thanksgiving feast. After a week living out of our trucks in the desert, our appreciation for the combat outpost luxuries was at an all-time high.

But Operation Steel Dawn was not finished with us yet.

*   *   *

The ABP Zone commander came down from Lashkar Gah on January 12, 2013, to oversee what we prayed was the final phase of Operation Steel Dawn: a joint ABP clearing operation with the district's local Afghan Uniform Police (AUP). Though Captain Quinn and Major Select did all of the planning and coordination, I was appointed patrol leader for the 1st Kandak advisors pushing forward with some ABP to establish a northern blocking position. The 2nd Kandak's Marine advisors would execute a helicopter insert at a blocking position south of the Helmand. The main force of the AUP and ABP would then clear the villages along the Helmand from Gherdai to Khyrebad. We linked up with the ABP outside the gates of Taghaz Station and then made our way up the Shelf, just above the forbidding Route Uniform.

From the Shelf, we saw three men digging, and the ABP asked us to send a truck with them to check it out. By the time we reached Bobo-6 for his approval to descend the Shelf toward Khyrebad, the ABP had decided to go on their own. But as soon as the ABP dismounted, the men hopped in a truck and left. An hour or so later, the ABP claimed to identify some men on motorcycles about twelve hundred meters away as Taliban. For once displaying some realistic weaponeering, the ABP acknowledged that they could not range the bikers with their AK-47s, so they asked us to engage with our turret-mounted machine guns. While I wanted to help, I saw nothing even close to positive identification of a legal target. Under our rules of engagement, we had to first establish that our targets had performed some hostile act, such as shooting at us, or demonstrated hostile intent, like pointing a weapon in our direction. We could not apply deadly force on mere suspicion. I tried to explain this to the ABP without much success, but they accepted that Marine rules were different and we moved on.

Rolling down off the Shelf and along Route Uniform to stay parallel with the ABP clearing the village to our south, we spotted two patches of disturbed earth in the road in front of our lead truck. Each time, I called up our EOD technicians from the middle of our convoy. Each time, they carefully extracted a pressure-plate IED. They blew one in place and disarmed the other to bring back for intelligence analysis.

From the sounds on the radio and the stories we heard a few days later, BAT-2 had a hell of a day with the 2nd Kandak. On top of managing all the expected challenges, they believed they might have been under fire at one point, as gunfire broke out in their general vicinity. In the confusion, their extraction helicopter initially refused to land, believing it to be a "hot LZ," and was scanning treelines and compounds for Taliban to engage. There were none.

By the ABP's account, they had discovered that the AUP had tied up eight civilians on suspicion of being Taliban, and were in the process of beating them so savagely that two had fractured bones in their skulls. The ABP were outraged and fired warning shots at the AUP, who escalated with reciprocal displays of tribal bravado. The ABP bragged that they had disarmed the AUP at gunpoint before the respective Afghan unit commanders intervened to settle everything.

The one good thing to come out of Operation Steel Dawn was a new recruit for 1st Tolai. On our next trip to PB Gherdai, we were greeted by a little white fluffball, an Anatolian shepherd about eight weeks old that was determined to sniff and chew everything we put on the ground. Sergeant Max, as the ABP introduced him, had been "liberated" from a local compound during the clearing operation in Khyrebad. After he completed his training, they told us, Sergeant Max would be tasked with sniffing out IEDs and standing guard at the gate to the patrol base. They weren't joking, either. In a rare act of administrative housekeeping, Baddar Gul updated his personnel roster to reflect the addition.

Chapter Twelve

Edge of the Empire

23 JAN 2013
1622 AFT (UTC + 4.5)

During a break in the gunfire, Lance Corporal Malone removed his helmet and sat down inside the clinic's central room. Sher Ali broke out a pack of Esse brand cigarettes and passed it around. Doc lit one for himself and then held out his lighter to the dart dangling from Malone's lips. Malone had seen the future.

"I knew I was gonna get shot at on this patrol because I puked twice and my fuckin' back is killin' me."

"Hey, can I get one of those?" Sergeant Polk wanted in. "Nothing like getting shot at to remind you why you smoke."

Corporal Palacios and Staff Sergeant Pulst were holding down the courtyard, so I stuck around inside with Sher Ali and Ahmed, who seemed a little jittery. Like all our interpreters, Ahmed was not armed, so I tossed him my camera to give him something to do with his hands. Sher Ali was beginning to feel quite of bit of pain from the gunshot wound now that the adrenaline surge was wearing off, so Doc prepared a shot of Toradol for him while we chatted. Sergeant Karim jogged over with another patrolman from the compound to our south. Sher Ali agreed we needed to consolidate with the rest of the ABP to our south, but neither group wanted to move. I pushed him to make a decision and give the order.

"Do you want to go to those ABP or bring them here?"

Sher Ali wanted to wait for reinforcements. Doc stuck his butt cheek with the inter-muscular painkiller. Feeling impatient and stir-crazy, I drew a smoke of my own from the pack of Esses and climbed up to the roof to get a better view of the battlefield while we waited for the Afghan QRF.

"ABP Inbound!"

Corporal Palacios called out from the courtyard that the Danger Rangers were coming in from the east. One rolled right over the suspected IED and pulled up to the north side of the clinic along Route Virginia to position their truck-mounted .50 caliber DShK "Dushka" machine gun about five meters to my right. Old Boy was up on the roof with me, arm's-length off my left shoulder with his PKM, a 7.62mm medium machine gun.

The Taliban must have been watching. Right as the Danger Rangers pulled up, we took incoming fire once again. A round caught the lip of the roof right in front of me, and despite the splash of dried mudbrick it sent into my face, I clocked some dirt kick up from the ridge of a berm four hundred meters away and so did the ABP. Judging my identification of the enemy position to be positive enough under the circumstances, I returned fire. The forgotten plastic muzzle cap that had been keeping canal water and debris out of my barrel got a 5.56mm holepunch. A combination of Dushka fire on my right and Old Boy with the PKM on my left exploded in my ears. I couldn't even hear the rounds I fired from my rifle, only a high-pitched ringing.

Dust soon clouded my sight, machine-gun fire reverberated through the mud roof rumbling beneath my body, and the smoke of the cigarette on my lips tingled in my lungs. A feral cat scurried out of some nook in the clinic and startled Malone, who drew down on it reflexively but caught himself before pulling the trigger. Aside from sporadic bursts from the ABP, the symphony of gunfire subsided after a minute or so. The ringing in my ears lasted a bit longer, and I yelled a curse I couldn't even hear. Sergeant Polk and Doc came up to take my position on the roof so I could check in on my guys in the courtyard and try to get the ABP moving.

When my hearing returned, I heard Malone call out from behind a wall in the courtyard.

"Hey, sir, are you busy?"

We were in a firefight, albeit a lull. It may have been the busiest I'd ever been in my life. What the hell was he asking?

"Define 'busy.'"

"I can't get up," came his meek response.

Like most veteran infantrymen, Lance Corporal Malone suffered from chronic back pain, and humping the low-band THOR for us on that mission had put him over the edge. I peered around the corner and saw him sitting down on a pile of rubble with his back against a crumbling wall.

"'Are you busy'. . . ," I grumbled, and grabbed his hand to yank him up while he laughed at himself.

Staff Sergeant Pulst and Corporal Palacios had both heard the exchange, and since Palacios was already humping the mid-band, Pulst took the low-band THOR from Malone. Everyone hunkered down while I struggled to get the ABP to make a move. Sergeant Polk filled the silence between himself and Doc.

"This is the Edge of the Empire, bro, legit right here." The slogan we chose for our team shirts and patches never seemed more appropriate.

"This is right where they set all their ambushes in, like, I'm not surprised at all. As soon as we left TCP 3, I betcha they were already fuckin' waitin'."

"I'm surprised they hit us up with *us* here." Sergeant Polk, like the rest of us, assumed the Taliban would wait until after the Marines departed to attack. It was the whole premise for my stay-behind plan.

Doc agreed. "I am, too, but . . ."

"That means they had more than just a three- or four-man team."

Doc fell silent for a moment at the thought, then changed the topic.

"Hey, Staff Sergeant," Doc shouted across the courtyard, "does it still count for quitting smoking if I smoked one today?"

"No, I think you earned one. You want one?"

"Nah, I already had one."

"I'm still counting that I quit and I smoked." Sergeant Polk threw his support behind Doc's logic.

I had followed Sher Ali out to the medevac truck on the east side of the clinic and flagged him down before they whisked him away on the Danger Ranger.

"Who is in charge now?" I needed to talk to someone who could make a decision.

"Sergeant Karim."

I found Karim and tried to *Inception* him into moving west in pursuit of the Taliban. He shrugged it off.

"The *dushman* all left."

As Karim told it, the ABP in the compound to our south observed one civilian vehicle and two motorcycles egressing from the area where we had taken fire. But it appeared they left behind one motorcycle in the field two hundred meters to our west. We figured it was probably where a Talib or two had staged their ride before falling back to more solid cover when they observed our patrol advancing toward the clinic. Karim wanted to steal their motorcycle, and he asked me for permission.

"If you want that bike, you go get it. You don't need to ask me."

In retrospect, my nonchalance could have green-lighted them into a booby trap. Thankfully, it was not an IED—just bait. As soon as they got to the motorcycle, the Taliban opened up on us with a few bursts of automatic fire. Malone and I had trailed Karim back out in the field west of the clinic to look for a 40mm grenade round that had bounced out of my belt during the initial contact. The Taliban gunfire from the west was soon joined by the ABP shooting back at them over our heads from the east with the Dushka next to the clinic. Under fire from both sides, I grabbed Malone and we ran back to the clinic, chalking up the 40mm grenade round as a combat loss that was not worth getting shot over.

Karim and another patrolman met us back at the clinic with the bike. I pressed him to pursue the Taliban and at least check out their fighting positions, but Karim just wanted to take the bike and leave. My advice to return to base by a different route also fell on deaf ears. As a compromise, I requested a satellite patrol to our south to guard where we were most vulnerable to another ambush. "Okay, no problem," Karim relented and shouted for a few patrolmen to move south. They made it about fifty meters and then pivoted back to converge with the rest of the patrol. Not quite what I'd had in mind.

You would think Karim had announced an armistice from the way the ABP patrolmen reacted to his order with celebratory cheers, loud banter, and a swift parade back to base. Bemused by their utter lack of tactical posture, Sergeant Polk called out the command meant to signal the end of a training exercise.

"All right, ENDEX!"

* * *

The ABP were not the only ones to revel in retreat. In mid-December 2012 we put the war on pause for a couple of hours to throw a breakfast potluck. We each contributed whatever we could from private stashes or items we'd received in care packages to make it a memorable party. I chipped in some eggs that Sher

Ali had bought for me at the Bazaar and a pound cake I'd gotten in the mail. Sully manned a pancake station, while Doc cooked up the eggs. Lieutenant Teller offered up some peanut M&M's for the pancakes, a summer sausage, and a random Tupperware full of butterscotch fudge that someone had sent him in a care package. (Even the weirdest care packages were appreciated.) Our EOD buddies came over with an extra burner and pan to join us for the meal. We brewed up pot after pot of coffee, put on some Christmas music, and donned all the Santa hats we could muster for the festive occasion.

We were celebrating the end of our stay at COP Taghaz. The base demilitarization planners had determined that the war in Taghaz was either won enough or not worth winning anymore. Either way, its scheduled demolition was imminent. Carnage packed up the COC into hard-shell Pelican cases, folded down all the tents, and resettled at FOB Payne. The contractors reeled in the aerostat balloon one final time and deflated it to be hauled away with their trailer. Combat engineers showed up and gradually knocked down all the plywood, emptied all the Hesco, and hauled away the fuel station. By Christmas, all that remained of COP Taghaz was a small berm enclosure adjacent to the eastern wall of Taghaz Station, and our team had a new home thirty kilometers east at COP Castle.

Appropriately named, Castle towered over the river valley with its mud-wall perimeter, thirty feet high and ten feet thick. The fortress dated back to the seventeenth century, or, by some Afghans' accounts, the campaign of Alexander the Great in 330 BC. An incongruous collection of architectural improvements attested to all the various invading armies that had occupied Castle over the years, including the Soviets, the Taliban, and most recently the Marines. Old guard towers were turned into Marine posts with only a few modernizing improvements, and concertina wire filled the gaps where the walls had decayed or been destroyed. An outer perimeter of Hesco barriers and more C-wire formed an entryway that enclosed our vehicles, extra supplies, and a massive pit of smoldering garbage.

My section was assigned half of a semi-permanent climate-controlled tent. It was the same size as our old home, except here we didn't also need to cram in two interpreters or Lieutenant Ramsey. We also found a discarded stash of heavy fleece blankets left behind by a psychological operations unit with messages promoting Afghan unity printed in the local lingua. From then on, I caught my Zs beneath a giant baby-blue fleece that boldly proclaimed "Afghanistan has a bright future," in Pashto on one end and Dari on the other. They were a significant upgrade from our standard-issue sleeping bags, and I slept well under the insulation of that comforting lie.

COP Castle offered several other enhancements to our living conditions, to include foam mattresses on bunk beds, luxurious contractor-serviced shower trailers, a laundromat, porta-potties, and recreational tents with exercise equipment, computers, and a slow but reliable satellite-based Internet service. It was a novelty to be able to connect to the world back home so easily, but that world was not a font of joy. The connection brought us some of the expected deployment heartbreak—Lieutenant Maynard got dumped by his fiancée; Lieutenant Teller found out his girlfriend was cheating and broke up with her via satellite phone— but also the unimaginable. Late on the very day of our move to Castle, news reached us of an attack that had murdered twenty elementary-school students and six of their teachers and staff in Connecticut. While we were spinning our wheels in the desert on the other side of the world, American children were being massacred in their classrooms by some deranged monster with his mother's gun. It sucked the purpose out of our mission like a gut-punch, and I felt the gravity of the atrocity tugging me back toward home.

* * *

Up until the day before we vacated Taghaz, the ABP had only heard unsubstantiated rumors of our impending departure, presumably leaked by our interpreters. Major Select had instructed us to wait for the ABP's chain of command to inform them of the base closure, but that never happened. So, the morning before we left, Major Select and some other headquarters advisors went over to Taghaz Station to break the news. All too predictably, every officer in the Kandak was home on leave after the latest phase of Operation Steel Dawn except the financial officer. Far from alarmed, he was already resigned to the Kandak's fate.

"We, too, will be gone, not two months after you leave." He presented the facts: Without the aerostat balloon, enemy activity would skyrocket. ABP casualties and desertions would follow proportionally. Already the Taliban had exploited the opportunities afforded by high winds and precipitation to emplace IEDs while the balloon was down. Every Afghan and Marine on the ground knew that once that balloon was reeled in for the final time, the Taliban would operate without a fear of being caught. The ABP simply were not prepared for that yet. Rather than risk the piecemeal disintegration with casualties and desertions, the financial officer speculated, the Kandak would most likely move back to Lashkar Gah, where the unit had originated.

As rational as it was, the financial officer's prediction depressed me. I recalled Tim's final words to me:

This war is a lost cause.

The Afghans would withdraw nearly as soon as we did. And who could blame them? Not for a second did I pretend that Taghaz was key terrain in the battle for Afghanistan's future, or that Marines should be posted there indefinitely. Likewise, Taghaz was not a hill the ABP wanted to die on; everything and everyone they were fighting for was back home in Lashkar Gah. Given their chronic manpower shortages, logistical and maintenance issues, and complete dependence on the Marines for higher-level casualty care, I myself might have advised Colonel Nasrullah to redeploy to Lashkar Gah before the unit could fall apart. Without adjusting the plan to extend the Marine presence long enough for the ABP to stand on their own, the ABP's foray into Khan Neshin was doomed to end in failure. I discounted the even more depressing possibility that no matter how long the Marines stayed, the ABP would never be ready to stand on their own. Whoever believed as much, maybe they were right, but the ABP at least deserved an honest chance. Marines had only supported the ABP of 1st Kandak for one year since they first deployed down from Lashkar Gah. To expect that they would be operating independently in that time frame didn't seem honest to me.

From a remote combat outpost, I could only guess how our assessments, and those of other advisors, made it up the chain of command to inform policy. The truth had to pass from the advisor teams assessing the Afghans' progress to the field grade commanders and staff officers, who reported up to the generals; then from the Pentagon to civilian overseers on Capitol Hill; and finally from politicians and bureaucrats to the media and the American public. If the truth somehow survived this arduous journey intact, and even if it were believed, it still had to matter enough to influence decision-making. Alas, it did not. *The Onion* transcended satire that November in its article titled "Nation Horrified to Learn About War in Afghanistan While Reading Up on Petraeus Sex Scandal."[18] For American civilians, the war where so many bade a farewell to legs was, to borrow a another phrase from Ernest Hemingway, "as far away as the football game of some one else's college."[19]

Reaching out from Afghanistan to my own college that December, I wrote to a mentor and former professor, "Merry Christmas." I was feeling far from merry.

My experience thus far has been good, and you'll be happy to know that almost all my stress stems from the generals and politicians way above me in the chain of command. . . . All these reports about Afghans excelling, ready to take the lead on security—it's a load of horseshit, and it's soon to show. What the higher-ups are reporting is so far detached from reality, it feels like Goebbels is running this thing.

We're conceding ground to the enemy, and there's nothing I can do about it. . . . I imagine the Marines on the tail end of Vietnam felt similar frustrations. . . . It's all very depressing to me now.

My frustration with the direction of my work here is still fresh, but I'm getting over it. I know I'll be able to call this a successful tour if I can just bring my men back in one piece. And I know I am very blessed to have my foremost concern be our premature withdrawal.

In response, that mentor called to mind the congressional testimony of a prominent Vietnam veteran in 1971, his indictment of the generals and political leadership for abandoning their men, and his troubling rhetorical query, "How do you ask a man to be the last man to die for a mistake?"[20] This was not the same war, and I did not, nor do I now, believe our fight in Afghanistan was a mistake. Yet, in the commitment to a deadline-based withdrawal, shaping facts to support it rather than the converse, and asking men and women to fight for a foregone conclusion, a variation of that question haunted us.

I wrote that email when our team was at FOB Payne for a week, waiting for repairs on our trucks. The repairs were even more important now that we had to make a three- to four-hour convoy just for our Headquarters Section to meet with their Kandak counterparts back in Taghaz. On Christmas Eve our MRAP was finally ready to go, but not before the commandant of the Marine Corps flew into Payne with his wife in tow to inspire us with his leadership and share in the hardships suffered by the Marines on a FOB who were all required to attend his speech. I knew the commandant and his wife meant well, but it reminded me of the exhortations of Joseph Heller's Colonel Cargill, commanding the officers in Yossarian's squadron to "voluntarily" attend a USO show and have a good time:

> These people are your guests! They've traveled over three thousand miles to entertain you. How are they going to feel if nobody wants to go out and watch them? What's going to happen to their morale?[21]

The commandant and his wife each delivered a gracefully short speech standing on a mine-roller, and dismissed us for chow.

"Must be nice to fly your wife to Afghanistan to spend Christmas together," Staff Sergeant Pulst said, capturing our collective mood as we walked over to the DFAC.

After indulging in a Christmas Eve feast, we made the short trip up, across, and down the aptly named Route Tophat from FOB Payne to our home at COP Castle. As we settled in, I filled stockings for each of my guys, using two pairs of candy-cane-striped Stanford University socks I'd received in a package from one of my younger brothers, who was a senior there at the time. I stuffed the socks with holiday candies, hand-warmers, instant coffee pouches, Under Armour socks, cigarettes, chewing tobacco, and Slim Jims. I also threw a deck of cards in each stocking, as we received them in care packages in such abundance that hiding decks in random places became a running joke.

Major Select advised that we would be stepping in to cover as 3/9's Quick Reaction Force for two weeks, which meant being on call to respond to any units requesting assistance at a moment's notice, including to provide an armed escort for EOD to support any IED strikes and finds. Weapons Company 3/9 was stretched thin while they finished breaking down COP Taghaz, but as advisors we had no duties at the COP aside from the occasional radio watch in the COC. We were pretty much living there rent-free. As a professional courtesy to our hosts, and since we had no planned operations with the ABP, Major Select agreed for our team to be on the hook for any events in Khan Neshin District requesting QRF.

The repurposing of our team away from the advising mission bothered me. With my infantry background, I had no problem serving as QRF commander, but I believed our time was better spent with the ABP. I also found it irresponsible to task the many non-infantry Marines on our team to serve as the QRF for the battlespace. Alluding to the diverse military occupations of the team members, I wrote to a fellow infantry officer from 1/5 who was deployed on the 31st MEU, "You know this war is fucked up when they have five trucks full of butchers and bakers and candlestick makers heading out to save the day on QRF."

I wished QRF duty kept us busier than it did; an IED find on Christmas Day required an EOD escort, but other than that there were no other callouts. Between the week at Payne and standing by as QRF at Castle, we enjoyed a lot of downtime. I did my best to fill it with training. Doc refreshed our medical skills and had us practice giving ourselves IV drips. Corporal Palacios drilled us on disassembly, reassembly, and calibrating the headspace and timing of the M2 .50 caliber machine gun. Lance Corporal Malone supervised our preventative maintenance on all the trucks. I taught classes to the Marines in my section on how to plan for and lead a combat patrol, hoping to give them opportunities to practice in the near future.

I can't say I hated the showers, mattresses, DFAC, gym, and the time to tear through four books on my Kindle, but that was not how I wanted to spend my deployment. Even FOBbits had jobs to do. We were just being sidelined. I knew that a boring combat deployment was a good combat deployment, but I still was itching to get back in the fight, or else why were we even there? I felt like Captain Willard at the beginning of *Apocalypse Now*, languishing in misery between missions. But I had to catch myself; Willard prayed for a mission, and for his sins he got one.[22] It was peaceful, even cozy, at COP Castle. One morning between Christmas and New Year's, just after sunrise, I stepped out of the exercise tent into an Afghan snow globe. We were red air due to the weather forecast, so no one was going out on missions and the COP was dead quiet. As the 20° morning air froze my sweaty clothes and condensed my hot breath into clouds, I said a silent prayer of gratitude for the moment of boredom, beauty, and peace. After all, it was fleeting.

Chapter Thirteen

What Winning Looks Like

23 JAN 2013
1649 AFT (UTC + 4.5)

Our shadows stretched long in front of us as a full moon rose in the eastern sky over Route Virginia. Corporal Palacios alerted everyone to a group of men skirting our patrol six hundred meters to the north, across the road, a deep canal, and acres of farmland. I kept an eye on them, but I was more concerned with the south, where the Taliban could maneuver against us without crossing a deep canal. I continued to push Karim to send a satellite patrol in that direction, but he was certain that the Taliban had fled. He at least humored me by posting the Danger Ranger with the Dushka by the bridge to cover our withdrawal, but it took off toward TCP 3 when Karim reached the PCO. There, Karim waited for Ahmed and me to catch up, while the rest of the advisors and Old Boy straggled behind us along the road.

In the rear of the patrol, Doc O'Connor greeted a half dozen turbaned gentlemen as they rounded the corner of a compound wall to get out of the open field to our south.

"*Salaam Alaikum!*" Doc called out with a wave.

They responded with shit-eating grins. After all my failed entreaties to Karim, that was the final warning.

Incoming machine-gun fire zipped into the middle of our patrol. The first burst missed Sergeant Polk by mere inches. The second passed just over the heads of Ahmed and myself, both instinctively dropping to our bellies on the edge of the farmland. I crawled off the thick tilling and down to where the farmland was at its lowest as rounds snapped overhead into the berm behind me. I evaluated my situation: behind me and across Route Virginia to the north was the deep berm along the canal where Staff Sergeant Pulst, Malone, and Sergeant Polk had scampered down after the initial burst; in front of me to the south was open farmland for another seventy-five meters; back to the west was a compound where Doc and Palacios went firm with Old Boy; twenty meters to my east was the PCO, where Karim and a couple of other ABP had taken cover behind its thick mud walls.

"Get to the PCO!" I shouted to Ahmed and popped up on a knee to provide suppressing fire. After sending a few rounds in the direction of what looked like a Taliban fighter lying prone in a pine grove to the south, I followed Ahmed to the PCO in a dead sprint.

While I flew across the field, Staff Sergeant Pulst scanned to see where everyone was and, seeing me, shouted to the others.

"Lieutenant ran to the PCO!"

His phrasing set me up to bear the brunt of many jokes; my Marines all popped their heads over the berm to see their supposedly fearless leader hauling ass away from them. Once the jokes started, and they filled me in on what they'd seen, I laughed and razzed them.

"Why the hell didn't you lay down suppressing fire for me?"

"We were just in awe that our leader ran away!" Sergeant Polk said, displaying his characteristic smirk.

No one was laughing in the moment. When Ahmed arrived at the PCO, he turned back to see bullet impacts splashing dirt up at my feet as I ran through the field. One of the menacing goats who had stood down Corporal Palacios hours earlier was caught in that same field and did not survive in the crossfire.

I never quite made it to hard cover. In order to engage the Taliban and provide accurate suppressing fire for the rest of my team, I had to position myself at the corner of the building. There, instead of the thick mud walls I had expected, I found a thin screen of stick and straw patchwork. I would have much preferred the ballistic protection of hard cover, but the concealment was better than nothing. I sent some lead downrange to allow my team to maneuver, expecting to take some rounds through the screen at any moment, but the Talibs never got a bead on my position.

On the other side of the field, Doc talked Old Boy onto target.

"Dushman!" Doc pointed around the corner of the wall where he had taken cover. *"Dushman halta!"*

Old Boy strutted out from behind the compound wall and, beaming, fired his PKM from the hip in the direction Doc indicated. He looked to Doc for approval and received a thumbs-up. Corporal Palacios wrangled him in and tried to coach him into shooting from a supported position to engage the Taliban with accurate fire.

"Bipods! Use the bipods!" The English instructions and accompanying gestures proved futile.

From my position on the northwest corner of the PCO, I shouted—over the sound of gunfire whizzing in and popping out—to Staff Sergeant Pulst.

"Strongpoint the PCO!"

By that order, the team knew to consolidate at the hardened structure, which we could easily defend along our egress route. Pulst heard enough of my order to execute, and had the rest of our patrol bound laterally to the PCO from far to near. Each man along the berm would lay down suppressing fire for the man farthest to the west, who would scamper ten to fifteen meters east before dropping down to take a position on the defilade. "Next man!" he would shout after leapfrogging the others, and the process would continue. We'd only practiced such a maneuver once on a range with leftover ammunition and some free time during ATG at Twenty-Nine Palms. Impressed with the execution, which I learned afterward was coordinated by Corporal Palacios, I wondered whether or not I had communicated my intent for the "banana peel" over the radio. All Staff Sergeant Pulst had heard and passed back to Corporal Palacios was "bound to the PCO!" and it amazed me that from just that one live-fire event four months earlier, Corporal Palacios and I were on the exact same page. The maneuver stood for me as a testament to a fundamental tenet of infantry training: rehearsals.

There was only one minor flaw. In his dash from the berm to the PCO, Staff Sergeant Pulst went down.

Time stopped.

Those who saw thought the worst.

Was he hit!?

Then he picked himself up and kept running. Under the weight of his pack and the THOR he had taken from Malone, Pulst had merely lost his footing as he barreled across the dirt road. We might have felt more relief if we hadn't still been under fire.

While we shot back at the Taliban to our south, we noticed that we were also under heavy machine-gun fire from the north. When we alerted Karim that we were taking fire from both sides, he grew animated and started speaking with his hands and his best Pashtunglish. He pointed north and gestured: "No *dushman*! No *dushman*!—ABP!—Dushka bop-bop-bop!" He held out two fists and jerked them with each "bop," then pointed up in an arcing motion. The ABP were shooting over our heads with a .50 caliber DShK heavy machine gun.

"Overhead fire with a Dushka?! Fuck that, man."

Sergeant Polk said what we were all thinking. Due to the extremely narrow offset between the bullet trajectories and the position of friendly troops, overhead fire is considered too advanced for even Marine machine gunners to conduct without a proper safety offset and prior confirmation fire. For Malone and me, this was the second time in an hour.

Old Boy was still going strong with his PKM, and Corporal Palacios was still trying to be a combat advisor.

"Hey, Ahmed, do me a favor—let the guy know in order to get more accurate fire; tell him to put his bipods down."

"What?" If there was a Pashto word for bipods, Ahmed didn't know it.

"Bipods."

"The legs on his gun," Doc suggested.

Ahmed obliged.

Between the wild weaponeering of the ABP and our strolling right into the Taliban's sights, we were baffled that we all got to the PCO unscathed. I came back from my concealed position on the corner to advise Karim and make another attempt at requesting air support. Staff Sergeant Ortega relayed that ISR was coming on station, so I directed the unarmed reconnaissance drone to look between two hundred and four hundred meters to our south. I never heard back. As much as Sergeant Polk begged for it, we were not getting any armed aerial assets. Anyway, the fire from the south had died down by then.

"Well," I asked Karim, "are we going to go south and get these bastards?"

"Yes, but I need to ask for permission first."

His refusal to take decisive action was disappointing.

"It is better to ask for forgiveness than permission." I regurgitated one of my favorite military maxims, but to no effect. He insisted on clearing it first with Baddar Gul.

I passed on Karim's intention to go south so everyone could prepare themselves to maneuver on the enemy and swapped out my half-empty magazine for a full clip. I had everyone tighten up our already small perimeter on the north side of the PCO and told Staff Sergeant Pulst and Corporal Palacios to deactivate both THORs so Karim could use the radio.

"Karwan—Sarbaz—Karwan," Karim called back to Baddar Gul once we stopped blocking his transmissions. At the end of the lengthy discussion that followed, ten minutes had passed with no gunfire and the sun had reached the horizon. Ultimately, Baddar Gul followed Karim's example and pawned off the decision-making on me. I nudged Karim to a decision by framing the situation for him.

"How many ABP do you have with you right now?"

He looked around and counted, *"yawa, dowa, drey, tsalor . . ."* then jumped to *"las"* and gave me his fabricated total: ten. I had taken for granted that Sergeant Karim knew how to count past four.

"Right . . . and how much daylight do you think we have left?" I asked next.

"It's almost dark. What do you want me to do?"

Again, the infantryman inside me shouted *fire and maneuver,* but another voice was louder: Tim's. It wasn't fear of confronting the enemy or the chaos of a spontaneous night attack with the ABP shooting over our heads, but a growing fatalism toward our general mission there that pulled me toward prudence.

"My advice for you now is to return to TCP 3 and conduct a patrol tomorrow to survey the Taliban positions for evidence."

"Sha, dzoo," Karim said, as if taking an order. *All right, let's go.*

I knew if we weren't quick, we would get left behind; so I rushed to have my men check their own gear on the move. Ahmed had lost his ████████ radio, but rather than look for it in an open field where we had just been ambushed, I chalked it up as another combat loss.

"Hey, sir, what's the word on the air?" Sergeant Polk called out to me as I wrangled our section to mobilize. Despite my attempts to get something more useful than unarmed ISR, I gave him the update:

"We're not getting anything right now."

"Well, I guess I'll just go fuck myself then."

"Yep. We gotta get moving."

I started north. Paranoid about getting ambushed again on another predictable route of egress, we stepped off Route Mexico into the farmland and covered our movement in a bounding overwatch with our heads on swivels. As the sun sank below the horizon, we encountered a group of ABP with the truck-mounted Dushka behind a berm about five hundred meters to our north. Baddar Gul stood among them with a camouflage jacket draped over his robes. He was carrying only a radio.

I counted each member of my section into TCP 3 and we all popped off our helmets, drank water, and caught our breaths, grateful to be surrounded by Hesco and C-wire. The Marines and ABP were all smiles—this was the fun kind of fighting, and Sher Ali's grazed leg was the only casualty on our side. We switched our kits over for night operations, testing batteries, mounting night vision optics, and swapping out ballistic sunglasses for clear-lensed eye protection. One more quick round of accountability for our gear, and we began the final trek up to PB Gherdai.

Just as we filed out of TCP 3 into the dusk, I got word that an F-16 was coming on station. Sergeant Polk asked me if I wanted the fighter jet to perform a show of force—buzz over the village low and loud, spray some jazzy flares, that kind of thing. I was in no mood for theatrics.

"I don't think a show of force will do us any good right now."

"I don't think it'll make a difference at all," mumbled Doc, his helmet camera recording his agreement in the back of the patrol.

No one spoke as we climbed out of the river valley and up to the Shelf. Night fell to the sound of our heavy breathing, boots crunching earth, and the occasional loosened rock tumbling downhill behind us. At the gate of PB Gherdai I put a hand on each man to count everyone inside the wire and exhaled the tension I'd been holding for hours with the last man, Corporal Palacios.

When I had imagined how I would feel after my first combat experience, I expected a somber, contemplative mood in which to mull the gravity of my actions. The possibility that I had killed another human being and the reality that people had just tried to kill me and my men were both dead serious. The time for that, however, was later. As we dropped our gear at the safety of our truck enclosure, the endorphins of relief hit us like a palliative drug. We were jovial, nearly euphoric.

"Lieutenant became a man today!" Lance Corporal Malone beamed as he made the pronouncement to Bravo Section back at the trucks. The firefights were a first for Doc as well, but officers made for the better fodder. Malone was not done.

"Hey, sir, how'd it feel to finally become a man?"

I tolerated his insubordination; it clearly came from a place of pride and affection. I joked back and deflected, turning to Staff Sergeant Pulst: "Did I see you trying to buy cigarettes in the middle of the firefight?" I had clocked the transaction when we were holed up at the PCO.

He grinned. "Priorities, sir!"

We each lit one from the new stock, and my per diem rose to five.

Kidding around with my enlisted subordinates was a breach of protocol, but over several months living together in trucks and tents and fighting together that day, we had forged bonds of brotherhood that transcended the detached officer–enlisted command relationship that doctrine prescribed. The hypothetical risks of an unprofessional degree of familiarity seemed small in that moment, compared to my instinct to be human with these guys; we held each other's lives in our hands.

Sergeant Max came around and contributed in a more literal sense to our warm fuzzies. With that therapeutic canine instinct, Sergeant Max made his bed on top of Lance Corporal Malone that night. That was until Malone startled him awake with thrashing and desperate shouts in the sleeping bag beneath.

"Help! Please! Help me! I can't get out!"

On watch with me at the time, Staff Sergeant Pulst extracted Sergeant Max and comforted Malone with his baritone voice and a gentle hand.

"It's all right, buddy, you can get out."

Baddar Gul was sipping tea in his Hesco office when I finished squaring away our post-mission business and walked over with Staff Sergeant Pulst and Ahmed. I asked whether he'd conducted a post-mission inventory, which he told me was ongoing in one of the Hesco alcoves down the row from his. A cloud of marijuana smoke greeted us when we popped our heads in, and I saw a room with guns and ammunition stacked in various piles. We returned to his office, and with an almost certainly notional ammunition count, Baddar Gul read me his inventory report:

- 5 Humvees, all of which were in need of repair
- 4 Danger Rangers, two of which also needed repairs and the other two totally destroyed
- 26 AK variant rifles
- 8 PKM medium machine guns

- 2 DShK heavy machine guns
- 3 M203 grenade launchers
- 4 RPG rocket launchers
- 5 Motorola radios
- 1 officer (Baddar Gul)
- 5 sergeants (counting Sergeant Max)
- 23 patrolmen

Between the number of ABP on leave at any given time, and the assumed ghost soldier or two whose pay Baddar Gul was "holding for them until they returned from leave," and the three ABP wounded in the past week, they only had about fifteen bodies on hand. They were supposed to have eighty-nine.

"We are suffering," Baddar Gul told me.

With so few ABP on hand and five posts to staff 24/7 between the PB and the TCP, sleep was in short supply. In the dead of winter, temperatures dropped well below freezing at night—and there were no heaters on post.

"The patrolmen feel like nobody cares about them," Baddar Gul went on, "their higher command or the Afghan government least of all." Add to all that the recent Taliban ambushes and near-nightly harassing fire. I empathized with his position and promised to convey his complaints through the advisor chain of command, but there was little else I could offer.

Despite orders not to share meals with the Afghans—Bobo's intelligence unit warned of a possible foodborne green-on-blue attack based on an uncorroborated report that some Taliban had obtained mass quantities of poison in the neighboring province—we ate together and reviewed what had happened on patrol that day.

The two engagements with the Taliban offered valuable insights into 1st Tolai's combat readiness. As far as individual skills went, marksmanship training was a glaring deficit. What they lacked in accuracy and efficiency, however, they more than made up for in enthusiasm. Too much enthusiasm. While I admired their gung-ho attitudes and ballistic generosity, the risk to innocent parties in the surrounding area posed a moral problem and complicated the counterinsurgency mission. We all knew "collateral damage" was inevitable in warfare, and I had even had my own scare while following Escalation of Force protocols earlier in the deployment. Those kinds of accidents weighed heavily on the souls of the warriors with the fortitude both to acknowledge their victims' humanity and to overcome the instinct to repress it.

Not that the ABP were callous to civilian deaths, but they came from a culture with a tradition of celebratory gunfire that disregarded the hazards of gravity's bringing those bullets back down to earth. In their minds, the risks were merely hypothetical, until they were not. Dodging the cultural difference to make a more practical point, I explained how every noncombatant caught in the crossfire, goats included, could serve as a radicalizing grievance or be exploited by Taliban propaganda, which was all the more likely when the ABP left the area without conducting a battle damage assessment. Lastly, I added, there was the most obvious risk of all: running out of ammunition during a firefight.

Assessing the Tolai's small unit leadership under fire, it was hard to fault Sher Ali with indecision when he'd been shot and we were jamming his communications. As our own SOPs restricted us to an extent, we had to acknowledge where we got in the way: the THORs, and my refusal to deactivate them at the clinic, had crippled the ABP's ability to relay information to the Tolai headquarters, call a QRF, and coordinate a counter-ambush. But this was a foreseeable issue, and a predetermined no-comms plan would have saved the ABP a lot of time figuring out how to coordinate between units. At least we were able to mitigate the obstacles we created by calling out their QRF through our Marines at PB Gherdai.

Communications and succession of command issues aside, I had serious concerns about the ABP's tactical decision-making. The ABP showed a bias for inaction that allowed the Taliban to maintain the initiative. During the engagements, most ABP seemed content to shoot back and wait for it to be over. Then, once the QRF arrived, the runner made contact with the satellite patrol, and Sergeant Karim took control, all the ABP turned tail to head home. Without pursuing the enemy, knocking on doors at the nearby compounds to question the locals, or inspecting the Taliban fighting positions beyond where the motorcycle was recovered, the Taliban were able to maneuver and hit us again on the predictable route back to base.

Then, at the PCO, Sergeant Karim had to wait to get permission before he would maneuver on the Taliban ambush positions. Those kinds of decisions, I noted for Baddar Gul, needed to be delegated to the patrol leader, with a clearly established commander's intent to respond to Taliban ambushes with aggressive counterattacks. To empower his patrol leaders to make decisions without a conversation over the radio, I offered ideas for how Baddar Gul could reinforce his intent in other ways, like collective training, after action reviews, tabletop exercises, and tactical decision games with his sergeants. In the moment, however, when Baddar Gul could have articulated this intent to Sergeant Karim over the radio, he also declined to make an independent command decision and passed the buck to me. Since Sergeant Karim had just disregarded my multiple exhortations to protect our southern flank with a satellite patrol, I knew the deflection at the PCO was not about his preference to follow my advice. In light of their eager parade home, it seemed more likely that the ABP were tired, lazy, scared, or simply content with letting the Taliban shoot at them and get away. It did not bode well for the battles to come.

* * *

Around that time, a reporter came to Khan Neshin to write a story about the ANSF's ability to provide security in the region following the imminent Marine withdrawal. He was not the first journalist to come to the area for a story, and Major Select had given explicit orders not to respond to any press inquiries. When the *Wall Street Journal* published the article[23] on February 3, I could see why. Major Select, the AUP advisor team leader, the Regimental Combat Team (RCT) commander, the AUP district commander, and even Colonel Nasrullah all regurgitated the same talking points we pushed the ABP to spread among the local population in their information operations—i.e., propaganda.

"These guys are doing operations on their own. I, frankly, don't believe they need us anymore," the article quoted the RCT commander, Bobo-6's boss.

"We hear that the enemy is waiting for the full withdrawal of the foreigners to strike us," Colonel Nasrullah started out with honesty, then joined in the chorus, "but we are ready to defend our country on our own."

The elder of a village in Khan Neshin bore no such illusions. "The Taliban are very happy that the foreigners pull out. When the Marines go, war will come back." He planned to leave with the Marines.

As patrolmen and villagers all explicitly stated their intentions to flee the area to avoid Taliban reprisals when the Marines left, the district governor tried some shameless mental gymnastics, suggesting that once the American troops withdrew, the Taliban would lose their shared grievance and base of support among the population. This was demonstrably false, since, as the article noted, 1st Kandak saw an immediate increase in Taliban attacks after COP Taghaz was razed. But this, too, was spun into a positive sign; so far—less than one month—1st Kandak had accomplished the impressive feat of not being overrun.

The information operations campaign that these military leaders waged in their public statements came as no surprise for several reasons. The first was strategic: we would not want to publicly send a discouraging message to a unit we were trying to build up, even if privately we had grave concerns about their abilities. Secondly, it was about morale. Marine legends throughout the history of the Corps are celebrated for borderline delusional optimism, such as the lore of Colonel Lewis "Chesty" Puller, in response to being informed that his unit was surrounded: "Great! Now we can shoot in every direction!" Military leaders in Afghanistan fully embraced this attitude, disregarding how such bombastic arrogance, in the absence of a successful outcome, looks less like an inspirational *esprit de corps* and a whole lot more like criminal stupidity.

The most cynical explanation was that conceding a major policy failure or even expressing a hint of skepticism was no way for an ambitious officer to make full-bird colonel or to pin on a star. As the Special Inspector General for Afghan Reconstruction (SIGAR) John Sopko observed during his visits to Afghanistan:

> There seems to be an ingrained incentive to report progress—no matter how fleeting—and an inability or unwillingness to admit failure. No one wants to be the person who says they didn't accomplish their mission during their tour in Afghanistan. As a result, senior officials may not always receive candid reports from the field.[24]

Military culture rarely awards promotions and desirable duty assignments to the skeptic who cautions, "Sir, that's not possible."

The tragic consequence was that countless soldiers, sailors, air-men, and Marines throughout history have fallen victim to their own leaders. Despite a hierarchical structure meant to enable detached decision-making by severing bonds of friendship and loy-alty between officers and enlisted men, leaders have a duty to not be reckless with the lives at their command. Sending the faithful into danger on some quixotic adventure born in self-deception is not just poor leadership, it's treachery.

But the knowledge and intellect of Afghanistan policymakers made self-deception too charitable an explanation for all their fantastical public messaging. There were too many opportunities to confront the grim reality, as far back as the planning of the surge in 2009. The strategy might have worked if it had been implemented as General McChrystal designed it after six months of careful study. But just two days before announcing the adoption of the surge, President Obama added the eighteen-month timeline, baffling the senior diplomatic and military leadership.[25] Setting aside the obvious downside to informing the Taliban exactly when we would be out of their way, the notion that meaningful and lasting progress could be made on that schedule was ludicrous to any student of history, especially when it came to developing an independently functioning Afghan government. Years later, SIGAR would cite the unrealistic political timeline as a key factor that explained why the ANSF could not sustain their fight after the U.S. withdrawal.[26]

A few Cassandras had chimed in to be ignored. Retired Army General Barry McCaffrey warned back in 2006 that even in a best-case scenario, the ANSF would need continued support until 2020 before they could operate independently.[27] The Obama administration's war czar, Lieutenant General Douglas Lute, admitted, "You can't possibly build the [ANSF] that fast."[28] A State Department official mused: "We can't even stand up a sus-tainable local police unit in the U.S. in eighteen months. How could we expect to set up hundreds of them across Afghanistan in that time frame?"[29]

Yet, when President Obama gave top military planners the chance to object to the plan, now contingent on the eighteen-month timeline, not a protest was heard.[30] Quite the opposite: General David Petraeus, in charge of U.S. Central Command at the time, assured the president, "I'm confident we can train and hand over to the [Afghans] in that time frame."[31] Likewise, General McChrystal told Congress shortly after the announcement, "We are going to win."[32]

American generals' public optimism was "so unwarranted and baseless that their statements amounted to a disinformation campaign," journalist Craig Whitlock concluded after reviewing more than one thousand interviews, after action reports, and other records obtained by Freedom of Information Act requests.[33] It was easy to impute an intent to mislead the public when dishonesty was so blatant and pervasive. SIGAR described how "a strong odor of hubris and mendacity" surrounded the efforts to rebuild Afghanistan, not just in the military, but across government and non-government agencies. And the means of such deceit were many: deliberately over-classifying reports, withholding information, changing reporting metrics, exaggerating progress, and turning a blind eye to obvious failures.[34]

Then came the rebranding of the war to a "non-combat" mission, where American servicemembers would continue to fight and die in combat in the coming years. At midnight on December 31, 2014, the NATO-led International Security Assistance Forces combat mission ended; OEF was replaced by a new "non-combat" operation with an equally ironic name: Resolute Support Mission (RSM). On January 1, 2015, the ANSF assumed responsibility for security of the entire country, with NATO forces supporting only in "non-combat" advisor and trainer roles. All this was as if the Taliban had no vote in when the combat ended. This "grand illusion" is what Whitlock characterized as "among the most egregious deceptions and lies that U.S. leaders spread during two decades of warfare."[35] Our troops continued to be sent into active combat zones, but the new rules restricted them from conducting effective combat operations.

For example, a colleague of mine from 1/5, Maurice "Chipp" Naylon IV, advised a battalion of Georgian soldiers responsible for the security of Bagram Airfield from 2014 to 2015. When OEF transitioned to RSM, the security patrols still went forward, but now commanders repeatedly denied ground troops permission to secure the airfield through commonsense operations like clearing suspected IED caches, detaining known enemy combatants, and emplacing snipers where rocket fire frequently originated. Unable to proactively defend the airbase, the Georgians, Chipp, and his Marines spent seven months of "non-combat" dodging suicide bombers and ducking rockets, furious with the "Great Betrayal" that put them in such a dangerous, unwinnable predicament.[36]

All these statistical manipulations and rhetorical departures from reality were expected from politicos, but their impacts at the ground level went beyond the billions of dollars lost to fraud, waste, and abuse. Lives hung in the balance. And that was what infuriated me. I thought about my platoon of young men back at 1/5, the horrors they suffered, all the fallen, and their families. Maybe the generals and politicians thought spinning fairy tales of triumph would help ease the pain, resting assured that the illusion would not shatter until long after their watch had ended. But the men and women actually in combat with the Taliban insurgency—my Marines, coalition forces, and our ANSF partners—deserved better. In the end, the only victories we could claim in Afghanistan were personal: conquering our fears; doing our duty; looking out for one another; and speaking the truth. In the meantime, victory meant sticking to the schedule.

* * *

One week after the *Wall Street Journal* article was published, General John R. Allen relinquished his command of NATO forces in Afghanistan to General Joseph Dunford Jr. At the change-of-command ceremony in Kabul, General Allen made a bold assertion:

"This is victory. This is what winning looks like, and we should not shrink from using those words."[37]

By then, the generals had passed down the word that we, too, were victorious: our Kandak advising would be "mission complete" on the first of March. Some staff-level advisors would continue to deploy to Lashkar Gah, Camp Leatherneck, and other large bases throughout the country to advise the Afghans at the Zone command and higher, some even beyond the end of the combat mission in 2014. But after my team left, there would be no more Marine advisors embedded with the ABP units that conducted combat operations in Southern Helmand. As much as we all were eager to return home, the effect was demoralizing across the board.

With the ABP so underprepared and scared, leaving them in that state felt like a betrayal. And the ABP felt betrayed indeed. On that last visit to PB Gherdai, Ahmed warned us about one of the 1st Tolai patrolmen, whom we all called David Duchovny for his striking resemblance to the American actor from *The X-Files*. Ahmed had overheard him grumbling hate and discontent about the Marines, and worried that he might lash out. I empathized with David Duchovny's anger—I was mad, too—yet I also saw how the Marine uniforms we wore made us complicit in that betrayal, at least symbolically, even though in reality those of us with exposure to the risks had no power to influence the decisions that fueled them. Ever wary of a potential green-on-blue, I felt relieved not to be spending any more nights on the Afghan patrol base with tensions running at an all-time high. There was no honor in our premature withdrawal, but maybe we could find some safety.

Our humor darkened with our spirits. A meme circulated among the advisor community in early 2013, showing a Marine lieutenant gesturing toward a whiteboard in front of a few uniformed Afghans and the caption *Just so you know, you're fucked when we leave*. The irony was that the Afghans knew it all too well; our own leaders were the ones who needed to sit down in front of that whiteboard.

Chapter Fourteen

Final Exchanges

<u>24 JAN 2013</u>

"Fuckin' Malone." Major Select took a guess at who had launched a 40mm grenade when we passed our ammunition expenditure report over the radio that night. It was a fair assumption, but I had to set the record straight.

"Actually, sir, it was me—it fell off my belt and we couldn't find it."

Major Select recorded all the details I could give him on the firefights and passed them up through the 3/9 chain of command. Bobo-6 must have sensed that Alpha Section's morale was unacceptably high after our skirmishes, or maybe the radio really *was* that important, because I soon received orders to lead a patrol to search for the missing radio the next day with a squad of the Carnage Marines in support. Ahmed felt terrible about all the Marines going back into the ambush zone and frantically asked all the ABP if anyone had seen the scanner. Pointing to the 40mm grenade round that I had lost myself, I assured Ahmed that these kinds of things happen and started working on my plan.

In the morning, Carnage drove over from the Taghaz Annex with EOD and dismounted a dozen men, including a machine-gun section. EOD was under express orders not to interrogate the possible IED from the day before, but Bobo-6 required them to accompany us anyway. As we would be literally retracing our steps through an ambush zone, I was grateful to have the extra assets at my command, but we had never worked together before and were understandably skeptical of each other. I wondered whether they were pissed at us for losing gear or grateful for the opportunity to actually conduct a dismounted patrol in the battlespace—a first for them, since there were no more Marine-led patrols in Khan Neshin District by that point. Maybe they were also frustrated by Bobo's restrictive posture and longed for a chance to do something besides stand post and drive trucks around the desert.

I described to them the previous day's firefights and walked through the operation order on a makeshift terrain model in the dirt so everyone could visualize their roles. The only pushback I got was on my machine-gun emplacement.

"Sir, we are supposed to employ the guns in pairs."

If I had borrowed my leadership style from Major Select, I might have dished out an "is that all?" I was intimately familiar with the Marine Corps publication that bore my favorite title: *Machine Guns and Machine Gun Gunnery.*[38] But even without textbook knowledge, every infantry officer knows that P is the first letter of the acronym for machine-gun emplacement: PICMDEEP; and it stands for "pairs." Regardless of whether this Marine was testing my tactical decision-making or genuinely trying to help improve the plan, I figured explaining myself could both educate and inspire confidence. After the initial annoyance flashed across my face, I explained my rationale to the machine-gun section leader, pointing to the terrain model with my radio antenna:

"One gun will go on the near side of the bridge before the PCO, facing west. The second will cross to the far side and set up twenty meters away on the corner of the PCO, facing south. These were the two directions from which the Taliban fired at us yesterday. Trackin'?"

Nods and grunts. This was the natural rhythm for instructing a group of Marines: sentence, sentence, sentence; confirmatory prompt; some unintelligible but audible response.

"I want a gun on each side when we are most vulnerable crossing the bridge. If we take fire from either direction, the best-positioned gun can immediately engage, while the other can quickly break down and relocate to support. That way, they're still mutually supporting, but flexible. Make sense?"

A "Roger that, sir" from the section leader, mixed in with the babble of "rah," "kill," "err," and the like.

There were no more questions.

The patrol was successful, in that we were not ambushed, we did not hit any IEDs, and we even recovered my 40mm round after carefully inspecting the area around it for possible booby traps. The ███████ radio, however, was nowhere to be found.

When we got back to PB Gherdai and finished our post-mission actions, I went to talk with Baddar Gul. Lo and behold, he handed me the missing radio. In the chaos of the previous day, one of the ABP patrolmen had picked it up and either "forgot" he had it when Ahmed asked, or tried to hide it. Either way, when word of the missing radio reached Colonel Nasrullah at Taghaz Station, he personally drove to PB Gherdai and demanded Baddar Gul return it to the advisors. While we recovered the ███████ radio too late to save us from an unnecessary patrol, I thanked Baddar Gul for doing the right thing. It was not something I would have the opportunity to do again.

Bobo-6 was furious. He had canceled my stay-behind ambush, but we had proven ourselves warfighters nonetheless. Rumor had it that he had chewed out Major Select for even letting us patrol with the ABP on foot. Then, he not only forbade us from conducting any more combat operations with the ABP, but went so far as to bar us from even visiting the Tolai positions. With that order, aside from meeting with the Tolai's leaders when they came to Taghaz Station, my advising mission was over. There was no way to perform my role as a combat advisor when advising on combat operations was prohibited. My job was reduced to shuttling our team's Headquarters Section back and forth to Taghaz and providing physical security by standing post or serving as a guardian angel. It was still better than floating around the Pacific on an MEU, but I felt as though my purpose for being in Afghanistan was gone not even five months into the deployment.

Part of me resented Bobo-6 for preventing us from playing through the whistle, to give our mission its best chance at success. I wanted to keep fighting. Why? In the immortal words of Dave Chappelle's PopCopy employee training film, "Why? . . . 'cuz fuck 'em! That's why."[39] But another part of me acknowledged the responsibility he had for the Marines in his battlespace: Bobo-6 could see the writing on the wall, and did not want American blood on his hands in what increasingly appeared to be a futile enterprise. 3/9 had already lost one Marine in December, when Lance Corporal Anthony Denier was shot through the neck on a combat patrol in Marjah. Recoiling from danger in the wake of such loss was a natural impulse, albeit one that military officers are trained to overcome. I also knew that the pressure to rein in risk came from higher than Bobo-6, and he was just passing the same message Tim had months earlier: this cause is not worth any more American lives.

Though the conservative posture was far better than the opposite extreme—some Manchegan colonel leading a battalion of Sancho Panzas to slaughter—it was a bitter pill to swallow after all we had individually and collectively sacrificed for our mission. Candid communications from higher command would have gone a long way to alleviate the cognitive dissonance. I couldn't shake the feeling that I was being gaslit, wondering if I'd missed a footnote in my orders, or a wink from an admin clerk who gave them to me, as if to say, "Here's your mission, but not *really*." Everyone seemed to play along, with only Tim breaking character to give a hushed hint of caution in that darkened smokepit the night before he flew home. Perhaps it was an unwritten ritual, an informal requirement of the transfer-of-authority process, to lift the veil of deception, just a bit, to bring your replacement into the fold.

Venting to friends of mine who were also Marine officers in Southern Helmand, I learned that they, too, had read the chai leaves. One of my squadmates from Basic Officer Course happened to be 3/9's communications officer. He had already heard from Bobo about the case of the missing radio. In response to my lamentations over Bobo-6 axing my stay-behind plan, Lee summed up the cold truth in an email from Camp Dwyer:

> I know it seems like you would be helping the Afghans by doing what you want to do, but if they haven't learned to do it by themselves now, then they are pretty much fucked. Whatever we were going to accomplish in the past 12 years is done now.

Another friend of mine since my Officer Candidate School days was James, who had deployed to Khan Neshin District as a platoon commander with 3rd Light Armored Reconnaissance Battalion and returned stateside shortly before I arrived myself. James empathized with my frustration and added some perspective:

> The battalion commanders are being told by RCT and Division to just conserve gains and avoid loss of life, I think. It all comes from Washington, obviously: No one who makes the real decisions there thinks the war can be won at a cost acceptable to Americans, so we're just winding down. Maybe they're right, but

either way it's demoralizing for an organization like
the Marine Corps that prides itself on winning battles.
As you said, the best junior officers like us can do is
get the Marines home and try to kill a couple of bad
guys if we're lucky.

James and I agreed that every Marine we could bring home was
a win, yet doing so in retreat didn't feel so victorious. Killing the
Taliban, on the other hand, did. Every fighter we could remove
from the battlefield on the way out was one fewer terrorist to kill,
maim, oppress, and traumatize the innocent people we left behind.
But after Bobo-6's order to my team, this last reservoir of morale
evaporated.

We never returned to Gherdai. It was two weeks before we were
even allowed to drive back out to Taghaz. In the meantime,
my section had to move homes again, out of our fancy,
climate-controlled tent into a rudimentary nylon shelter pitched
on a plywood platform. The shower trailers, Internet access,
and laundromat disappeared too; COP Castle was next on the
chopping block, and the contractor-supported amenities were
the first things to go.

Our remaining trips to Taghaz were largely uneventful. A
squad of Carnage Marines accompanied us as a security escort
each time, per a new mandate from Bobo-6 after the gunfights.
They parked their truck at the entrance to the Annex, dragged a
metal gate and concertina wire across the gap, and stood guard in
the turret. We parked one truck on the southern end and posted
a Marine in the turret to peek over the berm behind a machine
gun. Another Marine stood radio watch in the back of a truck,
scanning the surroundings with the periscoping optic that rose up
from the steel pod that housed it.

The headquarters advisors still had engagements with their ABP corollaries, and I occasionally went over as a guardian angel, but I was little more than a bodyguard. Each night I took a two-hour shift on watch, shivering behind a machine gun, peering into darkness, making up songs in my head to stay awake. It was dull. Except for one night. I startled awake and saw the silhouette of a human figure on my one-man tent, backlit by red and white lights that flickered in rhythm with the sound of the wind.

"Who the fuck is that!? Who is this!?" I demanded of the figure who I perceived trying to break into my tent. I clutched my Beretta and took aim at the shadow.

"Sir, there's no one outside your tent," Sergeant Diaz called back from his post on radio watch.

His voice brought me down from the half-nightmare, half-hallucination in a mix of dismay and shame. I was no stranger to the anxiety-fueled dreams where my gun wouldn't fire, or all my bullets missed even from point-blank range, or no matter how many times I stabbed him with my Kabar, the cackling Talib in hand-to-hand combat with me just Would. Not. Bleed. Disturbing dreams like these were routine and had never before blurred into my waking reality. Not since I was a child had something spooked me like the hallucination at my tent, and I hoped the subconscious burst of paranoia was not the first of many.

The next day, the Desert of Death herself chased us out of Taghaz. As our trucks crested the edge of the Shelf to push up to Route 96, a towering wave of blustering brown rose up from the horizon and advanced eastward from our rear. The sun was setting and it was red air; if the sandstorm caught up to our convoy we would have to coil up our trucks in a defensive posture and ride it out through the night. I heard no cries for the lead vehicle to slow down on this movement. Nobody was counseled or threatened with a NiPLOC for exceeding the speed limit of twenty-five miles per hour.

As we approached COP Castle, we could see that its aerostat balloon had been reeled in and anchored down. God forbid it would rip away and Marines would have to venture out to locate and recover the expensive technologies in its undercarriage from whatever corner of the country they came to rest in. We made it through the gate with a few minutes to spare and barely had time to break down the machine guns from their mounts in the turrets and batten down the hatches of our trucks.

The storm descended upon us and turned day into tempestuous night. We strapped on goggles, grabbed flashlights, and clung to the aluminum support beams of our tent to resist the over-fifty-mile-per-hour gusts pulling it from the ground. When the seams started ripping, Staff Sergeant Pulst and Doc frantically made repairs with plastic zip ties while I held on to our plywood door with all my might. Outside our hooch, unoccupied tents and debris flew across the COP, snapping antennas and temporarily severing our external communications. Somehow there were no serious injuries. The hour of apocalyptic chaos consumed the remaining daylight and left an eerie twilight in its wake.

Undeterred by the ominous sandstorm, we returned to Taghaz once more in early March for what proved to be an illuminating final visit. We learned that the infamous Farid Khan had detained two individuals he suspected of working for the Taliban. When his physical interrogation bore unsatisfactory results, he raped them. The Marines from BAT-2 had once told us a story of some ABP in 2nd Kandak bragging about raping hundreds of Taliban, so the concept was not unfamiliar to us. Unlike some ABP officers, however, the 1st Kandak commander did not tolerate war crimes. Colonel Nasrullah stripped Farid Khan of his weapon and uniform, and sent him up to the Zone Command in Lashkar Gah where his fate would be determined.

Our jaws dropped when we heard the story. I was as surprised by the accountability as I was appalled by Farid Khan's cruelty. Staff Sergeant Pulst riffed on a line from *Dumb and Dumber*.

"Just when I didn't think he could get any dumber, he goes and does a thing like that . . . and totally redeems himself!"

We had all exchanged various theories about Farid Khan attempting to stage a coup with his loyal band of followers sometime after we left. But none of us had predicted that this was how the Kandak commander would finally neutralize that internal threat.

There was no plan for my section to advise anyone from 1st Tolai on that last trip; after Bobo-6's recent order, the advise-train-assist mission was only taking place at the Kandak level. I was adding wood to our bonfire in the Annex when a call came over the radio that there was an Afghan at the gate. I looked up and saw it was Sher Ali. I woke up Staff Sergeant Pulst from a midday snooze and took Ahmed with us to go meet him.

After the exchange of pleasantries and inquiries about his leg, which he showed us was healing nicely, Sher Ali shared some good news. Shortly after he arrived in Lashkar Gah to spend time with his family and let his leg heal, he received a call from his informant in Sre Kala, a village west of Gherdai known to be a bed-down location for the Taliban. This informant reported that between the two skirmishes on the day Sher Ali was shot, the Taliban had sustained three killed in action and two wounded. Furthermore, one of the wounded was the leader of that cell and had to be evacuated down to Pakistan for medical treatment.

"*Dair sha!*" I told him. *Very good!*

"Double good! Ha ha!" he agreed in English.

Since we neglected to perform the usual battle damage assessments that day, and Scan Eagle gave us nothing from up above, this was the first concrete feedback we received. Even if the numbers were fudged by a Talib or two, it was satisfying to know that we had made a concrete impact. Sher Ali invited us over to Taghaz Station for tea, where I was expecting to meet with Baddar Gul one last time. Sergeant Karim joined us. Fittingly, Baddar Gul was home on leave.

Here on our last visit, we were prepared for the customary exchange of gifts. I had packed a second watch for the deployment in case the Casio G-shock on my wrist got damaged, lost, or stolen. As soon as it became clear early on that Baddar Gul had trouble meeting time hacks, I had decided it would make a good parting gift to him. Staff Sergeant Pulst had also purchased one for Sher Ali during one of our visits from the PX truck. Since there was no Baddar Gul, Staff Sergeant Pulst and I instead bestowed our watches on the de facto leaders of 1st Tolai, two men who had fought with us that day in Gherdai: the Tolai's *mawin*, Sher Ali, and Sergeant Karim. I wasn't sure about their ability to tell time, but they appeared genuine in their appreciation for their new wrist adornments.

Sher Ali gave us a pair of sequined Kandahari skullcaps, commonly sported by the ABP, which we put on for a few photographs together. We also pawned off all our leftover care package contents, including several toothbrushes, which we knew were in high demand, and decks of playing cards, which were not. Between drags on cigarettes and sips of tea, we reflected on our experience and the future of the Tolai.

"What would it take for you to become an officer?" I asked Sher Ali. "I will happily recommend you for a commission through my chain of command to the Zone advisors."

He grinned back. "If you give me $2,000 I can go to Lashkar Gah right now and become a lieutenant."

There was no doubt in my mind that a commission had a precise dollar value if you knew the right official in Kabul. And as Tim had told me four months earlier, 1st Tolai's future hinged on the person in command. To some extent it's true of any organization.

But it's also an organizational failure if one leader can make or break the entire mission. If that was all that mattered, the only advice we needed to give the ANSF was about who to place in command. Between the countless shared meals, trading tobacco over a desert campfire, patrolling and fighting together, Staff Sergeant Pulst and I came to really like Sher Ali as a person and as a combat leader. Still, was I going to invest $2,000 in one person, at one Tolai, in one corner of the country, that could all be gone in a flash, as had been the case for Haji Samad and Lieutenant Zarif? Hard pass. It was enough to invest years of training and risk my own life trying to make a difference when the outcome was all but guaranteed.

When the last ashes fell in the tray and the teacups ran dry, we said our farewells. We never went back to Taghaz. We never even went back to Castle, which was fully transferred to the district government the following week. Everything we needed for our remaining weeks in Afghanistan was packed in our trucks for our move to FOB Payne, another temporary home where our sojourning team would spend our final days downrange, sleeping on cots in a plywood hut that the Shock Trauma Platoon had already vacated. Payne itself was scheduled for demolition two months later. Our team meetings where we used to plan operations turned into planning conferences for redeployment back to Camp Pendleton. My excitement to return home gradually prevailed over my depression toward how we were leaving the ABP alone and unprepared.

With ample time to address administrative items, I wrote up the Marines on my team for Navy Achievement Medals, and I put in Doc for a Navy Commendation Medal—one step higher. Major Select shot it down.

"NavComs are what company commanders get at the end of their tour. Just put in Doc for a NAM."

It took me a moment to move beyond my initial shock at Major Select's understanding of a supposedly merit-based awards system. Then I protested bitterly. Saving the life of that contractor on FOB Payne back in January alone merited a NAM; add to that his triage and medevac of the wounded ABP the day before that and his treatment of Sher Ali's gunshot wound in the middle of a firefight a couple of weeks later. Doc O'Connor deserved more. Awards were supposed to recognize individual conduct, not merely to acknowledge rank or position. Clearly annoyed at my argumentative response, a terse Major Select had one question:

"Is that all?"

* * *

Our initial date for redeployment back to the States was set for mid-March. All we had to do until then was kill our new enemy: time. After a week and a half at FOB Payne, we linked up with BAT-2 and made one last convoy up to Camp Dwyer, where we turned in our equipment and waited for our next move in a transient tent. A few days later, a pair of Shitters shuttled us up to Camp Leatherneck. One step closer to home, we settled into air-conditioned trailers with mattressed bunk beds and relished our newfound access to Wi-Fi, recreational softball tournaments, Pizza Hut, and the full-scale brick-and-mortar PX. Even seeing women was a welcome luxury after six months down south where it was exclusively male, save for the occasional "blue ninja" sighting of a fully-covered woman wearing the traditional *niqab*. We took turns teaching each other songs on the guitar I'd ordered on Amazon as a Christmas present for Corporal Palacios. We shared hard drives filled with television shows, movies, and adult content. We worked out in gyms that improved with each move to a larger base, and trained with an instructor to level up in the Marine Corps Martial Arts Program. And at some point, we said goodbye to our Embedded Police Mentors and our interpreters.

Most of our interpreters were reassigned to other units or returned home to the United States or Canada. For Ahmed, going home would be suicide. He needed a new job; but with the troop-level reductions across the country, interpreter positions in American military units became increasingly scarce and competitive. So Ahmed asked me for help.

The leader of Tim's advisor team had written Ahmed a strong letter of recommendation before they went home, and Ahmed asked for the same from Major Select as the officer-in-charge of the current team. Major Select demurred, citing how Ahmed had lost the ███████████ radio during the firefights in January, and an earlier incident when Ahmed forgot his first radio on top of a truck tire, which crushed the radio when the vehicle began to roll. Having learned not to hold Afghans to Marine Corps standards, especially not civilian interpreters, I was honored to write for Ahmed. He was an excellent asset to our team and performed reliably, even under enemy fire. He guided us in cultural practices and tipped us off to potential insider threats whispered among the ABP. Ahmed risked his life, and his family's lives, for our mission there. I believed we had a moral duty to do everything in our power to give him a safe place to live after he completed his service. Though Major Select's endorsement would have carried far more weight, mine seemed to carry just enough. While Ahmed waited for the State Department to review and adjudicate his SIV application, he landed a new assignment with the Zone-level ABP advisors in Lashkar Gah.

The nefarious Good Idea Fairy also took a trip to Lashkar Gah, which we surmised from the Zone advisors' decision to delay our departure from Leatherneck so we could fly down to Taghaz for yet another iteration of Operation Steel Dawn. Major Select seemed powerless to say no, and our dreams of going home early were dashed. Family members had already made plans, and some had even purchased flights, to meet us at Camp Pendleton on the date of our original homecoming.

Everyone was pissed. Even Sully, our team's yoga enthusiast and zen master, whose catchphrase "it's whatever" became such a mantra for the many frustrations our team faced that he had our interpreters teach him the local slang to use with the ABP: *heech netab*. His wife was near the end of her pregnancy's third trimester, and naturally he did not want to miss such a monumental event just because the Zone advisors couldn't make up their mind about whether the Afghans needed another partnered operation before we abandoned them.

I had trouble embracing the *heech netab* mindset. The smallest decisions in a combat environment carried life-or-death consequences, and I took the time sacrificed by Marines and their families nearly as seriously. I valued emotionally detached decision-making as much as the next officer; but not *caring* felt impossible, even when I had no authority in the matter. So, even though I enjoyed Leatherneck's first-world amenities and the financial benefits of tax-free combat-zone pay, I joined the lobby for Major Select to take a more firm stand against Zone's needless theatrics. Major Select then figured out a way to place Sully on an early flight home and went to bat for us to finalize our itinerary without further interference from Zone.

With a new redeployment date for early April, we still had another two weeks to burn at Leatherneck. I spent my nights sharing rapport-builders and telling stories with my best friend from Infantry Officer Course, Justin. He was posted in a nearby transient tent, inbound to Sangin with his platoon from 3rd Battalion, 4th Marines. With commendable discipline, I held to my six-cigarettes-per-day limit, and on our final night overlapping in Leatherneck I passed Justin the torch. After sharing Tim's wisdom with some perspective of my own, I presented him the more tangible gift of my leather shoulder holster. It was the preferred method for carrying an M9 Beretta and extra magazines while filling a wag bag; and, thanks to the *sabzi* and the rest of the Afghan food, I had become an expert on the matter. I hoped Justin wouldn't need it quite as often as I had.

The day before the C-17 whisked us away from Leatherneck, an outbriefer from the divisional headquarters passed on some words of wisdom: try not to swear so much around your families and "be an adult" when it came to drinking on the long journey back to the States. Despite all our diminished alcohol tolerances, every member of our team behaved responsibly. I had a couple of beers at the pub in Manas, Kyrgyzstan—it had been off limits during our inbound visit. We spent a few days there overcoming the strange feeling of not carrying weapons everywhere we went. Our next layover was in Frankfurt, Germany, where I upgraded from that nasty excuse for an ale in Manas with a rich hefeweizen.

There was no booze when we landed in Bangor, Maine, in the dead of night, but rather there was a tunnel of military families and supporters holding welcome banners, waving flags, smiling, and cheering. One kind woman from the crowd handed me a homemade chocolate chip cookie as I walked through the terminal to our connecting flight, and it was only when I took a bite to discover the Oreo baked inside that Afghanistan melted from my mind and my eyes welled up in recognition: we were home.

Five days later, two IEDs constructed of nails, gunpowder, and pressure cookers detonated amid a crowd of civilians, killing two women and an eight-year-old boy. Hundreds were wounded. Thousands more were traumatized. These blasts weren't in Helmand Province, or anywhere in Afghanistan, but on Boylston Street at the finish line of the Boston Marathon. The bombs were Made in the USA. And these terrorists were at large in the city of many friends, my alma mater, and my future wife, whom I'd become "engaged to be dating" once I returned home. There I was, stuck at Camp Pendleton with the rest of BAT-1 and BAT-2, slogging through half-days of medical screenings, gear turn-in, weapons cleaning, and administrative tedium. As I frittered away the hours with cheeks full of Red Man to combat the monotony, I worried that Boston's citywide shutdown for the ongoing man-hunt could extend to the airport and dash my plans to start my post-deployment leave the coming weekend with my soon-to-be girlfriend and later-to-be-wife.

Friday finally arrived, and we were dismissed for post-deployment leave. I made a quick stop at my storage unit in Oceanside to toss my .45 caliber handgun into my checked luggage and set off driving north on the Five to catch my flight out of LAX. The radio distracted me from my anxiety about the rush-hour traffic around Los Angeles; I listened intently with a mix of horror and relief as the news described the murder, car chase, pipe bombs, and shootout that finally ended my first week back in America.

The Boston Marathon Bombing twisted the knife where I had already felt a stabbing pain over our abandonment of the Afghans and on self-defeating time constraints that made our mission futile. We could leave Afghanistan, but there was no withdrawing from the Global War on Terrorism. For all we invested and risked to fight our enemies abroad, they still grew from within and attacked us at home. If my service in Afghanistan made any difference, I couldn't see it. Only this sign, clear as day, to redirect my efforts elsewhere. I tried consoling myself with what I knew cognitively to be true: if all I accomplished was to bring home each of my men intact, then that was enough. But it wasn't. There were no laurels to rest on, just the final page to turn over at the end of that chapter and a blank page starting the next.

Chapter Fifteen

After Such Knowledge

"Remind me where you were again?" Dave asked me after a respectable amount of whatever whiskey we were pouring that night. One of my oldest Marine Corps buddies from Officer Candidate School, recruiting duty in Boston, Basic Officer Course, and Infantry Officer Course, Dave had deployed to Southern Helmand as a weapons platoon commander with 2nd Battalion, 8th Marine Regiment, which replaced 3/9 about a month after I got home. We kept in close touch, especially after we both moved back to Boston post-discharge. When I told him "Taghaz," his eyes widened, and he proceeded to tell me what he had witnessed there in September 2013.

With all his machine-gunners, mortarmen, and assaultmen attached out to rifle platoons, Dave started his deployment at Camp Dwyer training Jordanian troops and supervising base security during the reduction of Dwyer's perimeter. When 2/8's battalion commander fired one of the platoon leaders, a game of musical lieutenants left Dave in charge of Echo Company, 2nd Platoon. An order came down for Dave's platoon to fly into Taghaz in support of a joint Afghan National Army (ANA) and ABP clearing operation from southern Garmsir District down to the Helmand's Fishhook and westward through Khan Neshin District. Based on intelligence that the Taliban were gaining ground in Khan Neshin, the intent of the plan was to disrupt the Taliban's supply lines running from Pakistan into Southern Helmand. Dave's platoon was tasked to provide QRF for the 1st Kandak ABP at Taghaz Station, where he was reinforced with a radio reconnaissance team to collect signals intelligence, a captain from the Zone-level ABP advisors in Lashkar Gah with Ahmed as his interpreter, an EOD team, a mobile medical team, and a section of 60mm mortars to provide indirect fire support. Just for the one operation, Dave brought more assets into Taghaz than we'd ever had when Marines called it home.

The operation was almost canceled. During a coordination meeting at Camp Leatherneck a few days before, the Marines learned of a bloody green-on-green incident within 1st Kandak. A certain ABP lieutenant had fallen in love with a teenager from the village and kidnapped him to serve as a "chai boy." This was a common cover role given to the victims of child sexual exploitation, an insidious relic of Pashtun culture called *bachabazi*, "boy play." No one on my team ever observed anything suspect, but the Afghans had learned over the years that their American partners' tolerance for cultural differences did not extend to the sexual abuse of children. We'd all heard the urban legend of "Man Love Thursdays," when the Afghans were rumored to celebrate the end of every Islamic week with each other. But that was the same day most Afghan units reserved for administration and maintenance, so, whether by design or by chance, Marines were routinely absent from the Afghan bases then. I had noticed how a youthful ABP patrolman served Baddar Gul his tea at PB Gherdai, and I assumed this was just a function of seniority. Baddar Gul may have been incompetent and corrupt, but I never saw any indications of something so vile.

Dave continued:

This ABP lieutenant had also set up a vehicle checkpoint on the main road leading out of the village and forced every traveler to pay a toll. The villagers were outraged and complained to the Kandak commander, who was unable to effectively intervene. Personnel decisions involving officers had to be cleared by the Ministry of Interior; not even the Zone commander could remove the lieutenant from his post despite the blatant kidnapping and sexual abuse. Powerless to enforce the rule of law through the chain of command, an ABP commander (Dave couldn't remember whether it was Zone or Kandak) took a crew out to demand the boy's release, which ultimately escalated into an armed standoff with the lieutenant and his posse of loyalists. The ABP commander got the jump and killed the rogue lieutenant along with every mutineer by his side. The results were gruesome: one of the rebels took a direct hit in the torso from a rocket-propelled grenade and scattered his flesh and bones everywhere; the lieutenant's corpse was riddled with bullet holes from the ABP commander and his men unloading their magazines in fury. The ABP commander cleaned house, and having done so, proceeded with the joint operation.

Everyone in Khan Neshin knew the operation was happening, so there were few surprises. But it was still stressful for Dave, his platoon, and all the Marine attachments due to the recent inter-Afghan shootout. While the op was uneventful for the most part, the clearing force encountered a few Taliban ambushes and IEDs. Per Dave,

> The ambushes got snuffed out quickly. The Afghans blasted a Taliban RPG team set up next to a house. They brought a body to the Taghaz Station where it was out on display as a war trophy for a few days. The Marines enrolled it in biometrics and we made them remove it. It smelt like shit (literally, the dude defecated) and was oozing from all the bullet holes. . . . They brought it 300 meters outside the ECP and dumped the body. . . . My Marines on post had to watch it get eaten by dogs.

The operation also provided Dave a chance to observe the ANA's EOD technician in action (the ABP still didn't have one).

> Some sorry bastard in a fucked-up interceptor vest, a 2XL helmet, and a 5-gallon jug of JP8 [kerosene fuel] . . . walked up to the IED, dumped the fuel on it, lit it on fire, and just watched until it blew up.

Notwithstanding Dave's graphic descriptions, I felt my face form a big, stupid smile. I had a pretty good idea of who the rogue lieutenant was, so I asked Dave and Ahmed to send me all their pictures from the operation to check which lieutenants were still around and do some process of elimination. I recognized Lieutenant Yaqub and Lieutenant Zarif's replacement. Baddar Gul was nowhere to be found. It appeared that 1st Tolai's lame-duck lieutenant, who turned out to be even worse than I thought, had finally met his end. And the Afghans conducted a successful operation, almost on their own.

This was the last good news I heard out of Taghaz.

*   *   *

In May 2013, one month after our return home, the DOD inspector general released an official assessment of the NATO coalition's mission to advise, train, and equip the Afghan Border Police.[40] While recognizing the significant progress we'd made in developing the ABP into a self-sustaining force, the report issued dire warnings that undercut the figurative "mission accomplished" banners waved by field- and flag-grade officers as they rotated home from Helmand. In summary, the IG findings matched what we knew from personal experience: the ABP were unlikely to develop critical capabilities prior to the coalition's withdrawal deadline of 2014. There were two main reasons.

The first was our timing. Coalition leaders had made a deliberate choice to focus the initial priority for the advisor mission on building combat capabilities. Secondary functions like explosive ordnance disposal, intelligence, logistics, and casualty evacuation were to come later, once the ABP units had matured into a capable fighting force. Until then, the ABP, like the other ANSF forces, would rely on the coalition forces for support.

Advisor teams like mine observed how the ABP were approaching proficiency in planning and conducting a range of combat operations to varying degrees of success. However, in these operations—take Operation Steel Dawn or 2/8's clearing operation witnessed by Dave, for example—the IG report observed that the ABP were entirely dependent on us for enabling assistance. Providing this type of support was increasingly challenging due to the reduction in coalition troop levels and base closures. By the IG's assessment, the ABP were unlikely to develop critical secondary capabilities by the end of 2014. Accordingly, the NATO coalition needed to plan for continued support to the ABP beyond the 2014 withdrawal deadline. Failure to do so, the IG warned, put the entire ABP mission at risk.

The second challenge came from within the Afghan government. The ABP was fielding poor battlefield leaders due to the Ministry of Interior (MoI) policy that withheld the authority to transfer ABP officers between units. In addition to fostering cronyism and nepotism within the ranks, the policy hampered field commanders' ability to professionalize their forces by removing corrupt officers and replacing them with those who demonstrated real leadership abilities. One example from the report sounded all too familiar:

> ABP officials reported that unqualified candidates presented themselves for officer positions using letters of introduction from MoI, while the qualified officer

candidates the zone leadership presented to MoI for appointment or promotion were not advanced. The ensuing dysfunctional personnel system and command relationships had a palpably negative effect on morale.

The IG held out the exact leadership dynamic I observed in 1st Tolai as a problem with profound implications for the ABP's mission. This policy was why it took a green-on-green shootout for the Zone commander to remove a problem leader like Baddar Gul. It was why Sher Ali needed $2,000 before he had a chance at receiving a commission as an ABP officer.

Between the IG's assessment and my personal experience, it was clear how bureaucratic corruption caused tangible harms for the frontline war effort. But the NATO coalition had no power to make a branch of the Afghan government change its policy. The best we could do was lobby MoI to delegate the authority to hire, reassign, and remove officers down to the Zone level. Would the leadership at MoI adopt such advice to change a policy against their own fiduciary interest? Even then, would the Zone commanders inherit the irresistible opportunity to line their own pockets in exchange for officer assignments? The problem was institutional and cultural, not one that could be solved by foreign military advisors.

In addition to these two major obstacles, the IG assessment also voiced concerns about the ABP's vehicle maintenance, staffing levels, logistics, training, property accountability, and vetting of personnel, among others. Uncertainty over the funding of the ABP's explosive and narcotics detection canine program also made the list. As much as we all loved Sergeant Max, we had to concede that stealing a puppy meant to guard livestock from the local village was no substitute for the German police's formal training program that was due to end in 2014.

Though they never visited a Kandak, the IG's team validated my own concerns and demonstrated that these issues were being reported up the advisor chain of command with candor. The IG had been able to sound the alarm by slicing through the thick layers of bullshit that our colonels and generals smeared over the reality on the ground. *Perhaps*, I thought, *this was the warning that the public and policymakers needed to hear.*

Learning of Baddar Gul's undignified death even gave me hope that 1st Tolai might flourish under a new commander with Sher Ali as *mawin*. And having personally been on the receiving end of the intimidating bark of an Anatolian shepherd guarding his property while I was on patrol, I even held out hope that Sergeant Max could make something of himself as long as he detected the IEDs by scent rather than by digging. Despite my pessimistic attitude toward the viability of the ABP at Taghaz and Gherdai in particular, I took comfort in the possibility that at least the ANSF stationed in population centers and other key terrain might be adequately equipped, staffed, motivated, and led. Anticipating their eventual return to Lashkar Gah, I believed the ABP of 1st Kandak would at least be able to defend the city where their families and friends lived, even if Taghaz was "a bridge too far" for the ANSF.[41] With all these hopes, I left the Marine Corps and focused on the new civilian life before me, only occasionally checking in with an old advisor teammate and scanning the news out of Helmand.

The warnings went unheeded. Within a year of our departure, the Taliban had firmly reestablished themselves in Khan Neshin District.[42] In 2015, the neighboring Dishu District fell under official Taliban control.[43] By that time, al-Qaeda in the Indian Subcontinent had relocated its base of operations from Pakistan to Helmand Province, to include the establishment of an al-Qaeda training camp in Bahram Chah.[44] Then in March 2016, COP Castle changed tenants once again as the Taliban overran Khan Neshin, the fifth of Helmand's fourteen districts to fall.[45] In October that year, the Taliban ended their summer offensive with a siege of the provincial capital of Lashkar Gah, where the ANSF mounted a costly defense over several days. Only by withdrawing ANA units from more remote areas to reinforce the city, reinforcing the defense with a surge of Afghan commandos, and calling in American air support could the ANSF hold onto the city.[46]

Even as the depressing reports of the Taliban advance in Helmand trickled in over the years, I took for granted that the coalition had either adequately prepared the ANSF to defend Lashkar Gah or would continue to intervene to ensure that the provincial government would stand. General Nicholson promised as much during that 2016 battle.[47] The Taliban launched another major offensive to take Lashkar Gah in October 2020, inflicting heavy casualties and triggering the exodus of tens of thousands of civilians. Retreating from posts at the perimeter of the city en masse, the ANSF again battled to a stalemate only with the assistance of U.S. airstrikes.[48]

A few months later, a DOD congressional report pointed to the October 2020 siege of Lashkar Gah as a prime example of how tenuous the situation was for the Afghan government.[49] The report also detailed how the ANSF continued to struggle with the exact same issues cited in the IG's 2013 report on the ABP. Yet top Defense Department officials still pretended that the policy of scheduled withdrawal was grounded in reality:

> Our strategy in Afghanistan is conditions-based; our commanders on the ground continually evaluate the current conditions and make recommendations on the appropriate force levels.

That was the right answer, but not the true one. It echoed President Obama's promise to consider more than the ticking clock at the announcement of the 2010 surge:

> Just as we have done in Iraq, we will execute this transition responsibly, taking into account conditions on the ground. We'll continue to advise and assist Afghanistan's security forces to ensure that they can succeed over the long haul.[50]

The comparison to Iraq was like the tragic prophecy of a Greek oracle; armed with the American weapons and Humvees left behind by fleeing Iraqi military and police units, the Islamic State of Iraq and ash-Sham rose to prominence after U.S. forces withdrew. In Afghanistan, even before the withdrawal of U.S. troops was complete, ISIS-Khorasan Province—its regional franchise— had sprouted up, several thousands of fighters in strength. While the Obama administration pushed back the deadline for complete withdrawal beyond its original goal of 2016, the remaining American military presence was a paralyzed force, a mere gesture without motion.[51]

Whether by willful blindness, cold indifference to the certain consequences, or dogmatic adherence to the kitschy slogan "end the forever war," the political commitment to terminate American military involvement in Afghanistan was bipartisan. Excluding the Afghan government from the negotiations, the Trump administration reached an agreement with the Taliban in February 2020 that effectively exchanged a drop in violence against coalition forces for an escalation of targeted attacks against ANSF forces and assassinations of government officials across the country. Calculating as ever, the Taliban shifted their attacks to both encourage the complete withdrawal of U.S. forces and attrit the ANSF and Afghan government in the meantime. SIGAR ultimately concluded that the Trump administration's bargain with the Taliban to withdraw U.S. forces, through its decimating consequences on ANSF's effectiveness and morale, was the single most important cause of the collapse of the Afghan government.[52]

Despite the Taliban's building momentum, al-Qaeda gaining footholds in ungoverned pockets of the country, ISIS-K on the rise, and the U.S. intelligence community's persistent public warnings against a precipitous withdrawal, President Trump directed a reduction in U.S. troop levels down to a meager twenty-five hundred by the time he left office in January 2021. That February, the general in charge of U.S. Central Command cautioned that the scheduled withdrawal would lead to the collapse of the Afghan government. In March, the overall commander of Resolute Support Mission warned that the U.S. pullout would leave the ANSF without vital air support and maintenance.[53] Nevertheless, that April, President Biden set the complete withdrawal deadline for September 11, 2021. The Taliban went on to exploit the opportunity they'd patiently nurtured for years while Americans watched on, pretending not to see the future.

In May 2021, the Taliban launched what would become the final campaign for Lashkar Gah.[54] The ANSF scrambled, consolidating forces who retreated from the neighboring Garmsir and Marjah Districts, deploying hundreds of Afghan special forces as reinforcements, and calling in aerial bombardment by American B-52s, C-130 gunships, and unmanned drones. It all proved too little, too late. The Taliban chipped away block by block, checkpoint by checkpoint, police district by police district, until all that remained were a few hundred holdouts holed up in the governor's compound. After months of grueling urban combat, the helicopter evacuation of senior government leaders, and the surrender of the remaining ANSF, the Taliban finally toppled the government in Lashkar Gah on August 13, 2021.

The reinforcements sent to the city only spread the country's defenses thin, allowing simultaneous Taliban sieges to knock down the remaining provincial capitals like dominoes. By the end of the weekend, President Ashraf Ghani had fled the country, and the Taliban's white flag flew over Kabul.

Epilogue

Was it worth it? I hate that question. Most days, I just find it patronizing, as if I possessed some revelation or insight beyond the obvious and depressing truth. But if I let myself get to thinking, it torments me. Years ago I might have just shrugged, but not anymore. Not as a parent. Not now that I have felt the sublime joy of children and shudder to consider that they might not have been. It maddens me to be reminded of how much I gambled when the risks were merely hypothetical. And it maddens me further to know that I would still do it all again. I had to volunteer. We had to try; it was our fight. We all just hoped our time, treasure, limbs, lives, and the thousands of children that may never be would purchase more than a momentary disruption of al-Qaeda and a few short years of modernity for the people of Afghanistan. None of us bargained for disgrace and defeat.

Nobody puts the question to a fatherless child or a widowed spouse or a bereaved parent, and therein lies the answer. Now, maybe the Gold Star families would feel the same even if we'd won the war—my great-grandfather might have let the Nazis have Europe if it meant he could get his son back. But whatever the outcome, the worth of a war is better measured by those who paid full price. So don't ask me. I was lucky. I got out. I got my men out. Then each of us got out of the Marine Corps. Ahmed even got out of Afghanistan.

Just months before deploying for the fifth and final time on a route-clearance mission back in Helmand Province, Staff Sergeant Pulst pinned captain's bars on me at a small ceremony at the 5th Marine Regiment's memorial garden in Camp San Mateo. I was medically separated a few months later after my permanent scourge of Osama's revenge was diagnosed as inflammatory bowel disease. Lieutenant Teller and another officer from BAT-2 also received medical discharges after developing autoimmune disorders in the years that followed. There must have been something in the water, some feces in the farmland, or some toxic fumes emanating from the open-air burn pits.

Brian Pulst Jr. was passed over for promotion to gunnery sergeant one time too many, and it was up or out. He left the Marine Corps with a 100 percent disability rating for the countless TBIs he suffered from proximity to hundreds of explosions over his years as a combat engineer.

Fonz Palacios made sergeant and took one last assignment, training classes of Navy corpsmen to prepare them for "green side" service with the Marines. He remarried—a keeper this time—and moved home to Los Angeles to start a new life in peace as an electrician.

Zach O'Connor did one more tour at a Navy hospital in Pensacola, Florida, and then accepted an honorable discharge. After graduating from Baylor University, Zach moved back home to Michigan and fought his next battle against the coronavirus pandemic as an emergency room nurse.

Cory Malone finished his enlistment, whizzed through both college and business school as his family grew to four, then worked his way into a position as a supervisor at a Fortune 500 company. His night terrors strike less often these days. And when they do, a Labrador retriever is there to nuzzle and comfort him without words: *it's all right, buddy, you got out.*

A fortunate outlier in a shamefully broken system, Ahmed received his long-awaited Special Immigrant Visa and moved to the United States in 2014. After attempting to enlist in the U.S. Army as a linguist, Ahmed found better luck starting his own business, and helped other Afghans resettle by translating for Catholic Charities. But as the Taliban marched through Afghanistan in the coming years, his family was forced to flee the country as well. He helped them register with the United Nations High Commissioner for Resettlement, and they managed to find refuge in a nearby country. His cousin had been killed and his entire family sacrificed their home for our mission advising the ABP in Helmand, yet the only sentiment Ahmed ever expressed to me was gratitude. He had his life. It was the bare minimum of what he deserved, but still more than many others received in the frenzied rush to evacuate our Afghan allies.

Where the ABP of 1st Tolai landed in all this is anyone's guess. Like thousands of ANSF fighters in those final weeks, some undoubtedly gave their last breaths defending their country, their families, and their honor. Almost certainly among them were cynics or opportunists with a wet finger in the wind, and perhaps a few reluctant warriors stewing with resentment at the Americans who abandoned them, eager to turn coat. Those with the means—the officers—likely fled to Pakistan, Tajikistan, India, or Qatar. In a common but improvident act of desperation, some might have leveraged the local tribal elders to mediate a surrender in exchange for the Taliban's promise of amnesty for themselves and their families. Far too many were dragged out of their homes, with worthless amnesty papers in their pockets, and "disappeared" or shot to death in the street by Taliban hit squads targeting former ANSF.

One night in late August 2021, for instance, three Taliban in a pirated Danger Ranger visited a compound in Lashkar Gah shared by two brothers, both former ABP.[55] The Taliban executioners dismounted from the former ANSF truck with guns in hand and, ignoring the pleas of the women, dragged the brothers out, fired several times into their faces and chests, and left their lifeless bodies in the street. A former intelligence officer looked on from the roof of his neighboring compound to bear witness.

Against the very real likelihood that those brothers were Sher Ali and Omar, I like to imagine that the latter two are still alive and still fighting. And I like to imagine that Sher Ali sweeps wide into the jungle to flush out the enemy before crossing a danger area, just as I taught him. I like to imagine that Sergeant Karim pushes satellite patrols to protect where he is most vulnerable to ambush, like he learned the hard way on that cold January afternoon. I even like to imagine that Sergeant Max stands steadfast guarding the hideout of the ANSF now waging their own insurgency from the shadows. I also like to imagine all that could have been if only we'd been more honest or shown more resolve. And I like to imagine that the time we spent, the risks we took, and the sacrifices we made would have been worth it after all.

Acknowledgments

My heart is full of gratitude for all the people who helped me tell this story. First and foremost, I thank the Marines and corpsmen I served with in Afghanistan: Brian Pulst, Fonz Palacios, Cory Malone, Zach O'Connor, and the rest of Border Advisor Team 1. I am eternally grateful for the service of our interpreters as well, especially Ahmed, who assisted coalition forces for years at great personal risk to himself and his family. While countless other Marines supported me along the way, David Hull and Justin North in particular were there for me through the hardest times in training, the best times in the years that followed, and throughout the process of putting these words to the page.

Until the Veterans Writing Project took me into its mentorship program, I had nothing but a raw narrative and no idea what to do with it. So I give a sincere thank-you to my mentor, Dan Hudson, for his help in refining my work and his encouragement in discerning a route to publication. I also thank my other early readers whose feedback helped give this story the telling it deserves: Tomás Magaña, Jeffrey Izant, Margaret Gabriel, Lee Jacobs, and Katy Dacey. That I can write intelligibly at all is a credit to my years at the seminar table under the tutelage of Professors Mark O'Connor and Susan Mattis. For the education in the Middle Eastern history and languages that informed my deployment experience and has served me well in the years since, I thank Professors Kathleen Bailey, Franck Salameh, Ali Banuazizi, and Sassan Tabatabai.

I also want to thank my agent, Greg Johnson, for championing my story and my ability to tell it. And to my editor Keith Wallman goes my appreciation for recognizing the importance of my message and for applying his vision and experience to make it come to life.

With a day job, a working spouse, and a toddler bringing home every daycare virus known to man, free time is not something I have had in abundance. I could only scrounge the hours and energy necessary to write and publish this book with the steadfast support of my wife and the patience of our daughters. To my girls—you have my deepest gratitude and all of my love.

A final thank-you to the rest of my family, and my parents in particular, for their ultimate support of my service and their forgiveness for the stress it has caused them.

List of Military Abbreviations

ABP	Afghan Border Police
ANA	Afghan National Army
ANSF	Afghan National Security Forces
ATC	Advisor Training Cell
ATG	Advisor Training Group
AUP	Afghan Uniform Police
BAT	Border Advisor Team
CCP	Casualty Collection Point
CMD	Compact Metal Detector
COA	Course of Action
COC	Combat Operations Center
COP	Combat Outpost
CREW	Counter-Remote-Controlled IED Electronic Warfare
CVRJ	CREW Vehicle Receiver/Jammer
DFAC	Dining Facilities Administration Center
DOD	Department of Defense (U.S.)
DShK	Soviet Design 12.7mm Heavy Machine Gun
EOD	Explosive Ordnance Disposal
EPM	Embedded Police Mentor
FOB	Forward Operating Base
Frag-O	Fragmentary Order
GLE	Government-Led Eradication

IED	Improvised Explosive Device
IR	Infrared
ISAF	International Security Assistance Forces
ISIS	Islamic State of Iraq and ash-Sham
ISIS-K	ISIS-Khorasan Province
ISR	Imagery, Surveillance, Reconnaissance
JTAC	Joint Terminal Air Controller
MATV	MRAP All-Terrain Vehicle
MEU	Marine Expeditionary Unit
MoI	Ministry of Interior (Afghan)
MRAP	Mine-Resistant Ambush Protected [vehicle]
NAM	Navy Achievement Medal
NATO	North Atlantic Treaty Organization
NDS	National Directorate of Security (Afghan)
NiPLOC	Non-Punitive Letter of Caution
OEF	Operation Enduring Freedom
PB	Patrol Base
PCO	Public Call Office
PFC	Private First Class
PKM	Soviet Design 7.62mm Medium Machine Gun
POG	Person Other-than Grunt
PTSD	Post-Traumatic Stress Disorder
PX	Post Exchange
QRF	Quick Reaction Force
RCT	Regimental Combat Team
ROTC	Reserve Officers' Training Corps

RPG	Rocket-Propelled Grenade
RSM	Resolute Support Mission
RTB	Return to Base
SIGAR	Special Inspector General for Afghan Reconstruction
SIV	Special Immigrant Visa
SOP	Standard Operating Procedure(s)
TBI	Traumatic Brain Injury
TCP	Traffic Control Checkpoint
USO	United Service Organizations

Afghan Border Police Organization

ORGANIZATIONAL STRUCTURE

Ministry of Interior
Afghan National Police
Afghan Border Police
Zone (regional command)
Kandak (battalion equivalent)
Tolai (company equivalent)

AFGHAN BORDER POLICE OF 1ST KANDAK, 6TH ZONE
Colonel Nasrullah
1st Sergeant Amanullah

1ST TOLAI

Lieutenant Baddar Gul
Sergeant Sher Ali
Sergeant Karim
Sergeant Walid
Omar
Nur Muhammad
Abdul Aziz
Old Boy
David Duchovny

2ND TOLAI

Lieutenant Yaqub
Sergeant Farid Khan
Ibrahim

Holey Moley
Abdul

3RD TOLAI

Lieutenant Zarif

In December 2017, most ABP were transferred to a new Afghan Border Force under the Ministry of Defense, leaving only four thousand ABP under the Ministry of Interior to guard airports and border points of entry.

Notes

1. Thomas Barfield, *Afghanistan: A Cultural and Political History* (New Jersey: Princeton University, 2012), 68–70.

2. Rajiv Chadrasekaran, *Little America: The War Within the War for Afghanistan* (New York: Alfred A. Knopf, 2012), 236–248.

3. Barack H. Obama, "Remarks by the President in Address to the Nation on the Way Forward in Afghanistan and Pakistan," December 1, 2009, *Obama White House Archive*, https://obamawhitehouse.archives.gov/the-press-office/remarks-presiden t-address-nation-way-forward-afghanistan-and-pakistan.

4. Dan Lamothe, "Taliban Making Gains as Marine Presence Tails Off," *USA Today*, November 3, 2012, https://www.usatoday.com /story/news/world/2012/11/03/taliban-gains/1675141.

5. U.S. Department of State, Office of the Inspector General, *Review of the Afghan Special Immigrant Visa Program*, AUD-MERO-20-35, June 2020.

6. Barack H. Obama, "Remarks by the President on the Way Forward in Afghanistan," June 22, 2011, *Obama White House Archive*, https://obamawhitehouse.archives.gov/the-press-office/2011/06/22 /remarks-president-way-forward-Afghanistan.

7. "Vincent Paul Oatis," *The Men of the Second Oxford Detachment*, accessed January 1, 2022, https://parr-hooper.cmsmcq.com/2OD /the-biographies/vincent-paul-oatis.

8. "Jonathan G. Izant," *The Hall of Valor Project*, accessed January 1, 2022, https://valor.militarytimes.com/hero/44063.

9. Lyndon. B. Johnson, "Remarks in Memorial Hall, Akron University," October 21,1964, *The American Presidency Project, University of California-Santa Barbara*, https://www.presidency .ucsb.edu/documents/remarks-memorial-hall-akron-university.

10. Bill Roggio and Lisa Lundquist, "Green-on-Blue Attacks in Afghanistan: The Data," *Long War Journal,* updated June 17,

2017, https://www.longwarjournal.org/archives/2012/08/green-on
-blue_attack.php. Accessed January 1, 2022.

11. Dexter Filkins, "The Definition of a Quagmire," *New Yorker,*
September 30, 2012, https://www.newyorker.com/news/news-desk
/the-definition-of-a-quagmire.

12. Graham Bowley and Richard A. Oppel Jr., "U.S. Halts Training
Program for Some Afghan Recruits," *New York Times*, September 2,
2012, https://www.nytimes.com/2012/09/02/world/asia/us-halting
-program-to-train-afghan-recruits.html.

13. Fyodor Dostoyevsky, *The Idiot*, trans. David McDuff (New York:
Penguin Classics, 2003), 69.

14. Mattheiu Aikins, "Enemy Inside the Wire: The Untold Story of the
Battle of Bastion," *GQ Newsletter*, September 3, 2013, https://
www.gq.com/story/battle-of-bastion-taliban-afghanistan-air-base.

15. E.B. Sledge, *With the Old Breed at Peleliu and Okinawa* (New
York: Ballantine Books, 2007), 249.

16. Craig Whitlock, *The Afghanistan Papers: A Secret History of the
War* (New York: Simon & Schuster, 2021), 254–256.

17. Roggio and Lundquist, "Green-on-Blue Attacks," https://www
.longwarjournal.org/archives/2012/08/green-on-blue_attack.php.

18. "Nation Horrified to Learn About War in Afghanistan While
Reading Up on Petraeus Sex Scandal," *The Onion*, November
13, 2012, https://www.theonion.com/nation-horrified-to-learn
-about-war-in-afghanistan-whil-1819574188.

19. Ernest Hemingway, *A Farewell to Arms* (New York: Scribner,
2003), 291.

20. Legislative Proposals Relating to the War in Southeast Asia, Before
the Senate Committee on Foreign Relations, 92nd Cong., 1st Sess.
(1971). (Statement by John F. Kerry, Vietnam Veterans Against the
War.)

21. Joseph Heller, *Catch-22* (New York: Simon & Schuster, 2011), 28.

22. Francis F. Coppola, et al. *Apocalypse Now: Redux*. Santa Monica,
California: Lion Gate Films, 2010.

23. Yaroslav, Trofimov, "Afghans Gird to Go It Alone as U.S. Shuts
Down Bases," *Wall Street Journal*, February 3, 2013, https://www.

wsj.com/articles/SB100014241278873239261045782781109860
47572.

24. John F. Sopko, "SIGAR's Lessons Learned Program and
    Lessons from the Long War" (prepared remarks, Project on
    Government Oversight, National Security Strategy Retreat,
    January 31, 2020), https://www.sigar.mil/pdf/speeches/SIGAR
    _POGO_Speech_2020-01-31.pdf.

25. Whitlock, *Afghanistan Papers*, 153.

26. SIGAR, Collapse of the Afghan National Defense and Security
    Forces: An Assessment of the Factors That Led to Its Demise, May
    12, 2022, SIGAR-22-22-IP/Collapse of the ANDSF, iv, 24, 26.

27. Whitlock, *Afghanistan Papers*, 98.

28. Whitlock, *Afghanistan Papers*, 220.

29. Whitlock, *Afghanistan Papers*, 220.

30. Whitlock, *Afghanistan Papers*, 153.

31. Jonathan Alter, *The Promise: President Obama, Year One* (New
    York: Simon & Schuster, 2010), 390.

32. Whitlock, *Afghanistan Papers*, 153.

33. Whitlock, *Afghanistan Papers*, 94.

34. John F. Sopko, remarks (January 31, 2020), https://www.sigar.mil
    /pdf/speeches/SIGAR_POGO_Speech_2020-01-31.pdf.

35. Whitlock, *Afghanistan Papers*, 228.

36. Maurice L. Naylon IV. *The New Ministry of Truth: Combat
    Advisors in Afghanistan and America's Great Betrayal* (Ashland,
    Oregon: Hellgate, 2020).

37. Bengali, Shashank. "Gen. Joseph Dunford Becomes U.S.
    Commander in Afghanistan," *Los Angeles Times*, February
    10, 2013, https://www.latimes.com/world/la-xpm-2013-feb-10
    -la-fg-afghan-command-20130211-story.html.

38. U.S. Department of the Navy, *Machine Guns and Machine Gun
    Gunnery*, Marine Corps Warfighting Publication 3-15.1, September
    1, 1996.

39. *Chappelle's Show*, Season 1, Episode 1, "Popcopy & Clayton
    Bigsby," segment directed by Peter Lauer, written by Dave

Chappelle, Neal Brennan, and Norman Lear, aired January 22, 2003 on Comedy Central.

40. U.S. Department of Defense, *Assessment of U.S. Government and Coalition Efforts to Train, Equip, and Advise the Afghan Border Police*, by Kenneth P. Moorefield, Report No. DODIG-2013-081, May 24, 2013.

41. Chandrasekaran, *Little America*, Chapter 13, 246.

42. Bill Roggio, "Taliban Establish Training Camps in Southern Helmand," *Long War Journal*, February 12, 2014, https://www.longwarjournal.org/archives/2014/02/taliban_establish_training_cam.php.

43. Rod Norland, "Taliban Attack Police Base, Killing 17," *New York Times*, June 14, 2016, https://www.nytimes.com/2015/06/14/world/asia/taliban-police-base-southern-afghanistan.html.

44. Thomas Joscelyn and Bill Roggio, "Al Qaeda Operates in Southern Helmand, *Long War Journal*, October 24, 2015, https://www.longwarjournal.org/archives/2015/10/al-qaeda-operates-in-southern-helmand-province.php.

45. Rod Norland and Timor Shah, "A 5th District in Helmand Province Falls to the Taliban," *New York Times*, March 15, 2016, https://www.nytimes.com/2016/03/16/world/asia/a-5th-district-in-helmand-province-falls-to-the-taliban.html.

46. "On Their Own, Afghan Forces Strain to Combat Taliban Offensives," *New York Times*, October 10, 2016, https://www.nytimes.com/2016/10/10/world/asia/kunduz-afghanistan-taliban.html.

47. Pamela Constable, "Taliban Enters Capital of Helmand Province After Weeks of Fighting," *Washington Post*, October 10, 2016, https://www.washingtonpost.com/world/asia_pacific/suicide-blast-hits-southern-afghan-city-under-taliban-siege-at-least-14-dead/2016/10/10/7f1606da-8ee5-11e6-9c52-0b10449e33c4_story.html.

48. Mujib Mashal and Taiboor Shah, "Taliban Test Afghan and U.S. Resolve in Talks by Attacking a City," *New York Times*, October 12, 2020, https://www.nytimes.com/2020/10/12/world/asia/taliban-lashkar-gah-afghanistan.html.

49. U.S. Department of Defense, *Enhancing Security and Stability in Afghanistan*, Report to Congress, December 2020, https://media.defense.gov/2021/Apr/23/2002626546 /-1/-1/0/ENHANCING-SECURITY-AND-STABILITY-IN -AFGHANISTAN.PDF.

50. Obama, "Remarks," December 1, 2009.

51. T.S. Eliot, "The Hollow Men," in *Selected Poems* (San Diego: Harcourt, 1964), 77.

52. SIGAR 22-22-IP / Collapse of the ANDSF, 6.

53. SIGAR 22-22-IP / Collapse of the ANDSF, 14.

54. Bill Roggio and Andrew Tobin, "After Lengthy Siege, Lashkar Gah is Taken by the Taliban," *Long War Journal*, August 13, 2021, https://www.longwarjournal.org/archives/2021/08/after-length y-siege-lashkar-gah-is-taken-by-the-taliban.php.

55. Susannah George and Sudarsan Raghavan, "Taliban Wages Campaign of Targeted Killings Against Former Members of Afghan Security Forces," *Washington Post*, November 30, 2021, https://www.washingtonpost.com/world/2021/11/30 /taliban-killings-security.

INDEX

Afghan Border Police (*cont'd*)
  sexual abuse of children by,
    224–26
  in suspected
    IED-manufacturing site
    mission, 143–54, 157–60
  tactical decision-making by, 198
  Taliban attacks on, 15–16,
    33–34
  tobacco used by, 166–67
  Tolais, 8, 9, 11
Afghan forces
  after change in mission, 204–5
  coalition members killed by, 29,
    43–44
  insider threats from, 43–45, 102
  investing in/developing, 7
  see also specific organizations
Afghanistan
  advisors to, 24–25
  challenge from within
    government of, 227–28
  Taliban's post-withdrawal
    reestablishment in, 229–30
  withdrawal from, xv–xvii, 20,
    180–82, 213–14, 218–21,
    230–32
Afghanistan war
  attitudes toward, 28
  combat deployments in, 20
  cost of, in American lives, 210
  disgrace and defeat in, 235
  ground-level impact of, 203,
    210–12
  as lost cause, 180–82
  policymakers for, 201–2
  rebranding of, 202–3
  surge strategy for, 7
  troop-level reductions in, 24,
    49–50, 232
Afghan Local Police training, 44
Afghan National Police, 85–86

Afghan National Security Forces
  (ANSF), xv
  Afghan Local Police training,
    44
  collapse of, xviii
  combat readiness of, 199–201
  command positions in, 217
  continuing issues for, 230–31
  at final Lashkar Gah campaign
    of, 232–33
  in population centers and key
    terrain, 229–30
Afghans
  lack of technology access for, 142
  Special Immigrant Visas for,
    13–14
Afghan Uniform Police (AUP),
  170, 171
Ahmed (interpreter), 12–14,
  77–79, 81, 88, 90–93, 95, 96,
  110, 115, 134, 137–38, 143,
  148, 157–58, 173, 187–93, 195,
  204, 207, 209, 215, 219, 224,
  226, 235–37
air power, 50, 92, 160, 232
Ali, Sher, 79, 84, 89, 90, 101, 103,
  103–4, 108, 109, 115, 117, 132,
  134, 138–40, 142, 146, 147,
  153, 154, 157, 158, 160, 167,
  173, 173–74, 176, 178, 193,
  197, 215–17, 228, 229, 237–38
Alim, Haji, 113, 113–14
Allen, John R., 204
al-Qaeda, 6, 7, 229–30, 232
Amanullah, 1st Sergeant, 2
Ames, Lieutenant, 36, 88, 101
ANSF. *see* Afghan National
  Security Forces
ATC (Advisor Training Cell),
  37–42
ATG (Advisor Training Group),
  42–45

About the Author

CHRISTOPHER L. IZANT served as an infantry officer in the U.S. Marine Corps from 2010 to 2014 and deployed to Helmand Province as an advisor to the Afghan Border Police.

Chris attended Boston College for undergraduate studies prior to his military service, and afterward completed a joint degree program at Harvard Law School and the Kennedy School of Government.

Chris is a special agent at the Federal Bureau of Investigation. He lives in Maryland with his family.